Uncommon Controversy:
Fishing Rights of the Muckleshoot,
Puyallup, and Nisqually Indians

UNCOMMON
CONTROVERSY

Fishing Rights of the Muckleshoot, Puyallup, and Nisqually Indians

A REPORT PREPARED FOR THE
American Friends Service Committee

UNIVERSITY OF WASHINGTON PRESS
SEATTLE AND LONDON

Salmon design reproduced from a carving by Alex Jackson

THIS IS MY LAND

This is my land
From the time of the first moon
Till the time of the last sun
It was given to my people.
Wha-neh Wha-neh, the great giver of life
Made me out of the earth of this land
He said, "You are the land, and the land is you."
I take good care of this land,
For I am part of it.
I take good care of the animals,
For they are my brothers and sisters.
I take care of the streams and rivers,
For they clean my land.
I honor Ocean as my father,
For he gives me food and a means of travel.
Ocean knows everything, for he is everywhere.
Ocean is wise, for he is old.
Listen to Ocean, for he speaks wisdom.
He sees much, and knows more.
He says, "Take care of my sister, Earth,
She is young and has little wisdom, but much kindness."
"When she smiles, it is springtime."
"Scar not her beauty, for she is beautiful beyond all things."
"Her face looks eternally upward to the beauty of sky and stars,
Where once she lived with her father, Sky."
I am forever grateful for this beautiful and bountiful earth.
God gave it to me
This is my land.

—CLARENCE PICKERNELL
Quinault, Taholah

Preface

The impetus for this book comes out of nearly twenty years of American Friends Service Committee acquaintance with American Indian communities in the state of Washington. Constantly present with all of the fishing tribes are the problems of maintaining their unique fishing rights in the face of increasing pressures from an industrialized, populous society. In the AFSC's work in behalf of the Indian groups' community development efforts we inevitably have become concerned to understand the fishing rights question.

Perspectives of the state agencies in the controversy—the Department of Game and the Department of Fisheries—and the views of the sportsmen's organizations have been expressed extensively in the mass media and otherwise have been readily available, but reliable information on the points of view of the Indians has been difficult to come by.

The situations of three small tribes on rivers near the south end of Puget Sound have been especially puzzling—the Nisqually, the Puyallup, and the Muckleshoot. Each has been involved in active conflict over treaty rights, some of it very highly publicized. Each situation represents a unique set of circumstances.

Primarily in order to be able to decide what the attitude of the AFSC should be toward the issue and the particular disputes, in the fall of 1965 we began to assemble information. As our intent became known, inquiries and expressions of concern came from many parts of the country from citizens and organizations who wished to understand more about the problem than could be garnered from the mass media and other sources readily available; and as we pursued the task we became convinced that any fair resolution would require vastly increased public understanding of the Indians' points of view. Hence we felt compelled to consider public release of our information and conclusions. The National Congress of American Indians offered to publish the report, and in September 1967 it was released in mimeographed form. The present book is a revised, updated, somewhat expanded version of that report.

It should be understood that the report speaks only for the people who prepared it. The American Friends Service Committee, for whom the report was written, is pleased to facilitate its wide distribution. We do not speak for any of the Indians, Indian groups, public agencies, or private agencies or groups, although we have tried to be fair and accurate in our descriptions of their positions, feelings, and actions.

Because the Indian positions are not so fully recorded by them as are the other points of view we are particularly desirous to point out that we are only reporting our best understandings, which unfortunately are bound to be incomplete and probably somewhat distorted. The Indians' perspectives of history differ from recorded history; their views of legal positions in fishing rights often differ from those of the attorneys and the courts; and their views of current events differ from the views of those who generally report to the public. In this fishing rights matter, which is so much affected by public opinion, by national and state politics, and by the courts, we hope the Indians' own voices increasingly will be heard and that this book will serve to increase others' awareness of this gap in general knowledge which only the Indians themselves can fill.

So this book was not planned. Rather, it grew out of a set of circumstances. It represents the combined concern and effort of a great many people and organizations.

We are grateful to the many Indian people who have shared with us their knowledge about this problem. We will not name them individually here, because some of them felt that this report should not be taken to represent their full and accurate views. As indicated above, it is our interpretation.

The original study group, which did its work in 1966 for the report issued by the National Congress of American Indians, consisted of Mary B. Isely, William Hanson, Walter Taylor, Clarence Haggen, Joan LaFrance Lupson, Leo LaClair, and this writer. Pam Coe and Maria Pappalardo in the national office of the American Friends Service Committee performed monumental editorial functions. The work of these people produced the first, mimeographed edition from which body of material the present book has evolved. Acknowledgment also should be made of the interest and effort of Vine Deloria, Jr., then executive director of the National Congress of American Indians, in publishing that edition.

In the updating and rewriting for the present book Mary Isely and Joan Andersen have given most sacrificially of their time and skills. Joan Manzer has worked much beyond the requirements of duty in her copy editing function. Natalie Leberg and Barbara Remmerde have devoted many hours to the details of checking references; Mrs. Marian Gallagher and her assistants in the University of Washington Law Library gave invaluable aid. The maps were prepared by Gerald Petersen of the Department of Geography, University of Washington.

Special mention should also be made of the consultative assistance of Guy McMinds, Quinault Indian and fish biologist; and of Alvin Josephy's kindness in reviewing and advising regarding the historical material.

Personnel of the public agencies related to the problem all

have been gracious and accommodating in providing information and discussing their programs and policies: the U.S. Bureau of Indian Affairs, the Fishery Services Division of the U.S. Bureau of Sport Fisheries and Wildlife, the Washington State Department of Fisheries, and the Washington State Department of Game. In the text we have discussed all of these agencies frankly, sometimes critically, and, we hope, constructively.

Financial support for preparation and publication of the book has come from several organizations in addition to the American Friends Service Committee. The Indian Rights Association of Philadelphia, a nonpartisan organization seeking to promote Indian welfare and rights, kindly helped us with the study phase. Major assistance in both the initial study and the revision was given by the Harry Burks Memorial Fund, whose board felt it fitting that the special interest in Indians and their causes on the part of Harry Burks, former executive secretary of the Pacific Northwest Regional Office of the AFSC, be recognized in this way. As described above, the National Congress of American Indians published and distributed the first edition of the report.

A major financial contribution has been made by the American Indian Civil Liberties Trust, whose own statement of purpose and interest follows:

The American Indian Civil Liberties Trust, with headquarters in Washington, D.C., is the only all-Indian organization of its kind with funds for supporting causes involving the civil liberties of American Indians. Among the successes to which its subsidies have contributed are the defeat in a statewide referendum of the extension of state jurisdiction by South Dakota over Indian Reservations, the rejection by the U.S. Supreme Court of the state imposition of sales taxes on the Navajo and Papago Reservations, filling a need of the National Congress of American Indians at a critical period, and the slowing down of the movement of Government for the termination of federal supervision over Indians by reason of the opposition developed by the Ad Hoc Committee of Northwest Indian Organizations. Now it is supporting the fight of the Northwest Indians against state encroachments on their fishing and hunting rights as guaranteed in solemn treaties between the tribes and the United States. By way of appreciation for the work done, the names and tribal affiliations of its all-Indian trustees are given:

Dr. Paschal Sherman, Chairman (Colville Tribe); Robert B. Jim, Vice Chairman (Yakima Tribe); Mrs. Ruth Bronson (Cherokee Tribe); Francis McKinley (Uintah and Ouray Ute Tribe); Arthur Manning (Shoshone Paiute Tribes).

Thus *Uncommon Controversy* is the labor of many minds and hands.

CHARLES L. MCEVERS
Western Washington Indian Program
American Friends Service Committee

September 1969

Contents

Illustrations

MAPS

FIGURES

Introduction | Diversity: The Medicine
for Human Survival

WALTER TAYLOR

Salmon could become extinct during our century. Even American Indians might finally "vanish" after all within a generation or two—quite literally—along with the rest of mankind.
To be or to cease being—that is the critical question looming
over the human race during the final third of the twentieth
century. This book of "an uncommon controversy" over the
fishing rights of three small Indian tribes near Seattle, Washington, in the United States, deals with questions of survival
for salmon and for men everywhere.

"It is often assumed," writes René Dubos, professor of mi-
crobiology and experimental pathology at Rockefeller University, New York, "that progress depends on man's ability to
conquer Nature. In reality, there exist throughout mankind
biological and emotional needs that require not conquest of

Walter Taylor was National Indian Program Representative for the
American Friends Service Committee and then representative to the
Seneca Nation of Indians for Philadelphia Yearly Meeting of Friends
between 1960 and 1966; director of the VISTA training program at the
University of Wisconsin; and educational consultant to the Division for
Children and Youth, Wisconsin Department of Health and Social Serv-
ices. He is supervisor of placement for the Children's Aid Society of
Vancouver, British Columbia.

Nature, but rather harmonious collaboration with its forces." [1]
Unless the most powerful and affluent society in history soon
moves away from further conquest of nature toward harmonious collaboration with her, experts predict that within twenty
years the global atmosphere will start becoming unbreathable
for Indians and non-Indians alike, and all other living creatures; salmon and other life in the rivers and lakes will begin
to disappear; and plants will be dying of poison. That warning
emerged from the intergovernmental conference of experts on
the scientific basis for rational use and conservation of the
resources of the biosphere, a conference called by UNESCO
in Paris in September 1968.[2]

Man is destroying his own nest—the biosphere—that thin
layer at the earth's surface where the interaction of land, water,
and air makes life possible. There is no substance to any
dreams that modern scientific man could find refuge on another planet or move into the ocean depths if the biosphere
should become uninhabitable. We have no other nest. Man's
"progress" seems to be going backward toward destruction of
the environment upon which he must depend for survival.

While the world's population is growing explosively and
higher individual standards of living demand ever more raw
materials and heavier industrial production, the world's re-
newable resources are steadily decreasing. The waste products
of growth and technical development are accumulating faster
than we can dispose of them safely. All kinds of pollutants
threaten our mental health and our physical existence, including radiation, detergents, pesticides, heat, and noise. We now
have at our command more power and larger tools than ever

[1] René Dubos, "The Biosphere: A Delicate Balance Between Man
and Nature," *The UNESCO Courier* (Paris, Jan. 1969), p. 10.
[2] Published by UNESCO (Paris, Jan. 1969); and reported in *The
UNESCO Courier* (Paris, Jan. 1969), an edition devoted to the question
"Can We Keep Our Planet Habitable?"

before with which to mine, pave, or defoliate the earth, to consume oxygen from the air, and to pollute the water.

Professor Jean Dorst, of the Zoological Laboratory of the Museum of Natural History in Paris, and author of the book, *Before Nature Dies*,[3] urges a complete reappraisal of the whole problem of man's relationship to nature:

Despite technological progress and today's widespread belief in a machine-dominated civilization, man continues to be closely dependent on natural resources and especially on nature's primary productivity, of which photosynthesis is the first step. This basic fact links man closely to the entire living world. . . .

Even if we are only concerned with the utilitarian factor, we are forced to admit that man has nothing to gain by exterminating animals and plants, even those which at first glance are either "useless" or seem harmful. . . .[4]

The intrusion of urban life and industry upon the biological balance of waters has already been noted with alarm by scientists. There are many instances. In spite of a relatively low human population in the state of Maine, the rivers there are so polluted that most of them can no longer support a run of salmon. About seventy years ago fifty species of fish lived in the lower part of the river Seine, but now only a few diseased eels can be found there. Thousands of lakes in Finland are now completely polluted. Lake Zürich in Switzerland is "biologically dead," all its fish and other forms of life exterminated by pollution. Even the Great Lakes in the United States, the largest inland lakes in the world, are seriously threatened.

Against this background of world-wide damage to fish and to the rest of our biosphere, the "uncommon controversy" over the depletion of salmon in the Pacific Northwest takes on

[3] (English ed.; London: Collins, 1969); *Avant Que Nature Meurt* (French ed.; Neuchâtel, Switzerland, 1964).

[4] Jean Dorst, "A Biologist Looks at the Animal World (Beasts and Men)," *The UNESCO Courier* (Jan. 1969), p. 18.

extraordinary significance. This book indicates that the Indian fishermen have been made scapegoats and are not the cause of salmon depletion. If out of the controversy a sounder understanding of the true relationship between the Indians and the salmon could emerge, it could lead us not only toward a cooperative program to rehabilitate the fish in western Washington, but far beyond that toward some constructive approaches to global problems of human interaction, environmental protection, and human survival.

The common error which links this controversy to the question of man's survival on the planet is the persistent tendency of Western civilization to impose its values, its religion, its law, its education, and its technology on other cultures, whether they fit or not.

American Indians are not the only people to suffer from well-intentioned efforts to help them give up their own identity and to become homogenized in the mainstream of white, Western civilization. The Masai, for example, nomadic shepherds in East Africa, were successful in adapting their way of life to their environment by cooperating with nature instead of fighting it. With the "help" of Western veterinary medicine, however, their grazing lands became overstocked and nature's delicate balances were upset. Ecologist Frank Fraser Darling explains that

. . . wherever sedentary populations have impinged on nomad grazing there has been degradation of habitat for which the nomads are invariably blamed. Yet nomadism as a careful pastoral process is the least traumatic of human influences and as a form of husbandry utilizes areas which could not be utilized by man in any other way.[5]

[5] Frank Fraser Darling, "Man Against Nature," *The UNESCO Courier,* XXII (Jan. 1969), 26, 27. See also Thomas M. Fraser, Jr., *Culture and Change in India: The Barpali Experiment* (Cambridge: University of Massachusetts Press, 1968), especially pp. 261–79: ". . . the point to stress is that had either the technical and economic aspects

In reviewing its rural community development work in India during the 1950's, the American Friends Service Committee acknowledged that its technical assistance sometimes failed because of insufficient cross-cultural empathy and knowledge. Improvements in poultry raising and production, for example, unexpectedly created additional expenses and resulted in lower resistance to diseases against which the tougher native strains had been immune.

From his personal observation of pacification work in the Quang Ngai Province, Vietnam, Jonathan Schell, a graduate student in Far Eastern history, Harvard, writes about "the overriding, fantastic fact that we [Americans] are destroying, seemingly by inadvertence, the very country we are supposedly protecting." [6] A soldier from California explained very perceptively to Schell his own cross-cultural blindness—a handicap which so often turns philanthropy into imposition:

When I got here, some of the villages were wiped out, but quite a lot were still there. . . . Then every time I went out there were a few less, and now the whole place is wiped out as far as you can see. The G.I.'s are supposed to win the people's confidence, but they weren't *taught* any of that stuff. I went through that training, and I learned how to take my weapon apart and put it back together again, and how to shoot, but no one ever told me a thing about having to *love* people who look different from us and who've got an ideological orientation that's about a hundred and eighty degrees different from us. We don't understand what they're thinking. When we got here, we landed on a different planet. In Germany and Japan, I guess there was a thread of contact, but even when a Vietnamese guy speaks perfect English, *I* don't know what the hell he's talking about.[7]

A private from Texas told Schell, "No one has any feelings for

---

of the program or the existing sociocultural patterns in the villages been fully understood, it is unlikely that this particular program would have been undertaken at all."

[6] *The Military Half* (New York: Knopf, 1968), p. 3.

[7] *Ibid.*, p. 42.

the Vietnamese. . . . They're lost. The trouble is, no one sees the Vietnamese as people. They're not people. Therefore, it doesn't matter what you do to them." [8]

Perhaps it will be argued that one cannot expect much cross-cultural empathy under the brutalizing circumstances of war. While such an argument cannot justify a war in which deficient cultural understanding plays a major part, nevertheless let us consider briefly another example in which there is no war, but only a sincere and highly sophisticated concern by the United Nations to help an underdeveloped country achieve progress.

In his book, *International Aid to Thailand—the New Colonialism?*, Ronald C. Nairn, now president of Prescott College, Arizona, and a serious student of Southeast Asian affairs for more than twenty years, examines the culturally disruptive implications of technical assistance to underdeveloped nations. Although acknowledging that developing nations could benefit from some aspects of Western techniques, Nairn repudiates the presumption that "anything Western will bring a better life to Southeast Asia." In fact, he concludes that foreign aid "is interference in a nation's lifeways," imposing upon Asian people Western values and stresses, along with some benefits, much like the cultural disruption imposed by colonial powers.[9]

Nairn finds that foreign aid programs seeking ends which are "known" to be good tend to ignore or negate nonmaterial values:

In a recent study sponsored by the United Nations, a vivid example was given of this tendency. After describing (and indeed over-romanticizing) the charm and easy indolence of Thailand's people, the nonutilitarian beauty and the spiritual impact of its Buddhist temples, and the evident harmony between peasant, nature, and religion, the writer still concluded that modernization had to come to Thailand. "The transition is sure to be painful,

[8] *Ibid.*
[9] Ronald C. Nairn, *International Aid to Thailand—the New Colonialism?* (New Haven, Conn.: Yale University Press, 1966), p. 192.

sure to be unsightly, and the psychological impact will affect almost all of her citizens." But endure it Thailand must . . . "to get a better life." [10]

Noting the growing similarity beween Marxism and Western liberalism in respect to the material objectives of aid programs, Nairn was also impressed by their identical view of peasantry as a way of life: "Both despise it. . . . Both . . . see an industrialized, urbanized proletariat with a high standard of living as a laudable objective"—even though one of the major effects of urbanization was to produce a "rootless peasant." [11]

Are American Indians also victims of colonialism—and of "foreign" aid? The ugly history of destruction of Indian people by arrogant, acquisitive non-Indian intruders has now been well told by many writers. It should be more widely and honestly presented in our schools. However, without ignoring the significance of massacres, land thefts, buffalo slaughter, death marches, humiliation, and broken treaties, our purpose here is to emphasize the more benevolent imposition, the killing by kindness. "If I knew for a certainty that a man was coming to my house with a conscious design of doing me good, I should run for my life," wrote Henry David Thoreau.[12] Americans of good will and generous nature have for many generations wanted to help Indians to become civilized, to assimilate, to get into the mainstream of American life, to stop being Indians and to become more "like us." They have assumed that eventually the best hope for Indians would lie in becoming successful in the dominant, non-Indian society—in other words, giving up their Indian identity and "getting lost." That is the meaning of assimilation: making similar, not cultivating diversity.

[10] Ibid., p. 191. Reference is to James Morris, The Road to Huddersfield (New York: Pantheon Books, 1963), p. 134.
[11] Nairn, International Aid, p. 191.
[12] Walden, Modern Library Series (New York: Random House, 1946), p. 84.

These well-wishers suppressed native languages and took children away from home for cultural and academic training in white-style schools. They relocated young Indians from impoverished reservation communities to a new life—frequently less desirable, or even intolerable—in the crowded, inhospitable cities where many Indians felt completely alienated. Missionaries taught new religions and discouraged native religions which were deeply concerned with respect for nature and giving thanks for its many blessings. Benevolent Americans helped Indians, for example, to build a cattle industry after the buffalo were gone, but soon that new way of life was drowned beneath the waters behind a huge power dam. Dedicated people even now keep seeking better opportunities for Indian students to remain in school longer, just when we are discovering that most of our existing schools are not yet tuned in to the new values and learning styles required for human survival.

". . . Is there a deficiency in our system of education and communication which prevents us from understanding any other culture or ethos, apart from our own or that of Western Europe?" asks Arnold Beichman, writer and special correspondent for the *New York Herald-Tribune*, examining the American failure to understand the revolution in Vietnam.[13] Underlying these warnings against Western ethnocentric education is an exciting discovery—that other cultures contain wisdom, too. This truth has been well known to thoughtful Western people for many centuries, but it seems now to be coming clear to most of us only in the glare of our new awareness of impending doom.

In his provocative, hopeful book, *Education and Ecstasy,* George B. Leonard, who has received many national awards for educational writing and is a senior editor of *Look* magazine, recalls Thoreau's view of the American Indian as "the perfect

[13] "As the Cookie Crumbles in Vietnam," *Columbia University Forum,* VIII (Spring 1965), 5.

INTRODUCTION xxiii

lifelong learner." "Roving freely," writes Leonard, "interacting
directly with his environment, the hunter went on learning,
changing, all life long. He had no job except education. . . .
He planned, he maneuvered in concert with his fellows, he used
all of his senses. He grew wise with age. . . ." [14] With the
best of intentions, concerned Americans are inviting Indian
people to catch up with a way of life which has become danger-
ously obsolete—in school, in church, and in industry. The
pressure to change is familiar to Indians. For a hundred years
and more they have been urged to conform or die. Now it is
the powerful, affluent, dominant Space Age society which must
change or die. If it dies, it will take Indians and salmon with it.
We are nearing the end of "the long Dark Age called 'Civilization,' " in Leonard's words.[15] Our future, if we have any,
must take us into an Era of Ecology.

The first principle of ecology is the principle of diversity. In
respect to natural conservation, biologist Reginald E. Balch
advises, "We will make no mistake in aiming at the maintenance of as rich a variety of life as our soils and climate will allow." He acknowledges that the application of this principle
"may call for some sacrifice of short-term commercial interests
but in the long run should prove to be good economics." [16]
When we disrupt the balance of nature in the forest and reduce
its diversity, we endanger its occupants. For much the same
reason we need to preserve, even to cultivate, cultural diversity
among men in the world forest.

The basic issues discussed in *Uncommon Controversy* are
common throughout the world. The legal, practical, and moral
questions considered here apply to most of the cross-cultural
controversies which are currently threatening the peace and

[14] (New York: Delacorte Press, 1968), p. 73.
[15] *Ibid.*, p. 78.
[16] Reginald E. Balch, "The Ecological Viewpoint," a series of radio
lectures, CBC University of the Air, CBC Publications (Toronto, Ont.:
T. H. Best, 1965), p. 44.

even the continued existence of men on earth. The legal questions center around the meaning of non-Indian words in a treaty under study in a non-Indian court of law. Important decisions must be rendered by non-Indian officials. Even under these conditions, the weight of evidence in support of Indian interests seems impressive. The larger question pressed forward by this controversy, however, asks whether a dominant society's law can be made to fit a culturally distinct minority. If not, it may even serve the majority badly by its very tendency to impose conformity and to reduce the diversity upon which our future seems to depend.

The moral issues have always impressed some members of the dominant society but have not yet prevented violations of Indian treaties. We are only now beginning to teach honest history in some of our schools, history which includes the point of view of black people, Indians, and other minority groups. It is possible, however, for white men to learn. Those who do learn acquire a new dimension of freedom. Even deeply prejudiced people can escape from the bonds of racism to enjoy freedom.

Many sincerely concerned people finally arrive at cross-cultural appreciation only after passing through several intermediate phases. The beginning may be astonishment that Indians, as a culturally distinct people, have not yet vanished. Indians still exist! When non-Indians begin to learn, they are likely to be first incredulous and then shocked by the historical facts presented from a minority view. Next they may become angry, inspired perhaps by guilt inherited from the brutalities of previous generations and shared with contemporary decision-makers. From anger they may go on to pity, sympathy, charity, and even on to "helping them to help themselves." But there is such a long way to go. Paternalism can be so subtle. As Karl Gregory, professor of economics at Wayne State University,

Detroit, succinctly phrased it, "No matter how benevolent you are, you are still benevolent." [17]

The next phase is empathy. "Before judging a man," advises an old Indian maxim, "walk three moons in his moccasins." Three months is a short time, but with a culturally open mind it may be long enough to begin the last phase, appreciation of the Indian heritage and of its remarkable resistance to "vanishing." Appreciation means awareness of the positive qualities in another person or group. It is difficult because it requires one to climb out of his life-long cultural assumptions and to examine them along side of the different assumptions of another culture. It seems a long road from awareness of the very existence of Indian people to appreciation of their relevance to life in the twenty-first century. New generations of citizens of the world will, we hope, find that road more comfortable and familiar than their elders.

There have, of course, always been men gifted in crosscultural appreciation. Over a century ago George Catlin, noted artist and recorder of western Indian life, wrote about the Indians he visited before the impact of civilization hit them:

I love a people who have always made me welcome to the best they had . . . who are honest without laws, who have no jails and no poor-house . . . who never take the name of God in vain . . . who worship God without a Bible, and I believe that God loves them also . . . who are free from religious animosities . . . who have never raised a hand against me, or stolen my property, where there was no law to punish either . . . who never fought a battle with white men except on their own ground . . . and oh! how I love a people who don't live for the love of money.[18]

Indians take their treaty promises seriously and they expect others to do the same. When non-Indians feel strongly that

[17] "Thinking Black," quoted in *Newsweek*, LXX (Nov. 20, 1967), 38.
[18] Quoted in Harold McCracken, *George Catlin and the Old Frontier* (New York: Bonanza Books, 1959), p. 14.

some change in the provisions of a treaty or its interpretation is necessary, the whole climate for constructive consideration could be brightened significantly if non-Indian diplomats would approach Indian people in a spirit of mutually respectful negotiation.

One other aspect of the moral issue which even concerned non-Indians tend to ignore is the spiritual meaning of fishing among Indians today. Fishing is more than a right, more than a way to make a living. It is a way of life—a part of life itself, an integral part of the whole artistic, religious, economic, and social life of the Northwest Coast Indians.

We have little evidence to suggest that either legal or moral concerns will bring about a constructive solution to the "uncommon controversy" over Indian fishing rights in the near future. They are nevertheless important issues, and an understanding of them in this case will contribute in the long run to needed improvements in cross-cultural legislation, adjudication, and understanding throughout the United States and perhaps the world. The greatest hope, however, for salmon, Indians, and other living things on this planet lies in our growing recognition of some hard facts of life among the practical issues raised in this salmon controversy. A few lonely voices crying out in the wilderness for a more respectful, Indian-like attitude toward nature are now gaining strength from a new source. The white power structure is getting the message and sending it out with amplification never before available. For example, the Royal Bank of Canada devoted its February 1969 *Monthly Letter* to "Man in the Balance of Nature."

Nature maintained her balance for millions of years, but she is now up against something new. All other participants in nature live by habit and instinct but men try to manage things, to force things into new ways. Their conceited and arrogant interference has brought about the deterioration in living conditions which alarms us, the extinction of many animals and plants, and the defilement of air and water

Now that their continued existence is shown to be at stake men are called upon to rethink many things, to relearn lessons long forgotten. . . .
We face the hard task of putting natural forces to work in restoration and redemption. . . .
Man, part of nature, has become enticed into a nearly fatal illusion: that his skills in science and technology make him independent of the laws of nature. . . .[19]

Until recent years most Americans felt comfortably convinced that science could always find a new way to overcome any problems it might create in the course of progress. The very word "ecology" did not appear in the English language until 1873. Now experts are urgently warning us that there are limits to our natural resources and limits to the damage which science and technology can repair. Lynn White, Jr., professor of history at the University of California, emphasizes the practical issues, but insists that their resolution will require above all a spiritual change in our attitude toward nature:

I personally doubt that disastrous ecologic backlash can be avoided simply by applying to our problems more science and more technology. . . . What we do about ecology depends on our ideas of the man-nature relationship. More science and more technology are not going to get us out of the present ecologic crisis until we find a new religion, or rethink our old one . . . we shall continue to have a worsening ecologic crisis until we reject the Christian axiom that nature has no reason for existence save to serve man. . . .
In Antiquity every tree, every spring, every stream, every hill had its own *genius loci*, its guardian spirit. . . . Before one cut a tree, mined a mountain or dammed a brook, it was important to placate the spirit in charge of that particular situation, and to keep it placated. By destroying pagan animism, Christianity made it possible to exploit nature in a mood of indifference to the feelings of natural objects. . . .
The greatest spiritual revolutionary in Western history, St.

[19] *Monthly Letter,* Vol. L, No. 2 (Montreal).

Francis, proposed what he thought was an alternate Christian view of nature and man's relation to it: he tried to substitute the idea of the equality of all creatures, including man, for the idea of man's limitless rule of creation. Both our present science and our present technology are so tinctured with Christian arrogance toward nature that no solution for our ecologic crisis can be expected from them alone. Since the roots of our trouble are so largely religious, the remedy must be essentially religious, whether we call it that or not. We must rethink and refeel our nature and destiny. . . . I propose Francis as a patron saint for ecologists.[20]

This leads us back to the moral issue, but with new power drawn from the necessity to review our relationships and attitudes toward Indians, salmon, and all other living things in the light of ecological laws. Facing the practical issues squarely may bring about a finer resolution of the moral issues than Indians have experienced since the first European immigrants landed on their soil. Furthermore, even the legal issues can fall into place once we recognize the absolute authority of ecological laws and admit that they cannot be superseded by man-made laws.

One practical suggestion by Balch in respect to forest ecology might well be applied to stream ecology as well. In "The Ecological Viewpoint" he suggests:

One answer to unemployment seems to stare us in the face: more intensive management of our forests. The object should be to establish permanent communities in forested areas, communities of people skilled in the many arts of forestry, drawing their livelihood from the forest and taking a pride in it. This could be both the objective and the means of conservation, combining forest ecology with human ecology.[21]

We already have special communities of people with a whole heritage of devotion to the art of living in harmony with

[20] "The Historical Roots of Our Ecological Crises," 133rd Meeting, American Association for the Advancement of Science, Wash., D.C. (Dec. 27, 1966, mimeo), pp. 6, 8, 9.

[21] P. 44.

nature, namely the Indian reservations. It could benefit not only Indians, but all men, to recognize this inherent strength so pertinent to the desperate need of our time; to subsidize these communities for special conservation services rather than denigrating them; and thus to encourage their further development of expertness in fish conservation.

By recognizing the Northwest Coast Indians as legitimate fishermen and conservationists, we could even now—late as the hour may be—benefit from the traditional conservation wisdom of Indians. The spirit of Indian fishing illustrates the continuing tendency of many Indian people to integrate work, education, play, religion, and their relationships with their environment into a whole way of life. This could serve as a model for the survival of man suffering now from too much fragmentation and not enough community feeling among men.

We *must* move, in the opinion of George Leonard—"to learn delight, not aggression; sharing, not eager acquisition; uniqueness, not narrow competition." [22] Few Americans are better equipped than Indians to teach these values so familiar among Indians, so strange in the dominant society, and so necessary for human survival.

An intelligent application of new values, attitudes, and relationships is required for an Era of Ecology. We might find that by returning some of the salmon and the spawning rivers to the care of Indians, the state of Washington could increase the amount of fish available to all fishermen, including sport and commercial fishermen. In any case, the most hopeful approach to any similar uncommon controversies must include the cultivation of diversity and such fundamental attitudes as cross-cultural respect, dignity, and appreciation. We need a mutual exchange among culturally diverse peoples rather than the familiar one-way assistance from the "developed" nations toward cultural homogenization of the "underdeveloped."

[22] *Education and Ecstasy,* p. 132.

A generation ago John Collier, an anthropologist and former U.S. Commissioner of Indian Affairs, saw that Indians had the good medicine for human survival. He began his *Indians of the Americas* thus:

> They had what the world has lost. They have it now. What the world has lost, the world must have again, lest it die. Not many years are left to have or have not, to recapture the lost ingredient. . . .
>
> What, in our human world, is this power to live? It is the ancient, lost reverence and passion for human personality, joined with the ancient, lost reverence and passion for the earth and its web of life.
>
> This indivisible reverence and passion is what American Indians almost universally had; and representative groups of them have it still. . . .[23]

George Clutesi, artist, author, and Canadian Indian of the Tse-Shaht tribe, expresses the same thought in *Son of Raven, Son of Deer*:

> My father's generation was a happy, singing people. They were a proud people. . . . Quaint folklore tales were used widely to teach the young the many wonders of nature; *the importance of all living things, no matter how small and insignificant;* and particularly to acquaint him with the closeness of man to all animal, bird life and the creatures of the sea. The young were taught through the medium of the tales that there was *a place in the sun for all living things.*[24] [Emphasis added]

More than a century ago, in response to the whirlwind Treaty of Point Elliott, Chief Sealth, in Duwamish, told Governor Isaac Stevens' negotiating party:

> It matters little where we pass the remnant of our days. They will not be many. . . . A few more moons. A few more winters—and not one of the descendants of the mighty hosts that once moved over

---

[23] (New York: Mentor Books, 1947), p. 7.

[24] *Son of Raven, Son of Deer: Fables of the Tse-Shaht People* (Sidney, B.C.: Gray's Publishing, 1967), p. 9.

this broad land or lived in happy homes, protected by the Great Spirit, will remain to mourn over the graves of a people—once more powerful and hopeful than yours. But why should I mourn at the untimely fate of my people? Tribe follows tribe, and nation follows nation, like the waves of the sea. It is the order of nature, and regret is useless. Your time of decay may be distant—but it will surely come, for even the White Man whose God walked and talked with him as friend with friend, can not be exempt from the common destiny. We may be brothers after all. We will see.[25]

[25] Jan. 22, 1855. The speech is published in translation in Clarence B. Bagley, "Chief Seattle and Angeline," *The Washington Historical Quarterly,* XXII (Oct. 1931), 252.

Uncommon Controversy:
Fishing Rights of the Muckleshoot,
Puyallup, and Nisqually Indians

I | Before the Treaties

Before the advent of Europeans, the richest people in North America were the Indians of the Northwest Coast. They were among the few hunting and gathering societies in the world which produced wealth beyond that needed for subsistence. The basis of the aboriginal economy was fishing. However, salmon was not merely an important part of life—not a recreation and not solely a means of providing food—it was the heart of a whole way of life. It was the staple article of year-round diet, fresh, smoked, or dried, of which a Chinook man in the treaty days said that "if he was three days without [it] his heart failed him." [1] It was a major commodity in trade between tribes. Above all, it was a blessing for which the Indians always gave thanks.

All the tribes of the Puget Sound had a First Salmon Ceremony, usually in the spring when the fish came in prodigious numbers. Many religious beliefs and tales concerned salmon, and these were often presented in the rituals. Each group

[1] Edward G. Swindell, Jr., *Report on Source, Nature, and Extent of the Fishing, Hunting, and Misc. Related Rights of Certain Indian Tribes* . . . , Office of Indian Affairs, U.S. Dept. of Interior (Los Angeles, Calif., July 1942), p. 368 (hereafter cited as Swindell).

3

celebrated the first catch according to its own pattern. A Puyallup man, a descendant of those who participated, describes it:

Since the salmon was 80 to 90 percent of their diet the Puyallup Indians held a cultural festival or religious ceremony in honor of the salmon. At this ceremony they barbecued the first salmon of the run over an open fire. It is then parceled out to all, in small morsels or portions so all can participate. Doing this, all bones are saved intact. Then in a torchbearing, dancing, chanting and singing procession they proceeded to the river where they cast the skeleton of the salmon into the stream with its head pointing upstream, symbolic of a spawning salmon, so the run of salmon will return a thousandfold.[2]

The ceremonies, stories, and taboos exhibited a fundamental concept of the immortality of the salmon and the related desire not to offend it and endanger its return. The methods and skill of the aboriginal fishermen achieved extraordinary harvests but at the same time ensured continuation of the great runs.[3]

The land held other wealth than the fish. The beaches were full of clams and other shellfish, and game—deer, elk, and bear—was plentiful. Berries and certain roots were abundant in season. Among the great trees of the forests was the western red cedar, which in spite of its size can be split with a blow. Its wood is light in weight and easy to work, yet exceedingly tough and durable; its bark can be shredded almost to coarse thread size. It provided the all-important canoes, from river

[2] U.S. Congress, Senate, Committee on Interior and Insular Affairs, Subcommittee on Indian Affairs, *Indian Fishing Rights: Hearings on S.J.R. 170 and S.J.R. 171*, 88th Cong., 2d sess., Aug. 5–6, 1964; statement of Frank Wright, chairman of the Puyallup tribe, p. 105 (hereafter cited as *1964 Hearings*).

[3] It is estimated that 50,000 Indians took 18 million pounds of salmon from the Columbia each year before the white men arrived. *The Columbia River Comprehensive Report on Development . . . ,* Bureau of Reclamation, U.S. Dept. of Interior (Wash., D.C., 1947), p. 353.

canoes to the great sea-going canoes of the coastal people; and from it came the planks with which the longhouses, the gabled communal dwellings which amazed the early explorers, were constructed. Its bark supplied material for clothing, basketry hats, plaited mats, and baskets for storage, cooking, and burden bearing. And the climate was so mild that the starvation times of more severe regions were almost unknown.

The pace of life was hurried only during salmon runs. Then all in the community who were able spent long hours catching, preparing, and storing the fish. Men worked with weirs, canoes, spears, dip nets, and large fiber nets. Women cleaned the fish and spread them for broiling, or laid them on wooden racks to be smoked and dried, later to be stored in wooden boxes for the year to come. Children gathered wood and helped clean fish. In the off season, work was necessary to provide houses, clothing, and tools; but leisure time was still left for the development of complex ceremonies, potlatches, a rich oral literature, elaborate woodcarving, highly stylized art motifs, and some of the finest basketry in the world.[4]

For the Indians of the southeastern Puget Sound region, their fishing waters formed the basis of the relationships among themselves.

The Indians of this region were supremely conscious of the nature of the country in which they lived. They were completely aware of its character as a great water shed. From the geographical concept of the drainage system they derived their major concept of social unity. . . .

---

[4] For descriptions of various aspects of Indian life, see C. B. Bagley, *History of King County, Wash.* (4 vols.; Chicago, Seattle: S. J. Clarke, 1929), I, 653–57; James G. Swan, *The Northwest Coast* (New York: Harper & Bros., 1857), pp. 26, 56–93; Ruth Underhill, *Indians of the Pacific Northwest* (Riverside, Calif.: Sherman Institute Press, 1945), p. 17; and Robert B. Whitebrook, *Coastal Exploration of Washington* (Palo Alto, Calif.: Pacific Books, 1959), p. 58 (hereafter cited as Whitebrook).

. . . the tie which they recognized as most binding, as most closely paralleling what we know as political allegiance was based upon this geography of the drainage system. . . .

The Indians of the area lived in small groups, the members of which came together during the winter months, when life was sedentary, at certain sites which may be . . . called "villages." The village site was determined by strictly topographical considerations. . . . It was located either at the juncture of two streams or at the mouth of the stream where it entered the Sound. . . . The village frequently consisted of only one house, large enough for four or six families, and never of more than three such houses.

. . . [the village] was also the center from which radiated all of the year's food gathering and similar activities. Such activities were carried on by family groups which acted independently of one another. . . .

. . . A particular village site and the drainage connected with it bore the same name. The people called themselves by the name of the village site plus a suffix meaning "people of." When they spoke of themselves in relation to other people of the area they might use the term for the larger drainage of which their stream was part, plus the same suffix. Thus, the Puyallup River above its fork with the Carbon, and the village site at this point, were called *ts'uwa''*, its people were *ts'uwádiabc* or people of *ts'uwa''*, this term forming the true village name. In contrast to persons of the Nisqually, they were *spwiyä' la phabc* or people of the Puyallup River drainage. And they were, along with many persons from the Nisqually, *álebiuqu* or inland people of the Puget Sound drainage.[5]

While the river drainage was the primary unifying concept among these loosely organized groups, they recognized cultural differences. They distinguished among: (1) saltwater people who were skillful with canoes suitable for rough water; (2) river people who lived on river drainages above the Sound but spent some time on the tide flats; (3) inland people who

[5] Marian W. Smith, *The Puyallup-Nisqually,* Columbia University Contributions to Anthropology, No. 32 (New York: Columbia University Press, 1940), pp. 2–4, 6.

traveled back and forth in the country paralleling the Cascade range; and (4) prairie people who owned and made use of horses. While the inland groups relied more on hunting than the saltwater and river groups, all depended on salmon.[6] Territorial boundaries and identifications, in contrast to those in European society, had little effect on movement of people. "Movements were not restricted because of land ownership: the main considerations which determined them were always (a) convenience and (b) the state of feeling, whether friendly or inimical, which existed between travelers and the persons they might expect to encounter. However numerous other causes for disagreement were, there were no quarrels over land." [7]

An important method of maintaining peaceful and mutual-aid relationships among these groups was intermarriage,[8] which extended beyond the Puget Sound groups to tribes east of the mountains.

In contrast to more northern tribes, the Indians of the Puget Sound did little raiding except occasionally to take booty and slaves from defenseless groups. The slaves did the hardest labor and were excluded from the decision-making and prestige-gaining systems, although they were generally treated as members of the community.[9] The lack of wide political organization made larger war enterprises impossible. No warfare was ever directed toward the possession of land. The land was not thought of as a possession owned, or as something which could be alienated or exchanged for something else. Stachas, a Cayuse, explained the Indian concept of land:

My friends I wish to show you my mind, interpret right for me. How is it I have been troubled in mind? If your mothers were

[6] *Ibid.,* pp. 29–30.
[7] *Ibid.,* p. 24.
[8] *Ibid.,* pp. 32–33.
[9] *Ibid.,* pp. 150–61.

here in this country who gave you birth, and suckled you, and while you were suckling some person came and took away your mother and left you alone and sold your mother, how would you feel then? This is our mother, this country, as if we drew our living from her.[10]

The difference between the Indians' and the white men's view of the land was to be one of the greatest sources of misunderstanding at the time of treaty-making.

EXPLORATION AND TRADE: THE WHITE MAN COMES

Although the first Europeans may have set foot on the Northwest Coast a little before the Revolutionary War, until the early decades of the nineteenth century the only direct contacts the Indians of Puget Sound had with white men consisted of brief and infrequent encounters with explorers and traders. The Spanish and the British were the first to explore the Northwest Coast, searching for the mythical Northwest Passage that would have given enormous military advantage to the nation that found it.[11]

Spanish expeditions, under the press of English competition, worked their way up the Pacific Coast from Mexico. In 1774 the Perez expedition, charged with exploring as far north as 60°N, anchored at what may have been Nootka Sound on Vancouver Island, calling it San Lorenzo. A year later the Heceta expedition anchored off the coast of what is now the state of Washington and sent a landing party ashore. The members were killed by Indians of the area, probably at the mouth of the Moclips River.

[10] Swindell, p. 425. Quoted from official proceedings at the Council in Walla Walla Valley between Governor Isaac Stevens, Superintendent of Indian Affairs, Washington Territory, and Joel Palmer, Superintendent of Indian Affairs, Oregon Territory, during part of May and June 1855. Most historians refer to Steachas. It appears the "e" was left out in the copied material.
[11] Whitebrook, passim.

In 1778 Captain James Cook of England anchored in Nootka Sound, which he named, and traded with the Indians there. Cook observed and named Cape Flattery, but bad weather prevented him from entering the Strait of Juan de Fuca which leads to Puget Sound. The strait remained unexplored for more than another decade, when the Spanish Quimper expedition entered it in 1790. Manuel Quimper reported a number of encounters with Indians, some of which reflect a high degree of communication and cooperation. On June 30, at what is probably the present Royal Roads, near Victoria, B.C., he wrote:

After having made them some presents I asked them if there was a channel towards the east part of the strait. They answered with entirely understandable signs, that there was a large and wide one which trended somewhat towards the northwest, and that at the end of the range of mountains on the south coast there was another like it. They made a sign that this trended towards the southwest.[12]

Indians of present-day Dungeness Bay were friendly and generous to Quimper's expedition.[13] He took possession of Clallam Bay for Spain on July 8, 1790. The last Spanish expedition to explore the peninsula, that of Juan Francisco de Eliza, left a trading base at Nootka on May 4, 1791.

Russians had begun exploring the coast from the north much earlier, establishing trading posts in Alaska. Vitus Bering, a Dane sailing for Russia, on his second expedition in 1741 brought back furs from the Aleutian Islands and stimulated interest in fur trading. Russian traders, called *promyshleniki,* lived among the Indians with whom they traded. This position,

---

[12] Diary of Manuel Quimper, Archivo General, Mexico; trans. Henry B. Wagner, *Spanish Explorations in the Strait of Juan de Fuca* (Santa Ana, Calif., 1933), p. 105; quoted in Whitebrook, p. 56.
[13] Whitebrook, pp. 58, 61.

combined with fair treatment, put the Russians in a position to gain considerably in the fur trade. George Vancouver observed that "they appear to maintain their influence not by fear, as the conquerers [sic], but by having found the way to their hearts, and by securing an affectionate regard." [14]

When Captain Cook's *Voyage to the North Pacific Ocean* was published in 1784, describing the fabulous prices received in China for sea otter pelts, the rush to enter the fur trade began. Ships of all nations converged on the coast in a fiercely competitive exploitation of the sea otter. The trade was at its height from 1780 to 1790.

Predictably, conflicts arose among the several countries over jurisdiction of these lands. Don Esteban José Martinez, Spanish commandant of Nootka, seized the British ship *Iphegenia* in May 1789, later releasing her. In June he seized the *Northwest American,* then the *Argonaut,* and still later the *Princess Royal.* Martinez sent the commandeered vessels and prisoners to San Blas, New Spain. This treatment of ships of other nations led to the Nootka Sound Controversy, settled by a compromise which assured the English free access to the Northwest Coast.[15] Vancouver spent two years (1792 to 1794) exploring the Northwest Coast while awaiting word, which never came, to carry out the articles of compromise. They were finally implemented in 1795 by two newly assigned representatives of Spain and Britain.

Indiscriminate slaughtering of the sea otter,[16] which led to their near-extinction, together with a change in fashions, caused

---

[14] George Vancouver, *Voyage to the North Pacific Ocean* (1784), III, 199; quoted in Whitebrook, p. 41.

[15] Whitebrook, p. 35.

[16] The near extermination of the sea otter occurred some years before the buffalo was threatened. So almost the first appearance of white men on the Northwest Coast brought with it efficient and heedless destruction of a part of what they found. Fortunately the killing was not quite complete. A few isolated groups of sea otter survived, and under protection this unique and charming animal has been able to re-establish itself.

the trade in otter pelts to decline after 1821.[17] At the same time that the pressures from the sea were beginning to diminish, Americans and British were beginning to push overland from the east. Lewis and Clark reached the Columbia River in 1805. Five years later the Spokane House was built in the eastern part of what is now the state of Washington.

The competing fur companies were instrumental in opening the Oregon territory to non-Indians. The Astoria Company was formed in 1811–12 and built a trading post at the mouth of the Columbia River for the Pacific Fur Company. However, the Astoria Company found it was in competition with the Canadian North West Company, which was already doing business with many of the inland tribes. In 1813 the Americans sold all their interests on the Columbia to representatives of the North West Company, temporarily abandoning the area to the Canadians.[18] American fur traders did not return until 1824.[19]

Early in the nineteenth century Spain, Russia, Great Britain, and the United States reached agreements about the "Oregon Country." Spain in 1819 and Russia in 1824–25 accepted boundary adjustments under which they withdrew from the Columbia River drainage. In 1818 the United States and Great Britain signed a ten-year agreement which permitted citizens of either country to settle in the area without impairing the claims of the other; the agreement remained in effect until the boundary line was finally established in 1846. The United States Congress began to consider the Oregon territory during the 1820's, vigorously supporting the rights of the United States.[20]

---

[17] William Sturgis, "Memoir," *Proceedings, Massachusetts Historical Society,* Vol. VII (1863–64); quoted in Whitebrook, p. 43.

[18] Alvin Josephy, *The Nez Perce Indians and the Opening of the Northwest* (New Haven, Conn.: Yale University Press, 1965), pp. 46–51 (hereafter cited as Josephy).

[19] *Ibid.,* pp. 64–65.

[20] William Compton Brown, *The Indian Side of the Story* (Spokane, Wash.: C. W. Hill, 1961), p. 15.

All of these activities and agreements were carried out without consultation with the Indian inhabitants.

SETTLERS AND MISSIONARIES

The Canadian North West Company merged in 1821 with its chief rival, the Hudson's Bay Company. Governor George Simpson of the Hudson's Bay Company reorganized the Columbia Department. Naming Dr. John McLoughlin as chief factor, the governor ordered him to construct a new post on the north bank of the Columbia, which they assumed would remain British. Opposite the mouth of the Willamette River Dr. McLoughlin built Fort Vancouver, thereby encouraging settlers to enter the fertile Willamette Valley to the south.[21] The settlement had disastrous effects on the Indians of the valley, leaving them debilitated by disease and exploitation, an example which was to prove instructive to the Indians of Puget Sound.

Ten years later Flathead and Nez Perce Indians from the plateaus between the Cascades and Rocky Mountains traveled to St. Louis to request missionary assistance. In 1833 Jason Lee, a Methodist missionary, went to the Flathead nation to "live with them—learn their language—preach Christ to them and . . . introduce schools, agriculture, and the arts of civilized life." [22] But he found the Flathead country too uncivilized and moved his ministry to the Willamette Valley.

Marcus Whitman, a doctor, and his wife established a Presbyterian mission near the present site of Walla Walla among the Cayuse in 1836. Two years later, two Catholic priests, Fathers François Blanchet and Modeste Demers, entered the Oregon country.[23]

That Fathers Demers and Blanchet were aggressively on the offensive against all the American Protestant missionaries in Ore-

[21] Josephy, pp. 65–66.
[22] David Lavender, *Land of Giants* (Garden City, N.Y.: Doubleday, 1958), p. 158 (hereafter cited as Lavender).
[23] Josephy, pp. 666–67.

gon . . . is made frankly clear by their correspondence. . . . The two priests, instructed to "take possession of those various places in the name of the Catholic religion," moved vigorously into one area after another where the protestants had been trying desparately [sic] to instruct the Indians in Christianity, treated the Protestants as quacks and fakes, and turned many of the Indians against them, often splitting bands and villages into factions and creating added difficulties and dangers for the American ministers. The conflict must be viewed today with recognition of the bitterness and intolerance that existed between many Catholic and Protestant missionaries in the 1830's and 1840's, and it must be pointed out . . . that most of the Protestant missionaries in Oregon were also riddled with bigotry, and fought back against the priests in kind.[24]

During the 1830's, the Hudson's Bay Company retained major economic control of the Oregon territory. The balance was tipped by the "Great Emigration" of settlers along the Oregon Trail in 1843. The Protestant missionaries in the Oregon country seem to have been ambivalent in weighing their duty to Indians and their desire to see the country settled by people of their own kind. Whitman gave considerable time and effort to furthering the "Great Emigration." [25] Another missionary, Elkanah Walker, devoted a few afterthoughts to the Indians:

It seems the only [way] they can be saved from being destroyed from the face of the earth is by their yielding to the control of the whites, and nothing will induce them to do this but a cordial reception of the gospel, and how can this be done without the labors of the christian [sic] missionary.[26]

---

[24] Josephy, p. 672. See also Carl Landerholm, ed., *Notices and Voyages of the Famed Quebec Mission to the Pacific Northwest, 1838–1847*, Oregon Historical Society (Portland, Ore.: Champoeg Press, 1956), pp. 17, 18, 21, 22, 94.

[25] Lavender, p. 234.

[26] Paul C. Phillips, ed., "The Oregon Missions as Shown in the Walker Letters, 1839–1851," in *Frontier Omnibus*, ed. John W. Hakola (Missoula, Mont.: Montana State University, 1962), pp. 105–11; cited in Josephy, pp. 222–23.

The emigration of 1843 may have numbered not more than a thousand people, but it was only the beginning. With no established national sovereignty, the settlers found it necessary to set up a provisional government, which somehow survived the ensuing years of struggle between national, religious, and ethnic factions. In 1844 Polk was elected president of the United States on his slogan of "fifty-four forty or fight"; two years later a treaty settled the boundary between Great Britain and the United States at the latitude of 49°. In August 1848, Congress established the Oregon Territory.

HOSTILITIES

During these years the latent conflict between the missionaries and the interior Indian tribes burst into the open. Northwest Indians by now had learned what happened two decades earlier to the Delaware, Creek, and Seminole Indians, who had been driven into exile, and to the Cherokees on the "Trail of Tears" following the Indian Removal Act of 1830. A refugee Delaware Indian pointed out to them that the Indians in the Willamette Valley had nearly disappeared because of white men's diseases. In the summer of 1847 the camp of Peopeo Moxmox of the Walla Walla suffered an epidemic of measles which wiped out more than half the Cayuse tribe.[27]

Laws were imposed on the Indians. White officials hand-picked Indian leaders without regard for the internal disturbance this could cause in a tribe. The promise of justice in Indian-white conflicts was not carried out. When the son of Chief Peopeo Moxmox was murdered in California by a white man, the killer was not punished, the excuse being that United States jurisdiction did not extend into Mexican California.

Such practices increased the alarm of the Indians over the growing stream of settlers moving into the country. The con-

[27] Lavender, p. 261.

flict culminated with the destruction of the Whitman mission on November 29, 1847. The Indians "declared that Whitman had long been an abiding abomination in their midst; that they had patiently sought by peaceful means to induce him to leave, but to no avail, and that his obstinate persistence in remaining was what brought him to his fate." [28] Five hundred volunteer soldiers set out to take revenge:

The expedition caught no murderers. But the soldiers did serve their main purpose by preventing any general outbreak. They soundly whipped the Cayuses in the few skirmishes that developed; and in the process of marching back and forth across hundreds of miles of Indian territory they made a strong enough show so that the wavering tribes of the interior decided to listen to the overtures of the peace commission.[29]

Puget Sound remained a backwater during this period of conflict. The Indians welcomed the few settlers there for the trading opportunities they provided and for protection against the northern tribes. Ezra Meeker, who came to the Puget Sound area by oxcart in the early 1850's, wrote about the cordial reception of white men by the Indians: "The Indians, as a class, from the earliest settlements down to the time of making the treaties in 1854–55, evinced not only a willingness that the white man should come and enjoy the land with them, but were pleased to have them do so." [30]

Early in the decade of 1840–50 the Hudson's Bay Company established a dozen new trading posts on the pattern of Fort Vancouver. One was Fort Nisqually, located on the river that was the homeland of the Nisqually Indians and operated by the Puget Sound Agricultural Company, the local subsidiary of Hudson's Bay Company. The relations between the Indians and

[28] Brown, *The Indian Side,* p. 53.
[29] Lavender, p. 266.
[30] Ezra Meeker, *Pioneer Reminiscences of Puget Sound and the Tragedy of Leschi* (Seattle, Wash.: Lowman & Hanford, 1905), p. 214.

the "King George men" were close and cooperative, in contrast to those with the "Bostons." Some of the Nisquallys, including Leschi who later led the uprising of 1855, took up farming under the guidance of the trading post.

American migration to the Northwest was temporarily slowed by the gold rush in California. As late as 1850 less than five hundred whites lived in the Puget Sound area.[31] However, the Oregon Donation Land Act of September 27, 1850, again stimulated rapid settlement. The law provided that each adult United States citizen could receive 320 acres and made it possible for a man and wife to receive 320 acres apiece. Prior to this time Congress had followed a policy of recognizing Indian title to land, but the Indian claims had not yet been extinguished before the Land Act was passed and the settlers began to move in. The ground was thus laid for future trouble.

The same year Congress passed an Indian Treaty Act which authorized the purchase of the lands from the various Northwest Coast tribes, and the removal of the Indians to areas which were not wanted by settlers. Anson Dart was appointed to negotiate with the Indians. From 1851 to 1853 he arranged treaties with the tribes of the Willamette Valley.

The results did not reassure the Indians. White settlers moved onto the lands immediately without waiting for the treaties to be ratified. In the disputes which followed, the white treaty commissioners who tried to resolve them proposed terms unacceptable to the Indians. The Indians were usually willing to sell a portion of their land but insisted on retaining some for their own use. All Indians opposed moving the tribes from the west side of the Cascades to the east, those on the west because they did not want to go to the strange dry land where canoes were useless and horses a necessity, and those on the east because they feared the diseases common on the coast.

In the impasse the commissioners disregarded their instructions

[31] Lavender, p. 283.

from Washington and between 1851 and 1853 made treaties with a number of tribes in the Willamette Valley and along the Coast, in which the Indians ceded most of their lands but retained portions on which they could continue to dwell. . . . When the new treaties reached Washington, the Commissioner of Indian Affairs noted their deviation from what had been established Indian policy since the removal of the Southeastern tribes. The provision to allow the Northwestern Indians to retain sovereignty over a portion of their country, which would be reserved for their exclusive use, seemed to inaugurate a new policy, "the practical operation of which could not be foreseen," and the Indian Bureau sent the treaties to Congress without either recommendation or opposition. In turn, the Senate failed to ratify them, and the Bureau advised its Superintendent in Oregon to enter into no more treaties, unless forced to do so to preserve peace.[32]

The conflicts left unresolved by the failure of the treaties erupted into violence in southern Oregon and northern California. Some of the regular army, in particular General John Ellis Wool, came to the conclusion that the Indians needed protection from the settlers more than the settlers needed protection from the Indians. A United States Army investigation found the slaying and scalping of forty defenseless Modocs by the Oregon Mounted Volunteers a wanton massacre.[33] The Volunteers disputed the finding. "An emergency treaty brought the conflict to a temporary halt, but the ruthless violation of the Indians' rights by the miners served to heighten the fears of many other tribes on the western side of the Cascades." [34]

Although the Indians of Puget Sound did not participate in these events, they learned their first lessons in the governmental processes of the "Bostons." They were also feeling the pressure from an increasing white population, which numbered several thousand by the end of 1852. It was only a matter of time before new conflicts opened.

[32] Josephy, pp. 286–87. See also Francis Haines, "Problems of Indian Policy," *Pacific Northwest Quarterly*, XLI (July 1950), 203–12.
[33] Lavender, pp. 279–80.
[34] Josephy, p. 287.

II | Treaties and Reservations: 1854–57

Washington became a territory of the United States on March 2, 1853, without consultation with the Indians who still held title to most of the land. In that same month Congress authorized funds for the surveying of routes for a proposed transcontinental railroad. Isaac Ingalls Stevens had been appointed to serve both as governor and as superintendent of Indian affairs in the new territory, and he now received the assignment to survey the northernmost of the possible railway routes on his way there. A man of driving personality, he was to become the key figure in the development of Washington territory in the 1850's.

Still a young man of 35, a dynamo of energy who moved with speed and decisiveness, Stevens saw all three of his jobs complementing each other toward a single grand end. As a governor who would build up the population and prosperity of his territory, he was intent on winning Congressional approval for a railroad that would terminate at Puget Sound. . . . He bore no ill will against Indians, and even fancied that he admired and respected them. But as an instrument of advancing American civilization he had a job to carry out, and with a flair for publicity he expected to win notice in the East for what he would achieve. As Super-

18

intendent of Indian Affairs he would try to treat the Indians justly and peaceably, but he was determined to bend them to his wishes.[1]

The need to resolve the problems of Indian land rights was critical in both Washington and Oregon when Stevens took office as superintendent. Indian lands were rapidly being taken by whites, encouraged by the Oregon Donation Land Act. However, the prosperity of the country had been delayed by the uncertainty over peace with the Indians. Hostilities were already occurring because of the lack of treaties, and it was desired to "pacify" the Indians who lived along the proposed railroad routes. Joel Palmer, superintendent of Indian Affairs in Oregon, requested treaties with Indians on both sides of the mountains in this same year.[2]

When Stevens reached Washington in 1853, he acted vigorously to extinguish Indian ownership to the territory. The speed with which he pushed settlements with the inhabitants was remarkable. Six thousand Puget Sound Indians were involved in a period of a few months. Treaties signed at Medicine Creek, Point Elliott, Point No Point, Neah Bay, and Quinault River ceded most of the Puget Sound area and the Olympic Peninsula to the United States.[3] In less than a year "Governor Stevens had made treaties with more than seventeen thousand Indians and in doing so had extinguished the Indian title to more than one hundred thousand square miles [64 million acres] of land now making up much of the territory of Washington, Idaho, and Montana."[4] According to one writer, "the dazed Indians

[1] Josephy, *The Nez Perce Indians,* p. 293.
[2] C. F. Coan, "The Adoption of the Reservation Policy in the Pacific Northwest, 1853–55," *Oregon Historical Quarterly,* XXIII (March 1922), 6.
[3] See Maps—Washington 1 & 2, Northwest, Admiralty Inlet, in C. C. Royce, *Indian Policy of the United States and Indian Land Cessions in the United States,* Bureau of Ethnology, 18th Annual Report (Wash., D.C., 1899).
[4] Herbert Hunt and Floyd Kaylor, *Washington, West of the Cascades* (3 vols.; Chicago: S. J. Clarke, 1917), I, 143.

reserved less than 6,000,000 acres for themselves." Some feared that the palefaces "would push us into the ocean." [5]

A few months before he took action, Governor Stevens had outlined the goals he sought in treaties. In order to prepare the Indians to become citizens, they should have relocation areas of good land, enough to allow each family head a homestead; they should be supplied with farmers to instruct them in agriculture, although they should not be excluded from their fisheries; many bands should be concentrated on one reservation in order that control over them might be more effective; and the authority of the chiefs should be strengthened so they could be held responsible to the government for the conduct of their people. The policy was based on the assumption that the homestead farming pattern would encourage Indians to disappear into the American melting pot within the course of a generation of federal assistance (the twenty years specified in the treaties for payments on the purchase price of the land).[6]

William Brown appears justified in writing that "haste, high pressure, and no little chicanery on the part of the whites was predominant throughout the meetings from start to finish." [7] The minutes of the treaty conferences show that Stevens intended in one way or another to get signatures on his treaties as he dictated them. He met any reluctance to give up cherished homeland for reservation areas by reminding the Indians of trouble with "bad" white men who came to harm them. He pointed out that only with several tribes together on a small area of land could the Great Father offer them protection.

The original plan of the governor was to remove the various tribes and bands in the Northwest to one or two large relocation areas—not "reservations" in the sense of reserved portions

[5] Eva Anderson, *Chief Seattle* (Caldwell, Idaho: Caxton Printers, 1943), p. 223.
[6] See also Coan, "Adoption of Reservation Policy," pp. 13–14.
[7] Brown, *The Indian Side of the Story*, p. 64.

of their own land, but rather other land to which they would be relocated. The record of the negotiations at Gray's Harbor clearly shows his intent. Stevens told the Indians that the Great Father would choose a place for them. An Indian spokesman objected: "That little creek was the only place he cared for, as he always got his salmon there and he liked the place." Stevens replied, "If we gave you all the little spots you want, the great Father could not be your Father, though he desires to be so, for he could not take care of you." The representative of the Great Father in Washington would pick a spot and there he would protect the Indians; if they stayed where they were they would be swept away.[8]

Like Dart and Palmer before him, Stevens discovered that the Indians, though recognizing the necessity for selling much of their country, were adamant against being moved away from it, and refused to accept centralized reservations. A basic misunderstanding during the treaty-making lay in the differing concepts about land. White culture regarded it as a commodity to be owned, fenced, bought, and sold. To the Indians land was part of a religious heritage, not a chattel and not an article of trade. Stevens acceded to the reserving by tribes of a portion of their homeland. He did not achieve the degree of concentration he had desired, though it was more than the Indians wished.

The importance of the fish to the Indians seems to have impressed Stevens. He did not intentionally reserve to the Indians any more rights than he thought necessary, but he understood that the one indispensable requirement for securing agreement of any kind from Pacific Northwest Indians was to assure their continued right to fish. That right was as valuable to them as their lives: "It was also thought necessary to allow them to fish at all accustomed places, since this would not in any manner

---

[8] Council between Stevens party and bands of Upper Chehalis, Lower Chehalis, Quinault, Lower Chinook, and Cowlitz, Feb. 27 to March 3, 1885; cited in Swindell, pp. 354–74.

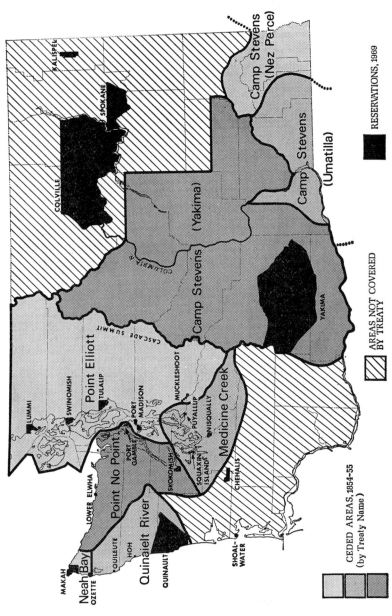

Map 1. *Areas ceded by treaties, Washington Territory*

CEDED AREAS, 1854-55
(by Treaty Name)

AREAS NOT COVERED
BY TREATY

RESERVATIONS, 1969

interfere with the rights of citizens, and was necessary for the Indians to obtain a subsistence." [9] An Indian spokesman said:

I hope the Governor will tell the Whites not to abuse the Indians as many are in the habit of doing, or ordering them to go away and knocking them down. We are willing to go up the Canal since we know we can fish elsewhere. We shall only leave there to get salmon, and when done fishing will return to our houses. I am glad to acknowledge you and the great father as our Father.[10]

No eager Indian agreement greeted even the first four treaties, which were signed with less protest than later ones. The Indians were not in such a hurry as the governor, and they were uneasy. The same tactics were used in each case—either they would let the Great Father choose the place or he would select it himself without asking them, "for it comes to that finally." [11]

Stevens insisted that the transactions take place in the Chinook jargon, a trade patois of about three hundred words from several Indian languages, with additions from English and French.[12] Colonel Benjamin F. Shaw was the interpreter. There is little doubt that he knew the jargon well, but some have questioned that he knew the Indian languages. Such a question is implied in the comment of Owen Bush of Stevens' staff:

I could talk the Indian languages, but Stevens did not seem to want anyone to interpret in their own tongue, and had that done in Chinook. Of course it was utterly impossible to explain the treaties to them in Chinook. Stevens wanted me to go into the war [which followed the treaty-signing], but I wouldn't do it. I know it was his bad management that brought on the war, and I wouldn't

[9] Council recorded at an evening session following the Treaty of Medicine Creek, signed Dec. 26, 1854, preparatory to further treaty negotiations with other Sound and Coast tribes; cited in Swindell, p. 330.
[10] Council between Stevens party and Clallams, Chemakums, etc., Jan. 25, 1855; cited in Swindell, p. 347.
[11] Cited in Swindell, p. 372.
[12] See Edward Harper Thomas, *Chinook: A History and a Dictionary* (Portland, Ore.: Metropolitan Press, 1935; reprinted by Binfords & Mort).

raise a gun against those people [Nisquallys] who had always been
so kind to us when we were weak and needy.[13]

Many, like Bush, and like Meeker who was quoting him, have
questioned the adequacy of Chinook (the jargon) for the proceedings. The questions of language and adequate interpretation were points raised in a claims case filed in 1926 in the
U.S. Court of Claims by the Duwamish and other tribes.[14] The
petition set forth

. . . that said Chinook jargon was used, and only capable of use,
in simple trade barter and simple transactions between those familiar with its words and use, and was wholly inadequate as a means
for communicating the terms of said treaty between the races and
persons present and entering into the same.[15]

The claimants' attorney, Arthur E. Griffin, stated in his brief,
"The interpreter did not understand the language of the Indians
or Indians the language of the whites." [16] An Indian witness,
Peter J. James, who considered himself to be fluent in the
Chinook jargon, testified: ". . . I don't hardly think you can
explain what you may call a business transaction. It would be
impossible to make a long stretch of a business transaction in
using the Chinook language." James testified further that only
forty-five to fifty words were in common use, and that the
treaty could not have been interpreted from English into
Chinook in such a way that the Indians would have understood it.[17] However, the findings of the Court of Claims in its
decision, rendered in 1934, were both that Colonel Shaw knew

[13] Meeker, *Pioneer Reminiscences,* p. 208.
[14] *Duwamish et al.* v. *U.S.A.,* 79 Court of Claims 530–613, June 4,
1934. The petitions, briefs, testimony, and other documents pertaining to
the case were separately printed in two volumes by Argus Press, Seattle.
Duwamish is also spelled Dwamish.
[15] Petition for the Claimants, *Duwamish et al.,* pp. 7–8 in Vol. I of
the documents printed by Argus Press (see n. 14 above).
[16] Attorney's Brief for the Claimants, *ibid.,* II, 902.
[17] *Ibid.,* pp. 713–14.

the Indian languages including the jargon and that the jargon was an adequate vehicle for the transactions.[18]

Whether or not either is literally true, in a wider sense the contention of the Indians and their attorney is surely accurate —neither the Indians nor the whites understood the language of the other.

TREATY OF MEDICINE CREEK

The Treaty of Medicine Creek, ceding the territory of the Nisquallys and Puyallups along with that of a number of other tribes and bands, was signed December 26, 1854. Altogether these tribes ceded to the United States about 2,240,000 acres for a price of $32,500 to be paid over a twenty-year period.

Article I describes the ceded lands, and Article II the three reservations of about 1,280 acres each which were reserved for the use and occupation of the tribes and bands which were party to the treaty. The Indians were expected to move within a year following ratification.

Article III secured to the Indians the continuing right to hunt and fish, without making reference to reservation boundaries:

ART. III. The right of taking fish at all usual and accustomed grounds and stations is further secured to said Indians in common with all citizens of the Territory, and of erecting temporary houses for the purpose of curing, together with the privilege of hunting, gathering roots and berries, and pasturing their horses on open and unclaimed lands: *Provided, however,* That they shall not take shell fish from any beds staked or cultivated by citizens, and that they shall alter all stallions not intended for breeding horses, and shall keep up and confine the latter.

Article VI was apparently written in the hope of reducing the size of the reservations.

ART. VI. The President may hereafter, when in his opinion the

[18] *Duwamish et al.,* pp. 536–37.

interests of the Territory may require, and the welfare of the said Indians be promoted, remove them from either or all of said reservations to such other suitable place or places within said Territory as he may deem fit, on remunerating them for their improvements and the expenses of their removal, or may consolidate them with other friendly tribes or bands. And he may further, at his discretion, cause the whole or any portion of the lands hereby reserved, or of such other land as may be selected in lieu thereof, to be surveyed into lots, and assign the same to such individuals or families as are willing to avail themselves of the privilege, and will locate on the same as a permanent home, on the same terms and subject to the same regulations as are provided in the sixth article of the treaty with the Omahas, so far as the same may be applicable. Any substantial improvements heretofore made by any Indian, and which he shall be compelled to abandon in consequence of this treaty, shall be valued under the direction of the President, and payment be made accordingly thereto.[19]

The treaty goes on to provide that the Indian signatories agree to be friendly to United States citizens, not to make war on other Indians except in self-defense, to accept the authority of an Indian agent, to forbid the sale or use of alcoholic beverages within the reservations, to free their slaves, not to trade with "foreign" Indians or allow them to live on their reservations without the consent of the agent. In return, the government agrees to establish a general district agency, to maintain a school for the children, to provide a smithy and carpenter's shop, to employ a smith, a carpenter, and a farmer to instruct the Indians in these occupations, and to provide the Indians with a physician.

The treaty-making commission had been organized December 7, 1854, with the major terms predrafted. On December 24, these terms were discussed with representatives of Nisqually, Puyallup, and at least seven other bands "who, for the pur-

[19] Full text of Treaty of Medicine Creek published by the Shorey Book Store, Seattle.

poses of this treaty, are to be regarded as one nation." On the following day the final wording was prepared; on December 26 it was read to the Indians and signed. According to the treaty minutes: "The treaty was then read Section by Section and explained to the Indians by the Interpreter and every opportunity given them to discuss it." [20]

During the negotiations, each chief was expected to make a map of his country so that one large map could be drawn up. Leschi of the Nisquallys is reported to have been so disturbed that he would not finish his map; it was only through the tact of George Gibbs, assistant to the governor, that the maps were prepared. Then the governor marked off the reservation sites: Squaxin Island for the Squaxins, the west part of Commencement Bay at the mouth of the Puyallup River for the Puyallups, and for the Nisquallys an area about a mile west of the mouth of the Nisqually River. There were serious drawbacks to both the Puyallup and the Nisqually reservations, particularly the Nisqually—it was a rough, rocky plain away from the all-important fishing waters. The land was not good even for pasture and certainly not for the farming the governor wished to institute. Gibbs was aghast at the plan, but Stevens was adamant. In seeking an explanation, Meeker wrote: "Governor Stevens was intoxicated and unfit for transacting business while making these treaties." He cited as evidence a letter written by Gibbs May 30, 1857, and published over his signature in the *Washington Republican,* June 5, 1857.[21] Later, Leschi and some other chiefs who were present at the signing declared that their

[20] Treaty minutes, Medicine Creek Signing Day, Dec. 26, 1854; cited in Swindell, p. 328.

[21] Meeker, *Pioneer Reminiscences,* pp. 258, 259. It should be noted also that Meeker (pp. 257–62) credits Stevens with sound impulse "while acting dispassionately and without excitement" and with commitment to constructive policy, but notes his failure to adhere to this policy for several reasons that were rooted both in his personality and in the extent of the duties assigned to him.

signatures were forged, that they had not signed. It is now too late to determine whether or not the thumbprint next to Leschi's name is his.[22]

The Treaty of Point Elliott, signed at Muk-il-teo, included many ancestors of the present-day Muckleshoot tribe. About 2,300 Indians convened on January 9, 1855, and two weeks later the treaty was signed. The terms were similar to those of the Treaty of Medicine Creek; the article relating to fishing is almost identical:

ART. V. The right of taking fish at usual and accustomed grounds and stations is further secured to said Indians in common with all citizens of the Territory, and of erecting temporary houses for the purpose of curing, together with the privilege of hunting and gathering roots and berries on open and unclaimed lands; provided, however, that they shall not take shell fish from any beds staked or cultivated by citizens.

Several areas of land, comprising altogether about forty sections, were reserved to the Indians.[23]

The major Indian figure at Point Elliott, Chief Sealth (Seattle) of the Duwamish, was dedicated to peaceful coexistence with non-Indians even though he saw with increasing clarity the tragedy befalling his people. His speech to Governor Stevens, an attempt to bridge the chasm between two cultures, is worth quoting:

Yonder sky that has wept tears of compassion upon my people for centuries untold, and which to us appears changeless and eternal,

[22] See C. A. Snowden, *History of Washington* (4 vols.; New York: Century History Co., 1909), III, 272. For other accounts of the treaty signing, see Meeker, *Pioneer Reminiscences,* pp. 240–42 and 258–61; and Della Gould Emmons, *Leschi of the Nisquallys* (Minneapolis: Denison, 1965), p. 186 (a historical novel).

[23] Full text of Treaty of Point Elliott published by the Shorey Book Store, Seattle.

may change. Today is fair. Tomorrow it may be overcast with clouds. My words are like the stars that never change. Whatever Seattle says the great chief at Washington can rely upon with as much certainty as he can upon the return of the sun or the seasons. The White Chief says that Big Chief at Washington sends us greetings of friendship and good will. This is kind of him for we know he has little need of our friendship in return. His people are many. They are like the grass that covers vast prairies. My people are few. They resemble the scattering trees of a storm-swept plain. The Great—and I presume—good White Chief sends us word that he wishes to buy our lands but is willing to allow us enough to live comfortably. This indeed appears just, even generous, for the Red Man no longer has rights that he need respect, and the offer may be wise also, as we are no longer in need of an extensive country. . . . I will not dwell on, nor mourn over, our untimely decay, nor reproach our paleface brothers with hastening it, as we too may have been somewhat to blame.

Youth is impulsive. When our young men grow angry at some real or imaginary wrong, and disfigure their faces with black paint, it denotes that their hearts are black, and then they are often cruel and relentless, and our old men and old women are unable to restrain them. Thus it has ever been. Thus it was when the white men first began to push our forefathers further westward. But let us hope that the hostilities between us never return. We would have everything to lose and nothing to gain. Revenge by young braves is considered gain, even at the cost of their own lives, but old men who stay at home in times of war, and mothers who have sons to lose, know better.

Our good father at Washington—for I presume he is now our father as well as yours, since King George has moved his boundaries further north—our great and good father, I say, sends us word that if we do as he desires he will protect us. His brave warriors will be to us a bristling wall of strength, and his wonderful ships of war will fill our harbors so that our ancient enemies far to the northward—the Hidas and Timpsions, will cease to frighten our women, children and old men. Then in reality will he be our father and we his children. But can that ever be? Your God is not our God! Your God loves your people and hates mine. He folds his strong protecting arms lovingly about the pale face and leads him by the hand as a father leads his infant son—but

He has forsaken His red children—if they are really His. Our God, the Great Spirit, seems also to have forsaken us. Your God makes your people wax strong every day. Soon they will fill all the land. Our people are ebbing away like a rapidly receding tide that will never return. The white man's God can not love our people or He would protect them. They seem to be orphans who can look nowhere for help. How then can we be brothers? How can your God become our God and renew our prosperity and awaken in us dreams of returning greatness. If we have a common Heavenly Father He must be partial—for He came to his pale-face children. We never saw Him. He gave you laws but had no words for His red children whose teeming multitudes once filled this vast continent as stars fill the firmament. No. We are two distinct races with separate origins and separate destinies. There is little in common between us.

To us the ashes of our ancestors are sacred and their resting place is hallowed ground. You wander far from the graves of your ancestors and seemingly without regret. Your religion was written upon tables of stone by the iron finger of your God so that you could not forget. The Red Man could never comprehend nor remember it. Our religion is the traditions of our ancestors—the dreams of our old men, given them in solemn hours of night by the Great Spirit; and the visions of our sachems; and it is written in the hearts of our people.

Your dead cease to love you and the land of their nativity as soon as they pass the portals of the tomb and wander beyond the stars. They soon are forgotten and never return. Our dead never forget the beautiful world that gave them being. . . .

Day and night cannot dwell together. The Red Man has ever fled the approach of the White Man as morning mist flees before the rising sun.

However, your proposition seems fair, and I think that my people will accept it and will retire to the reservation you offer them. Then we will dwell apart in peace for the words of the Great White Chief seem to be the voice of Nature speaking to my people out of dense darkness.

It matters little where we pass the remnant of our days. They will not be many. . . .

A few more moons. A few more winters—and not one of the descendants of the mighty hosts that once moved over this broad land or lived in happy homes, protected by the Great Spirit, will remain to mourn over the graves of a people—once more powerful and hopeful than yours. But why should I mourn at the untimely fate of my people? Tribe follows tribe, and nation follows nation, like the waves of the sea. It is the order of nature, and regret is useless. Your time of decay may be distant—but it will surely come, for even the White Man whose God walked and talked with him as friend with friend, can not be exempt from the common destiny. We may be brothers after all. We will see.

We will ponder your proposition, and when we decide we will let you know. But should we accept it, I here and now make this condition—that we will not be denied the privilege without molestation of visiting at any time the tombs of our ancestors, friends and children. Every part of this soil is sacred in the estimation of my people. Every hillside, every valley, every plain and grove, has been hallowed by some sad or happy event in days long vanished . . . the very dust upon which you now stand responds more lovingly to their footsteps than to yours, because it is rich with the dust of our ancestors and our bare feet are conscious of the sympathetic touch . . . even the little children who lived here and rejoiced here for a brief season, still love these sombre solitudes and at eventide they grow shadowy of returning spirits. And when the last Red Man shall have perished, and the memory of my tribe shall have become a myth among the white man, these shores will swarm with the invisible dead of my tribe, and when your children's children think themselves alone in the field, the store, the shop, upon the highway, or in the silence of the pathless woods, they will not be alone. . . . At night when the streets of your cities and villages are silent and you think them deserted, they will throng with the returning hosts that once filled them and still love this beautiful land. The White Man will never be alone.

Let him be just and deal kindly with my people, for the dead are not powerless. Dead—I say? There is no death. Only a change of worlds.[24]

Those most dissatisfied with the treaty were the inland groups,

---

[24] Chief Sealth, speech at signing of Treaty of Point Elliott, on Jan. 22, 1855; in Bagley, "Chief Seattle and Angeline," *Washington Historical Quarterly*, XXI (Oct. 1931), 243–75.

particularly the bands of the White and Green rivers, for they had been lumped together with the saltwater people of the lower Duwamish.[25] Although they all belonged to the Duwamish drainage, they were not united in feeling as were the groups which belonged to smaller drainages. The White and Green river people, in fact, thought of the saltwater people as traditionally hostile, and they were most unwilling to be placed in the homeland of their enemies and with them on a saltwater reservation. The attempted consolidation increased antiwhite hostilities.

OTHER TREATIES

While Stevens viewed the treaties as models of justice, the Puget Sound Indians were bitter with second thoughts. However, there was no time for reconsideration. Settlers moved quickly onto the lands even though the treaties were not supposed to go into effect until they had been ratified by Congress. The Indians had no right, by the treaties, to defend themselves, and were subject to much persecution by whites.

Chiefs who had concluded the agreements found themselves unpopular. Some followed Leschi's lead and declared that their purported signatures were forgeries. Others insisted that they had not understood the terms, which is quite possible.[26]

The tribes in the rest of Washington observed the situation with dread and determined to resist. Remaining groups on the Olympic Peninsula at first rebuffed Stevens, but his rough tactics

---

[25] Smith, *Puyallup-Nisqually*, pp. 32–33. Until 1906 the White River, which is now a tributary of the Puyallup, was a part of the Duwamish system as a tributary of the Green River. In that year, during a great storm and freshet (aided by some residents of the valley who dynamited a log jam and part of a bluff to facilitate the change), the White broke over the short distance lying between it and a small tributary of the Puyallup known as the Stuck River. The change was made permanent by diking and other channel control efforts. This part of the river, which flows through intensively cultivated agricultural and expanding industrial areas, is still usually called the Stuck River.

[26] Lavender, p. 299.

eventually gained their agreement to his terms. The last treaty in the area, the Quinault River Treaty, was signed in 1856. No treaties were concluded in the most southwestern part of the territory.

After the Puget Sound treaties, Stevens' envoys, A. J. Bolon, R. H. Lansdale, and James Doty, traveled among the tribes east of the Cascades—Yakima, Sahaptin, Salish, Shoshoni, Nez Perce, Wallawalla, Cayuse, Spokan, and Umatilla—and persuaded them to attend a treaty council. It opened May 29, 1855. The tribes were wary, and feared the promises being made to them in words like those of Joel Palmer:

We did not come here to scare you or to drive you away, but we came here to talk to you like men . . . if we enter into a treaty now we can select a good country for you; but if we wait till the country is filled up with whites, where will we find such a place? . . . If we make a treaty with you . . . you can rely on all its provisions being carried out strictly.[27]

The white men's determination to gain the Indians' land immediately was expressed in a passage in Stevens' diary:

A few determined spirits, if not controlled, might embolden all not well disposed, and defeat the negotiations. Should this spirit be shown, they must be seized; the well affected would then govern in the deliberations, and I anticipate little or no difficulty in negotiating.[28]

The commissioners had planned to lump Spokans, Cayuses, Wallawallas, Umatillas, and Nez Perces together in the Nez Perce country, and to place on a single reservation in the Yakima country all the tribes and bands along the Columbia River from The Dalles on the south to the Okanogan and Colville valleys on the north. Their purpose was to get the

---

[27] Josephy, pp. 321–22.
[28] Diary of I. I. Stevens, from Hazard Stevens, *The Life of Isaac Ingalls Stevens* (2 vols.; Boston: Houghton Mifflin, 1900), II, 29; quoted in Josephy, p. 315.

Indians off the land wanted by settlers or needed for the build-
ing of railroads. Spokesmen for the Wallawallas, Cayuses, and
Umatillas were won over after these tribes were offered a
separate place in the Umatilla Valley. Kamiakin and the
Yakimas held out. At this point Chief Looking Glass of the Nez
Perce arrived and "whipped scorn that night on the headmen
who had agreed to sign the treaty." Stevens ignored Looking
Glass, and Peopeo Moxmox eventually signed. Then came
Chief Lawyer of the Nez Perce and after him the other Nez
Perce chiefs, Looking Glass and Joseph; then the Cayuses. The
Yakima chiefs signed, but Kamiakin maintained that he had
only made a pledge of friendship.

Negotiations began with Flathead, Pend d'Oreille, and Kute-
nai on July 7. These tribes, long under the influence of
Christianity, were initially friendly to whites. But Stevens in his
haste made poor choices of areas, filling the Indians with bitterness. The Flathead leader Moses spoke for many when he
said, "You have pulled all my wings off."

In October Stevens held his council with the Blackfeet and
other tribes. For once the course was smooth, and on the
second day the tribes signed.

Stevens' sense of satisfaction was soon shattered. While he
was treating with tribes still further east, war had exploded in
both the Puget Sound region and eastern Washington.[29] The
Indians were dissatisfied not only with the treaties themselves
and the way they had been negotiated, but also with the flagrant
violations of their terms by white settlers. The Indians had been
promised that they would not have to move until the treaties
were ratified, perhaps as long as two years. However:

On June 23, 1885, only twelve days after the treaties had been
signed, the *Oregon Weekly Times* carried an article signed by
Stevens and Palmer, describing the regions ceded by the Indians

[29] The above discussion is based on Josephy, pp. 324, 327–28, 331,
339–40, 342, 343.

and announcing that "By an express provision of the treaty the country embraced in these cessions and not included in the reservation is open to settlement, excepting that the Indians are secured in the possession of their buildings and implements till removal to the reservation. This notice is published for the benefit of the public. . . . Oregon and Washington papers please copy." [30]

The feud between the Americans and the Hudson's Bay Company exacerbated the hostilities. In the Puget Sound area many of the Indians sided with the company. The "King George men" had come to trade, and for many years the Nisqually people had been in close cooperation with the Hudson's Bay post at Fort Nisqually. But the "Bostons" had come to take their land. The British publicly stated that Stevens had been responsible for the Indian trouble, as well as for the disruption of their own trade, in violation of the Treaty of 1846.[31]

Leschi was convinced that the whites would push all the Indians into "Polakly Illahe," a reservation of eternal gloom. Here the white men would torture them and sully all the lands and waters of the Indians, and they would die. He preached immediate war throughout the land—kill the whites before they become too many.[32]

Sporadic outbreaks flared in both the Puget Sound and the country east of the Cascades. On January 26, 1855, Leschi and the Nisquallys, with some Klickitats, initiated an attack on the city of Seattle, but they were driven off by cannon fire from a warship in the harbor. Chief Nelson of the Muckleshoots led the so-called White River Massacre.[33] Major Granville G. Haller's troops suffered a major defeat near the Toppenish River in early October 1855. When further skirmishes occurred in the

---

[30] *Ibid.*, pp. 337–38.

[31] *Ibid.*, p. 358.

[32] Snowden, *History*, p. 324.

[33] Evidence indicates that the Muckleshoots were not called by this name until after the move onto the reservation; see later discussion in this chapter.

Puget Sound, the white settlers believed that it was the start of an organized general uprising. Both regular troops and state militia, including units of the Oregon Mounted Volunteers and of volunteers from Washington, moved against Indians all over the region. Because of disagreements between the regulars and the militia, however, their actions were not coordinated.[34] Stevens was in bitter conflict with General John E. Wool, who was commander of the Department of the Pacific of the United States Army.

[Wool] had heard of the murder of Peopeo Moxmox [while a prisoner of the Oregon volunteers, taken in violation of a flag of truce] and the revolting indignities to his corpse, as well as other atrocities committed by the volunteers against Indians in the interior, and he condemned those actions to Stevens and in reports to Washington, stating in addition that their net result was to turn friendly and neutral Indians into hostiles. . . . Repeatedly, Wool argued that if the volunteers stopped provoking the Indians . . . the Indians would again become peaceful. . . . This so-called "peace policy" incurred the further wrath of Stevens and the settlers, who felt that the Indians had to be rendered powerless.[35]

The territorial governments of Oregon and Washington protested against Wool, and he was eventually replaced. Nevertheless, because of his influence, Congress delayed the ratification of all treaties except that of Medicine Creek until hostilities were ended. The Treaty of Medicine Creek was ratified on March 3, 1855, but the Treaty of Point Elliott not until March 8, 1859.

Not all the Indians were in agreement on war. Sealth rebuffed Leschi's appeal for help. However, the groups which had suffered most from treaty provisions—the Nisquallys and some ancestors of the present-day Muckleshoots—participated in hostilities. They could not win. By the middle of March 1856,

[34] Josephy, pp. 347–48.
[35] *Ibid.*, p. 362.

Stevens had succeeded in smashing the Indian war bands, and within a short time had executed some of their leaders.[36] Some headmen with their families fled across the mountains, and some died in the forests and swamps, resisting to the last.

FOX ISLAND COUNCIL

During the hostilities most noncombatant Indians stayed on Fox Island near Tacoma. In August 1856 Governor Stevens went to Fox Island and negotiated changes in the Nisqually and Puyallup reservation areas and the establishment of the Muckleshoot reservation. The Indians seemed to think the council was another treaty-making, but there is no evidence of formal treaty proceedings. Stevens negotiated the changes under the authority granted by Article VI of the Treaty of Medicine Creek, and recommended that the President put them into effect by executive order. A letter from George T. Manypenny, commissioner of Indian affairs, to Secretary of the Interior R. McClelland, dated January 19, 1857, detailed the recommended changes with no reference to the hostilities. Ironically, the changes set right most of the grievances which had originally contributed to the outbreak.

Sir: The treaty negotiated on the 29th [*sic*] of December, 1854, with certain bands of Nisqually, Puyallup, and other Indians of Puget's Sound, Washington Territory (article 2), provided for the establishment of reservations for the colonization of Indians, as follows: (1) The small island called Klah-chemin. (2) A square tract containing two sections near the mouth of the She-nah-nam Creek. (3) Two sections on the south side of Commencement Bay.

The sixth article of the treaty gives the President authority to remove the Indians from those locations to other suitable places within Washington Territory, or to consolidate them with friendly bands.

So far as this office is advised a permanent settlement of the Indians has not yet been effected under the treaty. Governor Stevens has formed the opinion that the locations named in the

[36] *Ibid.*, pp. 362–63.

first article of the treaty were not altogether suitable for the purpose of establishing Indian colonies. One objection was that they are not sufficiently extensive. He reported that 750 Indians had been collected from the various bands for settlement.

I have the honor now to submit for your consideration and action of the President, should you deem it necessary and proper, a report recently received from Governor Stevens, dated December 5, 1856, with the reports and maps therewith, and as therein stated, from which it will be observed that he has arranged a plan of colonization which involves the assignment of a much greater quantity of land to the Indians, under the sixth article of the treaty, than was named in the first article. He proposes the enlargement of the Puyallup Reserve at the south end of Commencement Bay to accommodate 500 Indians; the change in the location and enlargement of the Nisqually Reserve, and the establishment of a new location, Muckleshoot Prairie, where there is a military station that is about to be abandoned.

The quantity of land he proposes to assign is not, in my opinion, too great for the settlement of the number of Indians he reports for colonization; and as the governor recommends the approval of these locations and reports that the Indians assent thereto, I would respectfully suggest that they be approved by the President, my opinion being that, should it be found practicable hereafter to consolidate the bands for whom these reserves are intended or to unite other bands of Indians on the same reserves, the authority to effect such objects will still remain with the President under the sixth article of the treaty.[37]

The letter reached President Franklin Pierce the next day. He acted immediately with an executive order which carried out the recommended changes.[38] Creation of the Muckleshoot reservation settled the difficulty of attempting to amalgamate the inland and saltwater peoples of the Duwamish drainage.[39]

[37] In Charles J. Kappler, *Indian Laws and Treaties* (3 vols.; Wash., D.C.: U.S. Govt. Printing Office, 1903), I, 919.
[38] It is ironic that Article VI of the treaty, apparently included in the hope of reducing the size of the reservations, was immediately employed to enlarge two and create a third.
[39] Smith, *Puyallup-Nisqually*, pp. 32–33. The bands placed on the Muckleshoot reservation were parties to the Treaty of Point Elliott, but

That the purpose of the changes was primarily to "pacify" the tribes which had taken up arms is indicated by the very changes made.

Although the interior tribes were not "pacified" until 1858, hostilities in the Puget Sound were concluded with the capture of Leschi in the fall of 1856. He was accused of the murder of a white man at the beginning of hostilities, and was promptly tried. The jury deadlocked 10-2 for conviction.[40] In a second trial several months later he was found guilty.

Until 1855 Leschi had always been friendly to non-Indians, and a number of his white friends of the United States Army and Hudson's Bay Company worked feverishly to save him. They felt that even if Leschi had killed the man, it had been an act of war, not murder. Chief Sealth, too, tried to save Leschi, saying, "Leschi rebelled against bad treaty. White man gives Leschi's people new treaty. White man must know, in his heart, that first treaty was unfair. Or why give new treaty?" [41] Later great doubt was raised as to whether he had actually done the killing. But to the settlers Leschi had become the symbol of the "rebellion," and he was hanged February 19, 1858.

SETTLEMENT OF THE RESERVATIONS

The Nisqually and Puyallup reservations were occupied by the Nisquallys and Puyallups, the people of those river drainages. In the case of the Muckleshoot reservation, however, there was not the same direct relationship between the name of the reservation, the name of the river drainage, and the name of

---

the Muckleshoot reservation itself was created under the authority of Article VI of the Treaty of Medicine Creek. No reason was given, but it must have been that although the need to create the reservation was immediate, the Treaty of Medicine Creek had been ratified, whereas the Treaty of Point Elliott had not.

[40] Meeker, *Pioneer Reminiscences,* pp. 415–57; full description of trials.

[41] Anderson, *Chief Seattle,* p. 286.

the people. (See further discussion in chap. iv in section on Status of the Tribes.)

The Muckleshoot tribe today contends that the people who settled on the Muckleshoot reservation, their ancestors, were the Smalh-kamish, the Skope-ahmish, and the St-kah-mish. These were the three bands of the White and Green rivers, inland tributaries to the Duwamish basin. All three groups are named in the Treaty of Point Elliott, and Governor Stevens' reports support the contention that they were on the White and Green rivers. Anthropological research and other documents from the time of the treaties further substantiate the Muckleshoots' claim to having been descended from these three groups named in the treaty; and reports of Indian agents after the establishment of the reservation show that the Indians from the White and Green rivers were settled together on the Muckleshoot reservation. By 1870 they had come to be referred to as the Muckleshoot tribe.

Marian W. Smith's information gathered in the 1930's provides details of the village sites and their relationships to each other. Briefly, the drainage was divided into four sections, each of which was named and each of which included one or more separate villages. The Indians of the Muckleshoot reservation, primarily the people of the White River, included also Green River groups and the South Prairie Puyallup village.[42]

Such evidence shows that the majority of the Indians placed on the Muckleshoot reservation were from the White and Green rivers and were represented at the Treaty of Point Elliott. The United States intended to treat with all the Indians in the area, and Chief Sealth of the Duwamish drainage signed. The Muckleshoots hold that he signed for all the bands in the area. The few Indians on the Muckleshoot reservation who came from bands in the Puyallup drainage were represented at the Treaty of Medicine Creek.

[42] Smith, *Puyallup-Nisqually*, pp. 15–16.

III | United States Indian Policy and the Tribes

In 1865, Henry A. Webster, agent for the Makahs of the Olympic Peninsula, wrote in his report to the Commissioner of Indian Affairs:

I have been of the opinion for a long time that one of the most practical methods of directly benefiting these Indians is by aiding them in their fisheries. . . . I do not wish to be understood as wanting to do less to carry out the plan of agriculture; but I should like to do something more for the tribe, and think to encourage their fisheries is one of the wisest steps that could be taken.[1]

His suggestion was ignored. The prevailing concept in Indian policy was to make Indians into farmers on the family-farm homestead pattern which was then usual in the United States, and those in control expected it to be applied as indiscriminately in the Pacific Northwest as elsewhere. Before the treaties (except the Treaty of Medicine Creek) had even been ratified, Governor Stevens wrote in a letter dated October 15, 1858:

The Secretary intends to send out circular instructions to the Supts and Agents on the Western Coast in regard to making the reservations self-sustaining and he states that whilst he is disposed to

---

[1] Henry Webster, Makah Report, in *Annual Report of the Commissioner of Indian Affairs* (Wash., D.C., 1865), p. 259.

recommend large appropriations for another year, he will go no further. I suppose that they will become in a measure self-sustaining in about another year, after the present fiscal year. By that time the Indians will have their little homesteads on which they will be able to raise considerable crops.[2]

The single-minded emphasis on agriculture—even less appropriate in the Pacific Northwest than among some of the other diverse Indian cultures—and the complete disregard for the possibilities inherent in the existing situation reflect the rigidity of approach which has characterized most national policy toward Indian communities. Not until 1962, nearly a hundred years after the Makah agent's letter of 1865, did the trustee agency, the Bureau of Indian Affairs, direct attention toward assisting the "fish Indians" of the Northwest Coast to develop their most obvious resource—their fisheries.

TRENDS IN INDIAN POLICY FROM 1857 TO 1960

Congressional legislation and the attitudes of changing administrations have been the principal determinants of national Indian policy. Regional and local attitudes have also been fac-

---

[2] "Letters of Isaac Stevens, 1857–1858," ed. Ronald Todd, *Pacific Northwest Quarterly*, XXXI (October 1940), 452. It is doubly ironic that Stevens, writing before any of the treaties except the Treaty of Medicine Creek had been ratified, speaks of having the Indians settled where they would raise crops. The Treaty of Medicine Creek provided for three reservation areas—Puyallup, Nisqually, and Squaxin—each containing two sections of land, a total of six square miles. The reservation areas as finally established by executive orders under the Treaty of Medicine Creek, including the Muckleshoot reservation, contained a total of approximately 51.5 sections, a little less than 52 square miles, as follows: Squaxin, about 2 sections (unchanged); Nisqually, about 7.5 sections; Puyallup, 36 sections; Muckleshoot, 6 sections. It is impossible to determine with certainty the number of persons expected to be placed on those reservations (see later discussion in this chapter) but it seems safe to assume that it was between 1,000 and 1,500, perhaps more. These reservations were formed at the same time that settlers could establish claims under the Oregon Donation Land Act of 640 acres, or one section, per couple. The combined area of these reservations was thus somewhat less than the area which 52 families could homestead.

tors, and partly because of their influence the implementation of federal programs has varied across the country. The conflict between state and federal jurisdictions has also played a part, especially where the demarcation is ill-defined. Here the federal government has often been the protector of Indian rights.

In 1871 Congress passed a law declaring that it would make no more treaties with Indian tribes, which were no longer to be considered separate nations. The legislation specifically provided, however, that terms of all treaties which were then in existence were to be honored.

The Bureau of Indian Affairs had been established many years before. Created in 1824 in the War Department and transferred in 1849 to the new Department of Interior, it is the oldest bureau in the federal government. It is charged with the responsibility of managing Indian affairs, but the specific nature of the charge has reflected great variations in national policy. As a civilian agency it was not responsible for the control and "pacification" of Indians, although it often has had immediate responsibility for "law and order." It has operated principally as a provider of such services as education and medical care and as a manager of trust property.[3]

Indian reservation land is held in trust by the United States government for the Indian owners, with the Bureau of Indian Affairs as the trustee agent. Land so held is commonly referred to as trust land, or land in trust status, or restricted land. Trust land is not subject to federal, state, county, or municipal taxes; neither can it be sold, leased, or otherwise exploited without the approval of the trustee, the United States government acting through the Bureau of Indian Affairs. It cannot be transferred to a non-Indian and remain in trust status. At the present time, part of the trust land of the reservations is tribally owned and part of it is owned by individual tribal

[3] The Division of Indian Health was transferred in 1955 to the U.S. Public Health Service.

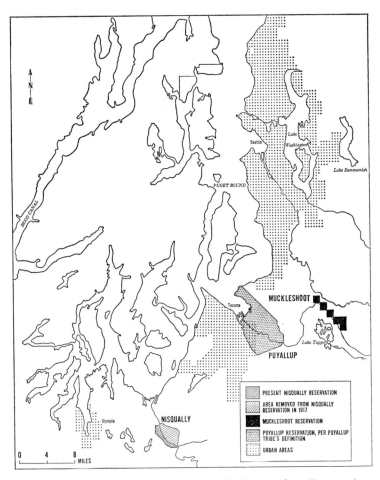

Map 2. *Nisqually, Puyallup, and Muckleshoot Indian Reservations*

members. The government through the bureau is the trustee in each case.

When the reservations were formed, the Indians held the land in common, and there was no such thing as individual ownership. In 1887 Congress passed the General Allotment Act, also known as the Dawes Act.[4] The land of the reservations was to be divided and "allotted" to individuals under presidential authority. This was a radical departure from the Indian concept of tribal land use; to Indians the land was a whole and individual parcels unknown. The allotments were supposed to be sufficient to enable a family to make a living by farming, but in practice little attention was given to the qualities of the land or the interests and talents of the families. Allotments were to be inalienable for twenty-five years, after which an allottee might apply to be declared "competent" to manage his affairs and receive title in fee simple. On his receipt of such title, his land passed forever out of trust status, and he could sell it to whomever he wished or do with it whatever else he saw fit. The bureau had no further interest in it. The land also passed onto the tax rolls of the jurisdictions in which the reservation was situated. However, it remained a part of the reservation.[5]

The General Allotment Act also provided that Indian land left over after the allotments had been made could be declared surplus and might be sold to the United States.

The majority of interested non-Indians supported this legislation—reformers did so because they felt it would force the Indian for his own good to adopt the white man's ways by becoming a farmer and property-owner, and profiteers because a great deal of Indian land would be opened for exploitation. A

---

[4] For a general discussion of the General Allotment Act and its results, see Harold Fey and D'Arcy McNickle, *Indians and Other Americans* (New York: Harper & Bros., 1959), pp. 70–79.

[5] Reservation land is still being alienated in this way.

few opposed it. Senator Henry Teller of Colorado described it as a "bill to despoil the Indians of their lands and to make them vagabonds on the face of the earth."⁶ A House committee minority report declared:

> The real aim of this bill is to get at the Indian lands and open them up to settlement. The provisions for the apparent benefit of the Indians are but the pretext to get at his lands and to occupy them. . . . If this were done in the name of greed, it would be bad enough; but to do it in the name of humanity, and under the cloak of an ardent desire to promote the Indian's welfare by making him like ourselves, whether he will or not, is infinitely worse.⁷

This assessment proved correct. Within forty-five years, Indians had lost ninety million acres—nearly two thirds of the land they had originally reserved.⁸ Since most Indians did not settle down to farming, the loss merely impoverished them. And, as most did not ask to be declared "competent," the trust functions of the Bureau of Indian Affairs became far more complex.

The Board of Indian Commissioners, whose members in 1887 had strongly supported the General Allotment Act, in 1921 issued a report which showed the failure of the allotment policy.⁹ In 1934 the further allotment of lands still in tribal ownership was forbidden by the Indian Reorganization Act for those tribes which voted to accept the organizational provisions of the act. (See discussion of the Indian Reorganization Act in the following pages.) Although the provision did not

---

⁶ Quoted in Fey and McNickle, *Indians*, p. 73.

⁷ *Ibid.*

⁸ *Ibid.*, p. 74.

⁹ Fey and McNickle, p. 81, describe the Board of Indian Commissioners as "created by act of Congress in 1869, . . . an independent body appointed by the President and consisted of ten men 'eminent for intelligence and philanthropy, to serve without pecuniary compensation.' The Board had no authority in the field of policy, but through the years it exerted great influence on the policy makers."

apply to tribes not officially accepting the act, in effect the allotment policy was ended.

However, the heritage of its results remains. While not all reservations have been individually allotted—in particular, those in the Southwest remain largely in tribal ownership— all reservations in the state of Washington have been allotted to some extent, and most of those in western Washington have been allotted almost in entirety, including the Muckleshoot, Nisqually, and Puyallup.[10] A great deal of the land has been alienated—has passed out of Indian ownership. In addition, much of what remains has been "fractionated" as the original allottees have died and their heirs have received fractional interests in the allotments without actual division of the land. These inherited fractional interests are in turn further divided with each successive generation. In this way a number of persons, sometimes a hundred or more, come to be part owners of a single piece of land.[11]

Indians were declared to be citizens of the United States by the Indian Citizenship Act of 1924. Because some states were unwilling to accept the idea, for many years its application over the country was uneven.

---

[10] The Puyallup Allotment Act of 1893 made allotment mandatory on the Puyallup reservation; also sale of surplus lands. See p. 54.

[11] No one of the part owners of such a "fractionated" holding can himself do anything with it. Without the formal agreement of the others, he cannot exploit any resource on it. He cannot sell or lease his share. Because of expenses with deeds and technical difficulties connected with trust status, one owner can rarely buy out the others even when they are willing to sell for the price he can pay. In practice the bureau manages such holdings (part of the increasing complexity of its functions). Income, as from bureau-arranged logging, gravel lease, agriculture, or mining, carried on by outsiders, is distributed by the bureau to the several owners in proportion to their respective shares. Fractionation has produced the so-called problem of heirship. For further discussion, see Fey and McNickle, *Indians,* pp. 75–77; and see Henry W. Hough, *Development of Indian Resources* (Denver: World Press, 1967), pp. 46–52.

Living standards had declined after the passage of the General Allotment Act. Conditions on many reservations were so bad by the time of the Hoover administration that Secretary of the Interior Herbert Work requested a private firm, the Institute for Government Research (Brookings Institution) to make a survey and propose a program. This study, commonly referred to as the Meriam Report, was published in 1928, and it provided reformers with badly needed factual information.[12] The report showed living standards for Indians to be far below those of the general population. It criticized the services of the Bureau of Indian Affairs, indicating that "too much reliance was placed on the sheer effect of individual land ownership and not enough was done to educate the Indians in the use of the land." [13]

In 1934 the Indian Reorganization Act, also known as the Wheeler-Howard Act, was passed by Congress, partly as a result of the Meriam Report. President Franklin D. Roosevelt declared that the time had come to "extend to the Indian the fundamental rights of political liberty and local self-government and the opportunities of education and economic assistance that they require in order to attain a wholesome American life." [14] The act allowed greater self-government to tribes, forbade further alienation of land, and encouraged tribal consolidation of fractionated holdings. It established a revolving loan fund and provided financial assistance to cooperative enterprises, expanded educational opportunities and encouraged the trend from boarding to day schools, and supported craft development. For the first time Indians were protected in the exer-

[12] Lewis Meriam and associates, *The Problem of Indian Administration* (Baltimore, 1928).

[13] Quoted from the Meriam Report in William T. Hagan, *American Indians* (Chicago: University of Chicago Press, 1961), p. 153; see also pp. 155–58, upon which the discussion here is based. See also Fey and McNickle, *Indians,* pp. 93–101.

[14] Quoted by Hagan, *American Indians,* p. 156. See also Fey and McNickle, *Indians,* pp. 91–101, for discussion of the Indian Reorganization Act.

cise of their own religions and ceremonials. The most revolutionary step allowed local option: Indian tribes voted on whether or not to accept those provisions of the act which related to tribal organization. Although some tribes did not do so, the Muckleshoots, Puyallups, and Nisquallys each voted to organize representative tribal governments in accordance with the act.

Conditions improved after passage of the Indian Reorganization Act. However, entrance of the United States into World War II in 1940 curtailed domestic spending. After the war, sentiment developed for the government to "get out of the Indian business." [15] The drive to reduce federal spending was part of the reason, and part was the revival of the attitude that Indians should be assimilated into American society and no longer regarded as a special group with distinct legal status.

In 1946 Congress established the Indian Claims Commission to expedite settlement of Indian claims against the government. Until that time the only recourse which a tribe had when it felt it had been wronged by the United States was to persuade Congress to pass special legislation allowing it to sue in the Court of Claims. The government hoped to make final settlement for past injustices and hasten the end of the special status of tribes. During the five years set for filing, 852 claims were filed. These were primarily on the basis of underevaluation of land ceded to the United States by the Indians under treaty. Failure to abide by treaty provisions was also cited.[16] The Claims Commission was created to function for ten years only; it is still in existence and has a great deal of work remaining on its agenda.

Other developments occurred which tended to reduce the

[15] This phrase was used by Senator Arthur Watkins of the Senate Subcommittee on Indian Affairs. See Hagan, *American Indians,* p. 160.

[16] See Hagan, *American Indians,* pp. 166–68. See also Fey and McNickle, *Indians,* pp. 104–6.

separateness between Indian groups and the rest of society. More use was made of public schools in place of bureau boarding schools, at first because of inadequacies in the boarding schools, and later with encouragement from the bureau to foster Indian "integration." At the present time, with few exceptions, Washington Indian children attend public schools. The last bureau school in the state closed in 1932.

Another development was the Social Security Act, passed in 1936. Its provisions, applying to all who enter "covered employment," brought Indians into the systems of Old Age and Survivor's (and now Disability) Insurance and Unemployment Compensation. Other terms of the act also brought them into those state public welfare programs which are financed in part by federal "matching funds"—by far the greater portion of all such programs.[17] The intent of the act was to assure equal treatment to all citizens; an effect for Indians was to involve them with the states and to reduce certain areas of special federal relationships.

During the 1950's pressure arose to end the special relationships between the tribes and the federal government. House Concurrent Resolution 108, passed in 1953, declared it to be the "sense of Congress" that the unique relationship between Indian tribes and the federal government should be terminated at the "earliest possible date"—hence "termination" became the common expression. For some groups such termination has brought about the end of all services of the Bureau of Indian Affairs to the tribe or its members, the end of the trust status of the land, and the end of the tribe as a legal entity. The Bureau of Indian Affairs was directed to prepare a list of tribes it considered "ready for termination," and to draft terminating legis-

---

[17] The state of Washington, unlike most states, has for many years made no distinction between Indians on reservations and other residents in any of its public welfare programs, whether federally matched or not.

lation. Termination was actually carried out for several tribes, though none were in the Puget Sound area.[18] In 1954 ten termination bills were presented to Congress and six were passed.

At the same time, as another aspect of the same emphasis, a number of programs of the Bureau of Indian Affairs were directed toward the relocation of individuals and families from the reservations to urban areas.

Developmental policies for tribes were in abeyance except as they would assist toward termination. Most tribal people, whether they liked the bureau or not, were much more afraid of the states, and wholeheartedly opposed termination. A great deal of the energy of tribal governments and national Indian organizations has been channeled into fighting it. Although termination as such no longer seems to be active national Indian policy, House Concurrent Resolution 108 stands unchanged on the books.

In 1953 Congress also passed Public Law 280, which gave permission to state governments under certain conditions to assume law and order jurisdiction on Indian reservations, in effect making way for the termination of one aspect of the unique Indian-federal government relationship. Hunting and fishing rights secured by treaty, however, were specifically exempted from the law's provisions.

The state of Washington passed legislation in 1957, Chapter 37.12 of the Revised Code of Washington, to take advantage of Public Law 280.[19] Chapter 37.12 provided that the state and county could assume law and order jurisdiction on a reservation on request of the tribe. The Nisquallys and Muckleshoots, as well as most of the other small tribes of the state,

---

[18] It is reported, however, that reservations in the jurisdiction of the Western Washington Agency of the bureau were high on the priority list for termination before the change in federal administration in 1961.

[19] This was done without amending the state constitution. See chap. iv for discussion of the law.

acted to make the request and are now under state and county jurisdiction on their reservations.

The Puyallups did not take action under Chapter 37.12 and have never requested state law and order. However, it had been imposed years before, probably on the basis that all but a few acres had passed out of trust status under the terms of the Puyallup Allotment Act of 1893.[20]

THE RESERVATIONS

The Puyallup Indians are definite in the conviction that in the treaty period they were not as few in numbers or as weak as portrayed in official documents.

According to anthropological testimony in a recent fishing rights case, in 1790 there were between 800 and 1,000 Puyallup Indians. Swanton cites an estimated 1,200 "Puyallup, Nisqually, etc." for 1780. By 1839 there were reported to be only 484 Puyallups.[21] Reports of numbers at the time of the treaty-making in 1854 vary considerably. The lowest figure is 100, from the same court testimony. M. J. Simmons, Indian agent for the Puget Sound District, suggests underestimation at the treaty time in his report of June 1858—that whereas all of the tribes and bands treated with at Medicine Creek in 1854 (Puyallup, Nisqually, Squaksun, etc.) were estimated at 650, by actual count in December 1857 they numbered 1,020.[22] A. H.

[20] See discussion in the following chapter.

[21] Memorandum Decision 158069 by Judge John D. Cochran, May 27, 1965, in *Departments of Game and Fisheries of Washington* v. *The Puyallup Tribe,* Pierce County Superior Court, Tacoma, Wash. John R. Swanton (*Indian Tribes of North America,* Bulletin 145, Bureau of American Ethnology [Wash., D.C.: Govt. Printing Office, 1952]), gives conflicting information (see n. 32 below).

[22] Letter from M. T. Simmons, Indian Agent, Puget Sound District, Washington Territory, to Colonel J. W. Nesmith, Superintendent of Indian Affairs, Washington and Oregon Territory, dated June 30, 1858; included in *Report of the Commissioner of Indian Affairs, Accompanying the Annual Report of the Secretary of the Interior, for the Year*

Milroy, Superintendent of Indian Affairs, Washington Territory, wrote in 1873 that although the number treated with at Medicine Creek had been fixed at 638, "in truth and in fact there were about 1,400 of them." [23] Meeker states that the Puyallups and Nisquallys numbered about four hundred each at the treaty time.[24]

The most recent tribal roll of the Puyallups, in 1929, counted 344. It is reported that they estimate their present number at 400.

The original Puyallup reservation—1,280 acres at the mouth of the Puyallup River—was soon recognized by officials to be too small for the number of people expected to live there. In 1857, following the Fox Island conference, the area was enlarged by executive order to contain a total of about 36 sections—approximately 23,000 acres—and in 1873 the boundaries were adjusted to correct a surveying error and give the Indians access to Commencement Bay.[25] At the same time, President Ulysses S. Grant approved alterations in the reservation to permit the Northern Pacific Railway free access across it, and the inroads on Puyallup lands had begun.[26] Three years later a branch line was approved; and in 1888 a right of way was granted, technically with the consent of the Indians, to the Puyallup Valley Railway. Five years later Congress acted to

---

1858 (Washington, D.C.: Wm. A. Harris, 1858), p. 226. "When these tribes and bands were treated with, (December 26, 1854,) their number was estimated at 650; at the payment of their annuity, last Christmas, it was ascertained to be 1,020—978 of whom were present. They consist of the Nisqually and Puyallup tribes, and the Squaksin, Squeit-letch, Stetch-as, and Chit-hut bands."

[23] Letter from A. H. Milroy to U.S. Commissioner of Indian Affairs, March 20, 1873.

[24] Meeker, *Pioneer Reminiscences,* p. 257. "The two tribes of Puyallups and Nisquallies [comprised] . . . about four hundred . . . each."

[25] Kappler, *Indian Laws and Treaties,* pp. 922–23.

[26] *Ibid.*

ratify another agreement between the Puyallups and the Northern Pacific.[27]

As already noted, all three reservations were individually allotted under the General Allotment Act of 1887. The Puyallup reservation, however, was under special pressure because it was directly in the path of non-Indian commercial and industrial development, lying entirely on land which has since been occupied by the city of Tacoma. In 1893 Congress passed a special act for the Puyallups, the purpose and result of which was to bring about the alienation of almost the entire reservation area. It directed that all Puyallup lands not required for the allottees' homes, the school, and the burying ground were to be sold, and it provided that those lands remaining in Indian ownership could be alienated after ten years (instead of twenty-five as provided in the General Allotment Act).[28]

Today no more than thirty-five acres of the Puyallup reservation remain in trust status as defined by the Bureau of Indian Affairs,[29] although two to three hundred acres still are owned by Indian heirs of the original allottees. None of the land officially defined as trust land touches Commencement Bay or the Puyallup River.[30] The state contends that the tribe therefore has no on-reservation fishing sites. The Puyallups, however, point out that while Congress authorized the sale of their lands, it has never extinguished the boundaries of their reserva-

---

[27] *Ibid.,* p. 465; 27 Stat. 468, Feb. 20, 1893, chap. 14.

[28] Kappler, *Indian Laws and Treaties,* pp. 487–88; 27 Stat. 633, March 3, 1893, chap. 209.

[29] The Indians do not concur in the bureau position, on the basis of alleged irregularities in conveying some of the land out of trust status.

[30] Here too there is dispute, as the Puyallup tribe has not accepted the legality of the condemnation procedure by which tribal land was conveyed to the state for construction of a highway bridge across the Puyallup River. The bridge was built, but the tribe contends that legally the land still is theirs in trust status; and according to the tribe's attorney it never has accepted the payment from the state.

tion; and they believe that the fishing from the sites they use which are within the original boundaries[31] is on-reservation fishing.

The Nisqually and Puyallup population together has been estimated at about 1,200 in 1780. The Nisqually figure given by Swanton for 1910 is 1,100.[32] In 1937 the Indian office reported 62 members, which suggests that the Nisqually band name was earlier given to a larger group. The 1965 roll lists 61 tribal members.

The Nisqually reservation was established in 1857 by executive order, a larger and better area than originally designated in the Treaty of Medicine Creek. It consisted of 4,700 acres on both sides of the Nisqually River, a few miles above its mouth. All of that part east of the river—3,300 acres or more than 70 percent of the reservation—was condemned in 1917 for the site of Fort Lewis. Twenty-one allotments were entirely taken and most of two others. The remaining reservation land consisted of 1,400 acres, and of this 835 acres remain in Indian ownership today.

The condemnation applied only to the land. It did not explicitly change the reservation boundary, nor did it apply to the river.

The Nisquallys whose land was taken were paid a total of $75,840 for the lands and improvements. Called a compromise settlement, it was accepted by the Department of the Interior "in view of the immediate war necessity" and with the understanding that Congress would be asked to make a supplemen-

---

[31] As established by the executive orders of 1857 and 1873.

[32] Swanton, *Indian Tribes,* pp. 428–29, 430. Swanton gives conflicting information, citing 3,600 Nisqually in 1780 (p. 430) and 1,200 "Nisqually, Puyallups, etc." in 1780 (p. 429). However, his source, James Mooney, *The Aboriginal Population of America North of Mexico* (Smithsonian Miscellaneous Collections, Vol. LXXX, No. 7 [Wash., D.C.: Smithsonian Institution, 1928]), gives only the figure of 1,200 Nisqually, Puyallup, etc., in 1780.

tary "gratuity appropriation." [33] In 1924 Congress gave them another $85,000 as compensation for the hunting rights lost with the land and loss of access to lakes and streams included in the land.

Some members whose allotments were taken for Fort Lewis chose to receive the money payment. Others elected to have their money used to purchase nearby land, some of which was on the west side of the river. It was given trust status although it was not within the reservation boundaries. The Nisquallys believe that such tracts carry all the rights of reservation land, and that fishing from sites on them is on-reservation fishing. The state holds that so far as hunting and fishing and any law enforcement are concerned, such places are subject to state law and that the fishing there is off reservation. This point has been bitterly contested at Frank's Landing, situated on an exchange tract bought for Billy Frank, Sr., one of the Nisqually tribal members whose allotment east of the river was taken in the Fort Lewis condemnation.

It is difficult to estimate the aboriginal population of the bands placed on the Muckleshoot reservation. Swanton thinks the Muckleshoots are probably included in the estimate of 1,200 "Nisqually, Puyallup, etc." in existence in 1780. The Skopamish numbered 222 in 1863 and the Smulkamish 183 in 1870. In 1937 the Office of Indian Affairs reported 194 Muckleshoots.[34] The official tribal roll in December 1968 named 383 persons.

The Muckleshoot reservation is situated about twenty-five miles southeast of Seattle, near the city of Auburn. It consists of five sections of land lying in a northwest-southeast diagonal and touching only at the corners, together with one more section adjacent to the sides of two others at the east end. The

[33] Letter from the Acting Secretary of the Interior, Alexander T. Vogelsang, to the President of the United States, Feb. 28, 1920, contained in Sen. Doc. No. 243, 66th Cong., 2d sess., pp. 1–4.

[34] Swanton, *Indian Tribes*, p. 429.

White River flows through the southern edge of a portion of it. The reservation does not touch the Muckleshoots' other river, the Green. Because of the unusual designation of the reserved area, Muckleshoot land has always been mixed with non-Indian land. The original acreage was 3,500. As of June 1968, 2,300 acres, or about two thirds, had passed out of Indian ownership, with 1,200 acres still in Indian hands. What remains is therefore even more intermixed with land owned by non-Indians.

THE TRIBAL ORGANIZATIONS

The Puyallup tribal constitution and bylaws were approved by the Secretary of the Interior May 13, 1936. Article II provides that membership shall consist of all persons of Indian blood on the roll approved in 1929 and all children born to any member who is resident on the reservation or within a twenty-mile radius of the Tacoma Hospital Reserve (the old Cushman Hospital).

The constitution grants the tribe the authority to determine who exercises the tribal fishing right. The Puyallup tribe allows members and spouses to fish. They have made regulations governing fishing, but the Bureau of Indian Affairs has not supported their authority over what the bureau has considered to be off-reservation fishing. Tribal officials contend that reservation boundaries are still valid, that fishing rights are not limited to the reservation in any case, and that the tribe has authority to regulate the behavior of members.

The Nisqually Indian Community Council, also organized according to the provisions of the Indian Reorganization Act, was approved by the Secretary of the Interior September 9, 1946. The 1965 membership roll is based on the Bureau of Indian Affairs census roll of 1945 and includes all children born on the reservation to persons on the 1945 roll.

Enrolled Nisquallys and non-Nisqually Indian men married

to Nisqually women have the right to fish. According to Indian sources, the council has also in years past given tribal fishing permits to non-Nisqually Indians who were born or reared in the community and identify primarily with that community, but those permits are no longer in effect. In the 1950's the Nisqually Community Council adopted fishing rules which, although not submitted to the Secretary of the Interior for his approval, apparently were operative in the community. Two tribal fishery patrolmen were employed, one for the reservation and one for the lower river. Confiscation of gear was the penalty for violations. The off-reservation patrol was discontinued, however, because orderly control by the tribe proved impossible in face of the actions by the state enforcement officers. New fishing regulations were passed by the council in October 1968, and subsequently were approved by the Bureau of Indian Affairs. They formed the basis of a 1969 off-reservation fishing agreement between the tribe and the state Department of Fisheries, but were not recognized for off-reservation fishing by the Department of Game (see Epilogue).

The Muckleshoot tribal constitution was approved by the Secretary of the Interior May 13, 1936, the same day as the Puyallups'. Membership is accorded all persons of Indian blood whose names are on the 1934 census roll or who were resident on the reservation at that time, and all children born to members residing on the reservation at the time of their birth. An adoption procedure has been established.

Muckleshoot fishing is restricted to tribal members, but the tribe has no active enforcement either of their own or from the Bureau of Indian Affairs. They depend on social pressure to induce conformity to their rules.

FISHING SITES

The Indians of western Washington formerly fished at many customary sites which they no longer use. Some Indians feel that they should reassert rights to such places by using them. George Gibbs, a secretary and staff member of the Stevens treaty-making party, wrote regarding Indians on Puget Sound:

As regards the fisheries, they are held in common, and no tribe pretends to claim from another, or from individuals, seigniorage for the right of taking. In fact, such a claim would be inconvenient to all parties, as the Indians move about, on the sound particularly, from one to another locality, according to the season.[35]

The Puyallups, Muckleshoots, and Nisquallys are certainly among those most affected by the loss of accustomed fishing sites. Within the memory of persons still living, the Muckleshoots fished not only the Green and White rivers but also the Cedar and the Black.[36] The Puyallups fished all around the mouth of their river and upstream, and some Indians contend that they also went as far as the Nisqually River.[37] The Nisquallys certainly fished below their reservation and probably upstream on the Nisqually and also on the Deschutes.

Several factors have influenced the reduction in fishing the "usual and accustomed" places. Land was taken by farms, towns, and cities, and the rivers became harder to reach. Early

[35] George Gibbs, *Tribes of Western Washington and Northwestern Oregon,* Vol. I, Pt. 2 of Contributions to North American Ethnology (bound together with W. H. Dall, *Tribes of the Extreme Northwest*) (Washington, D.C.: Government Printing Office, 1877), pp. 186–87.

[36] The Black River, which no longer exists, was the outlet of Lake Washington and a tributary of the Duwamish, and the Cedar River was a tributary of the Black. When the Lake Washington Ship Canal was opened in 1916, it lowered the level of the lake ten feet, and thereby eliminated the Black River. The Cedar River was diverted into Lake Washington, which it now enters, by utilizing part of the old channel of the Black, but reversing the direction of the water's flow. The only outlet of the lake is now through the Lake Washington Ship Canal. Thus the landscape, and the salmon rivers, change with industry, commerce, and engineering. See Victor B. Scheffer and Rex J. Robinson, "A Limnological Study of Lake Washington," in *Ecological Monographs,* Publication of the Ecological Society of America, IX (Durham, N.C.: Duke University Press, 1939), 98.

[37] From conversations with lower Nisqually fishermen.

court cases established the Indians' right to pass over non-Indian land to fish, but actual practice led to hostile and unpleasant relationships. Indians were disinclined to push the matter.[38]

Over the years the state fish and game authorities have asserted that Indian treaty-protected fishing exists only on the reservations, and have acted to enforce this position. Injunctions against off-reservation fishing by Indians of the Nisqually, Puyallup, and Muckleshoot tribes have been obtained and enforcement actions carried out even while the injunctions are being contested in the courts. Arrests of fishermen and confiscation of gear have seriously hampered the Indians. Valuable gear held by the state as evidence can effectively put the fisherman out of business during several runs of fish, even though he may eventually win his case. Unable to stand the costs of court action and replacement of gear, many Indians have limited their fishing activity.

Currently Muckleshoots fish openly in the White River within the boundaries of their reservation; and judging by reports of arrests, to some extent also off the reservation in the White and Green rivers. Recent Puyallup fishing appears to have been sporadic and limited to the lower Puyallup River and the adjacent part of Commencement Bay. The Nisquallys fish their river both on the reservation and below it. As evidenced by continuing arrests, off-reservation fishing has not stopped on account of the injunctions.

THE DEVELOPMENT OF FISHERIES IN WASHINGTON STATE

The Indian fishery was, of course, the original fishery, predating Washington Territory and Washington state. In the treaty and pretreaty times there was significant Indian commerce in fish in addition to those taken for their own consump-

[38] See 1964 *Hearings,* pp. 77–78.

tion. Coastal Indians traded regularly with those in the interior. In early contacts both Quimper and Vancouver recorded trade with Indians for fish and other commodities.[39] Sextas Ward, a Quileute who was born about 1852, is reported by Swindell to have testified:

. . . prior to the coming of the white men the Indians who lived in the villages along the various streams were able to catch much more salmon than those who lived along the ocean, whereas those along the ocean could obtain seal, whale and smelt; that as a result of this they were accustomed to trade amongst themselves so that they could have all kinds of fish and sea food for their daily subsistence; that after the white men came to the country they would trade fish to the white people for sugar, coffee, molasses and things like that; that the trade amongst the Indians and the white people amounted to quite a bit.[40]

Swan wrote in 1857:

The waters of the Bay, and all the streams that enter into it, are well stocked with fish. Salmon of several varieties abound, and are taken in great numbers by the Indians for their own food or for trading with the whites.[41]

He goes on to report also considerable oyster trade between Coast Indians and schooner captains out of San Francisco.[42]

When Washington became a state in 1889, there were no controls over any fishing except a requirement that trout could be taken only with hook and line.[43] Little organized information exists on the growth of competition for fish or on the rise of practices detrimental to them. However, Bagley's *History of King County* devotes a section to the commercial fisheries which gives a general picture. In the 1850's Dr. David May-

[39] Whitebrook, p. 58.
[40] Swindell, p. 221.
[41] Swan, *The Northwest Coast*, p. 26.
[42] *Ibid.*, pp. 59–63.
[43] *First Report of the State Fish Commissioner* (Olympia, Wash., 1890).

nard, a Seattle pioneer, asked Chief Sealth to show him a good location for catching salmon commercially. Sealth took him to the mouth of the Duwamish River. Maynard hired Indian fishermen, and the catches were salted and transported to San Francisco. For many years as many as sixty canoes at a time could be seen in Elliott Bay. Eventually, in the 1920's, the state prohibited any commercial salmon fishing there—an indication that industrial development had already affected the runs.[44]

Increasing regulation of fishing by the state, as well as other efforts to conserve the fish, developed as time went on. The beginning of the Department of Fisheries was in a law passed by the legislature February 2, 1890, which provided for a state commissioner of fisheries. The following year a Department of Fisheries was established. The first commissioner, James Crawford, held the office for seven years. His first *Report,* in 1890, did not mention Indians. In 1899 the department became the Department of Fisheries and Game, and the commissioner's title was changed to State Fish Commissioner and Game Warden. For many years the department had a Division of Fisheries and a Division of Game. Finally, by an initiative measure sponsored by sportsmen's organizations and approved by the voters in 1932, the two were separated and the present Department of Fisheries and Department of Game were established.

In 1947, the steelhead was defined by legislative action as exclusively a game fish. The Washington law, which forbids entirely the commercial taking or selling of steelhead, is to date the only one of its kind among the states. However, a similar measure, which did not pass, was introduced into the Oregon state legislature in 1967.

Steelhead is under the authority of the Department of Game, while salmon, as a food fish, is under the jurisdiction of the

[44] Bagley, *History,* pp. 653–58.

Department of Fisheries. In enforcement practices respecting sport fishing—the salmon is also a sportsman's fish—the two departments cooperate closely. In the rivers, the Department of Game carries the primary responsibility during the period when steelhead predominate (December 1 through April 30); during the time of the salmon runs (May 1 through November 30) the Department of Fisheries assumes it. When large numbers of officers are wanted, personnel from both departments may appear together.

The Department of Fisheries, an agency of the state, is supported by appropriations from state tax revenues. It also receives monies from the sale of licenses. In addition it receives a sizable and growing amount from "reimbursable services"— funds received for projects, including research, carried on in cooperation with or on behalf of other agencies. The greater part of such funds are from the federal government. The proportion from reimbursable services, as shown in the 1966 *Annual Report,* was 27 percent in 1963, and 36 percent in 1966. Total expenditures of the department in 1966 amounted to $3,900,000.

The Department of Game, also an agency of the state, is unusual in that it receives no funds from appropriations out of general tax revenues. Its funds come principally from sport fishing license fees and other license fees and tags. No doubt this is the basis for the sport fishermen's feeling that the game fish, especially the steelhead, belong to them. The department also receives funds from "reimbursable services." Its *Biennial Report* for July 1, 1966, through June 30, 1968, shows for the fiscal year July 1, 1967, to June 30, 1968, that about 78 percent of its revenues came from license fees and tags and about 13 percent came from federal reimbursements. Its total revenues in that fiscal year were $6,700,000.

Another kind of conservation agency, the Washington State

Pollution Control Commission, was established in 1945. The 1967 legislature, renaming it the Water Pollution Control Commission, enacted provisions to strengthen its functioning.

When the territory of Washington became a state, the Enabling Act passed by Congress required, and the state constitution contained, a clause disclaiming jurisdiction by the state over Indian lands and the Indians on them.[45] In spite of this, various documents show that the state early made efforts to control Indian fishing as it controlled the fishing of non-Indian citizens. Dr. Charles M. Buchanan, agent for the Tulalip reservation north of Everett, cited a number of state interferences with Indians fishing on their reservation.[46] In a written address to the Washington state legislature of 1915 he entered a vigorous defense of Indian fishing rights:

The natives' natural larders have been chiefly the shellfish and fishery locations adjacent to the mouths of the great rivers of this vicinity. These resources have been sufficient to subsist and maintain our Indian people hitherto. These resources have naturally lessened with the advent of the white man; more recently, the use of large capital, mechanized assistance, numberous [sic] great traps, canneries, etc., and other activities allied to the fishery industry, have greatly lessened and depleted the Indians' natural sources of food supply. In addition thereto the stringent and harsh application to Indians of the State game and fish laws have made it still and increasingly precarious for him to procure his natural foods in his

[45] Such a disclaimer was a usual requirement for a territory applying for statehood, and the pertinent clauses in a number of state constitutions are similar to Washington's. P.L. 280, discussed earlier in this chapter under Trends in Indian Policy from 1857 to 1960, gave states permission to change such disclaimer clauses. See also chap. iv on law.

[46] Two Lummi Indians, Patrick George and Dan Ross, arrested while fishing within the boundaries of their reservation, were tried in 1913. The state fish commissioner, when the case went against him, threatened to re-arrest the Indians again and again for the same offense. Casimir Sam of Tulalip was arrested for duck hunting in waters claimed as on reservation, and the ducks were forcibly removed from him and were claimed to have been killed off reservation. The jury acquitted him. See Charles M. Buchanan, "Rights of the Puget Sound Indians to Game and Fish," *Washington Historical Quarterly*, VI (April 1915), 110.

natural way. Much of this has been done under color of law. An empty larder, however, is an empty larder. The pinch of poverty and hunger are none the less severe because the man who has taken your means of subsistence has done so under cover of law and the appearance of legal right. The Indian is aware of no defect, default, or transgression on his part—*ergo,* he argues it must be that transgression is upon the part of the white man—*post hoc propter hoc.* One by one his richer and remoter fishery locations have been stripped from him while the law held him helpless and resourceless.[47]

The Indian fisheries seem never to have been looked upon by the state as genuinely legitimate fisheries, entitled to both a share of the resource and a share of the responsibility for managing it. They have been tolerated because of the accident of the treaties. At best, the state has accommodated to them by agreements between its agencies and some individual tribes; at worst, some of its officials and citizens have seemed intent on eliminating Indian fishing.

With a few perceptive exceptions the federal government has not done a great deal better. It has consistently upheld the fishing right at least on the reservations, and its agents and officers have not harassed the fishermen. But it has taken virtually no interest in the fishing, and it has adhered to the overall aim of remodeling the Indians into something else.[48] The view of both the state and the Bureau of Indian Affairs seems to have been that Indian fishing, although legal, is a nuisance and an anachronism, something which should be expected to disappear in the course of events.

No effort has been made by any agency to integrate the Indian fisheries as a separately defined category into an overall fisheries program, even theoretically. Salmon caught by Indians have entered non-Indian commercial markets for many years, and since 1935 they have been separately tabulated in the

---

[47] Buchanan, "Rights of Indians."
[48] See discussion in chap. v on very recent attention to fisheries.

statistical reports of the Department of Fisheries, but essentially as a special part of the commercial fisheries. The Indian fisheries have had a separate, isolated existence of their own, without aid or encouragement and without access to the growing body of knowledge about salmon or to assistance in regulation.[49] The reciprocal effects of all the fisheries upon each other, however, as well as the results of many physical changes in the environment, could not remain isolated.

In the meantime the job of the departments of fisheries and game has become increasingly complex and difficult, with many factors affecting the fish which are outside the control of the agencies. The state, as it has developed, has come under increasing pressure from the competing interests which make use of the rivers—irrigation, hydroelectric power, logging, manufacturing. The reduction or extinction of salmon in rivers elsewhere has brought increasing pressure on the rivers of Washington. Expanding population and rising prosperity have greatly increased the number of sport fishermen. It was perhaps predictable that in the many conflicts of interest, the fishery with the least understood basis for existence would be the object of attack.

TWO CULTURES

The style of life among the Puyallups, Nisquallys, and Muckleshoots, as well as other Indians in the Pacific Northwest, has changed enormously over the past hundred years. Marian W. Smith, an anthropologist, stated flatly in 1940, "Puyallup-Nisqually culture is gone." She described her book, *The Puyallup-Nisqually,* which was based on the information given to her by persons then still living, as a "monument to the culture into which they were born and which they saw vanish before their eyes." [50]

---

[49] Under the circumstances Indians have done remarkably well in their efforts at controlling their own fishing; and their practical knowledge and interest in the matter have served both themselves and others.

[50] *Puyallup-Nisqually,* p. xi.

It is certainly true that little overt trace remains of the way of life which she describes. Puget Sound Indians do not ordinarily wear any outwardly distinguishing articles of clothing or adornment. Few speak or know any Indian language—all speak English. Few seek any ritualized deep communication with the natural world, or set off on quests for spiritual power; children are no longer brought up to discipline their bodies and spirits in the manner necessary for such quests. The communal longhouse dwellings are gone, supplanted by conventional one-family frame structures. Canoes have been largely replaced by skiffs, with outboard motors added. Highly efficient fiber nets have given way to equally efficient nylon nets. The manner of making a living has been tied to the money economy.

In one of the recent fishing rights cases, Judge John D. Cochran of Tacoma asserted that "there is no Puyallup tribe which succeeds in interest to the rights of the original signers of the Treaty of Medicine Creek." Part of the basis was the statement of an anthropologist: "Puyallup culture is dead . . . the only thing that survives are memories. They are now Americans by 'cultural assimilation'; what was two cultures has become blended into one." [51] Judge Cochran's decision was reversed by the State Supreme Court, but the idea which underlay it remains—the widespread belief that Indians are "just like everybody else," that all differences have disappeared and Indians are "fully assimilated," that the two cultures have indeed blended into one, or more accurately that Indians have adopted the dominant pattern.

More of old Indian ways remain, however, than may at first be apparent, even of what is outward and visible. In many cases something new has been added to something old, or something old has been transformed into something new, and the connections are not always obvious. Gatherings not themselves derived from a specific tradition continue to serve the traditions

[51] Memorandum Decision 158069.

of feasting (on traditionally roasted salmon served on paper plates), dancing, singing, bone games, and the entertainment of guests, where ceremonial occasions, like the giving of names and the showing of respect, can be observed. People arrive in cars instead of canoes, but on top of the cars the beautiful traditional canoes also come, with Indian and other names in English letters on their bows. The canoes are used not for raiding or traveling, but for racing, for which the participants have spent weeks and months in practice and preparation, as participants once did for other quests.

There are "spirit dance" gatherings, rooted in ancient Indian beliefs. Indians still practice traditional arts and crafts, as well as the new developments growing out of them. People move about with the seasons, on a kind of circuit, as they always have, but today they travel to the berry and hop fields to work for the growers in the harvest instead of to their own summer camps to gather wild berries and roots. In the winter inter-reservation basketball tournaments take the place of earlier kinds of intertribal visiting. Out of reservation life itself have come distinctively Indian developments. One is the Shaker church. A religious movement widespread among Indians of the Pacific Northwest and recognized as a religious denomination, it incorporates some of the old guardian spirit complex, aspects of Roman Catholic symbolism, a profound belief in prayer for healing, and the use of movement and singing.[52]

And salmon remains. The river, the boat—whether skiff or canoe with outboard added—the fishing gear, continue to be the familiar setting of life. Fishing is a principal occupation, still providing the main basis of subsistence, whether for direct

[52] The Indian Shaker church started about 1880 on the Skokomish reservation at the lower end of Hood Canal. For history of its early struggles and development under persecution by whites and Indians alike, see Homer G. Barnett, *Indian Shakers* (Carbondale: Southern Illinois University Press, 1957).

consumption or for sale to acquire necessities which once were otherwise secured, sometimes by the trading of salmon. Salmon is still near the center of daily living.

Above all, attitudes survive. What finally remains is the set of mind, the frame of reference, the outlook. The details just described are perceived differently by Indian and white. The continuing difficulties in the relationships between the Indians and the dominant society, as pervasive and perplexing now as when the United States was negotiating treaties with the tribes, lie in fundamental differences in outlook. These go beyond the basic concepts about land which complicated treaty-making, and they persist in spite of the changes which have occurred during this time for both Indians and whites. The latter value enterprise, individual achievement, progress, and development. Time is for accomplishment, and is clearly divided into past, present, and future. For the Indians, "progress" and "development" were unknown concepts a hundred years ago, and are by no means the highest values now; and time, which is for living, is not sharply divided by what has already happened and what is going to happen. Chief Sealth's speech at the Treaty of Point Elliott, quoted in Chapter II, expresses the Indians' sense of continuity with those who have gone before and those who will come after.

Moreover, the Indians' view of life was, and is, oriented toward the group, as an organic, all-embracing body. A person's identity as part of the group is part of his individuality. He is this person, and part of him is the fact that he is attached to, belongs to, is part of, this particular group. He behaves as an individual, to be sure, but he behaves with reference to his group attachment. In general, such group orientation and group identification is foreign to non-Indian American society, and is virtually unintelligible in it. In the non-Indian society, persons think and behave in individual terms; their conformity, though great, is to commonly held norms, not to a group which they see as a part of themselves.

An illustration may help to clarify this point. In the dominant society, what a man is is what he has done, what he has accomplished—position gained, property acquired, books written, scientific discoveries made. If he has accomplished a great deal, at his death many people will come to his funeral; no skid road resident can expect much of a funeral. But among Indians, what a man is is who he is, such and such a person; what he has accomplished is comparatively irrelevant. And whatever he has done or not done, everyone will come to his funeral, because he was who he was.

It is as an aspect of the group that fishing takes on its significance, for fishing is part of the life of the group, and so is part of what and who a person is. With the disappearance of the old languages and of many practices and beliefs, and with increasing use of goods from the non-Indian world, Indian fishing remains a solid point of identification.

Non-Indians have been almost completely blind to the place of fishing in the Indians' conception of themselves. Though it has been anthropologically recognized and described, the fact that fish could be so intertwined with life has never actually been felt by non-Indians; the idea of fishing as the essence of the group, and so of a person's own essence, is hardly comprehensible.[53] White and Indian have lived side by side, but they have not known each other. They in fact live in different worlds, the worlds defined by their different perceptions. They speak with the same words, but they neither say nor hear the same things.

Furthermore, the history of one is not the history of the other. The white settlers occupied the country and became the

[53] It must be at least partly for this reason that the Bureau of Indian Affairs, among others, has never paid much attention to fishing in the programs through which it aimed to help Indians. See also discussion of Bureau of Indian Affairs in chap. v.

population of today. For them, after the reservations were established, the Indians were seen, like part of the scenery; then they disappeared. For the whites, history began with the coming of white men to the area, as the elementary history texts show; and in the present-day non-Indian world the sense of connection even with that time is tenuous.

For the Indians it is quite different. What has gone before is much more a part of them. It is less a sense of history, a march of actions and events, than a feeling of continuing relationship to the land and rivers, within the context of which events occur. The continuity extends far back beyond the days of the explorers and settlers, and all of it is still present. What happened during the times of the treaties is very much with Indians today. It is "to us" that those things were done.

Indians, a minority, are aware of a difference without necessarily analyzing it. But with rare exceptions non-Indians have not comprehended that there are two continuities, two time progressions, two histories, different in sense and feeling.

Fish, particularly salmon, still are an integral part of Indian life. As some other aspects of that life have disappeared, the role of fish and fishing has assumed even more importance—both economic and symbolic, and the symbolic may well be more significant than the economic. They still represent meanings and relationships so old and tenacious that even Indians who no longer fish will fight to preserve the accustomed rights in the rivers and streams with which they are traditionally connected. Fishing is the heritage of hundreds of years of use and development. It is a stronghold of the Indian person's sense of identity as an Indian. It is a remaining avenue of close relationship with the natural world. And in this modern world, it is at the heart of his cry for recognition and respect.

IV | The Law of Indian Fishing Rights in Washington

WILLIAM L. HANSON

Disputes over Indian fishing and fishing rights inevitably have led to legal tests and a search for answers in federal and state courts and legislatures. Few lawyers and laymen are familiar with Indian law in the United States, as it is both special and complex. It grew as the United States expanded westward, and adapted to a variety of relations with hundreds of tribes. It is unique. One seeks in vain a similar relationship in other societies, past and present: not in Brazil, South Africa, Russia, or China, with their important national minorities; not even in Canada.

A source of legal contradiction and conflict is the split concept of territorial expansion of this country. The books, elementary through college, show the familiar colored map, with the great wedge of the "Louisiana Purchase" and areas bear-

William L. Hanson, a Seattle, Washington, attorney and a Friend, has for many years been an advocate of full recognition for Indian fishing rights. He led the move in the Washington American Civil Liberties Union for involvement in the issue and was the first chairman of the organization's Indian Rights Committee. As an ACLU cooperating attorney he is one of those representing the Muckleshoots in *State of Washington* v. *Moses*.

ing labels such as Grant from the Crown, Treaty, Purchase, Mexican Cession, and for our area, "Oregon, divided with Great Britain." Absent is the map available through the Department of Interior showing almost the whole of the United States as actually secured from Indian tribes by conquest and/or treaty.

By one map Americans are shrewd empire builders; by the other they are aggressors. This literal doublethink has direct legal implications, the chief of which is the inconsistency of judges and legislators as to whether Indians *retained* property and rights, rather than *receiving* them from the United States.

Perhaps the doublethink has been produced and perpetuated by the sharp contradiction between the egalitarian principles of this country and actual conduct toward Indians. The settlers conquered the Indians, disparaged their culture, and took most of the land they used. These clashing values and attitudes cannot be separated from consideration of Indian law, for that law cannot be read without the realization of how personal prejudgment affects the legislator and the judge. It should also be noted that "law" is made not only by the courts but by administrators, like Washington's fisheries and game departments, and by the police, as well—for all of these administrative people have a certain leeway of judgment in the conduct of their work.

The Supreme Court of the United States has produced contradictory doctrines on Indian treaties; one being that they are part of the supreme law of the land and must be honored, the other that Congress may abrogate or modify treaties without Indian consent.

QUESTIONS OF JURISDICTION

The power of the federal government to deal with the Indians is found in the commerce power of the Constitution (Article I, Section 8), as well as the power to make treaties (Article II,

Section 2, Clause 2). Not only did the Constitution give the federal government the power to deal with Indians, but it gave that power exclusively to the federal government.

The United States government, as it made treaties with the Indians, regarded the tribes as organized political entities occupying certain lands and making use of other areas in a gathering economy. In early cases the Supreme Court declared that a treaty with an Indian tribe had the force and effect of a treaty with a foreign nation.[1] In *Worcester* v. *Georgia,* Chief Justice John Marshall described the Cherokee Nation as a distinct country, "occupying its own territory . . . in which the laws of Georgia can have no force, and . . . the citizens of Georgia have no right to enter, but with the consent of the Cherokee themselves, or in conformity with treaties, and with the acts of Congress." [2]

Although that doctrine has been discarded, nevertheless the concept of the residual sovereignty, however attenuated, of each Indian tribe, especially those with whom the United States has made treaties, has been preserved in decisions to the present day.

Congress has absolute power over Indians as Indians, as distinguished from rights of Indians as citizens. In *Gritts* v. *Fisher,*[3] the court declared: ". . . the members of this tribe were wards of the United States, . . . fully empowered . . . to assume full control over them and their affairs, to determine who were such members, to allot and distribute the tribal lands and funds among them, and to terminate their tribal government." [4] And in the case of *Lone Wolf* v. *Hitchcock,*[5] the Supreme Court presumed that when circumstances justify disregarding treaty

---

[1] *The Cherokee Nation* v. *Georgia,* 39 U.S. 1 (1831); *United States* v. *McBratney,* 104 U.S. 621 (1882).
[2] 31 U.S. (6 Pet.) 515 (1832).
[3] 224 U.S. 640 (1912).
[4] *Id.* at 642.
[5] 147 U.S. 553 (1903).

stipulations in "the interests of the country and the Indians themselves" the government should do so,[6] a criterion which is not borne out by Congressional practice.

In 1871 the making of treaties came to an end when Congress declared that no Indian tribe or nation within the United States should thereafter be recognized as an independent power with whom the United States could execute a treaty.[7] Existing treaties were preserved by the provision that this should not impair the obligations of any treaty previously ratified.

The legal status of Indian treaties would appear to be high. They are part of "the supreme law of the land." The Supreme Court declares that the language of treaties between the United States and the Indian tribes should be construed not to the prejudice of Indians but in the sense in which the words are understood by the Indians.[8] And any treaty entered into between the United States and another nation, including Indian nations, can curtail rights of individual states without consent by the state.[9] However, treaty rights are eroded and courts act inconsistently.

Both Congress and governmental departments exercise their powers to regulate Indian tribal activities. Congress passes laws found in Title 25 of the United States Code, which in its annotated version fills an 890-page book. Regulations established under these statutes, together with the interpretive cases and constitutional requirements, make up the basic body of Indian law: huge, technical, and unavailable to the Indians in any real way except through lawyers. The Department of Interior and its Bureau of Indian Affairs operate under these same laws. Consequently, Indians, both as individuals and as organized tribes, are generally governed under this great invisible structure.

---

[6] *Id.* at 566.

[7] 16 Stat. 566.

[8] *Minnesota* v. *Hitchcock*, 185 U.S. 373 (1901); *United States* v. *Shoshone Tribe*, 304 U.S. 111 (1937).

[9] *Missouri* v. *Holland*, 252 U.S. 416 (1919).

Until 1885 the federal government left criminal jurisdiction to the tribes in cases of offenses by Indians against Indians within confines of Indian country, which is generally reservation territory.[10] Starting in 1885 Congress extended federal jurisdiction to major crimes committed in Indian country.

Where special state jurisdiction acquired under Public Law 280 (see later discussion) does not pertain, criminal complaints and disputes between Indians, or between Indians and non-Indians on Indian reservations, or arising out of Indian tribal or reservation matters are under the jurisdiction of tribal courts where such courts exist.

The Wheeler-Howard Act of June 1934, generally called the Indian Reorganization Act, gave the opportunity to each tribe to organize and adopt a constitution.[11] Each of the three tribes which are the special subject of this fishing rights study—the Muckleshoot, the Puyallup, and the Nisqually—has adopted a constitution under the act. The Puyallup and Muckleshoot constitutions, of similar form and date, both specify power in the Tribal Council:

To promulgate and enforce ordinances, which shall be subject to review by the Secretary of the Interior, governing the conduct of members of the . . . Tribe, and providing for the maintenance of law and order and the administration of justice by establishing a reservation court and defining its duties and powers.

So far as the study group knows, none of the three has attempted to provide for tribal law and order, and the *de facto* situation is that state police power is in force at all these reservations.

In 1953, a time when Congress and the Department of Interior were acting under a policy pointed toward "termination" of the federal relationship with Indian tribes, meaning termination of the separate and peculiar status of Indian tribes in the

---

[10] Ex Parte Crow Dog, 109 U.S. 556 (1833).
[11] Act of June 18, 1934, Ch. 576, § 16, 48 Stat. 984.

United States, Congress passed Public Law 280.[12] This act provided, astonishingly, that certain named states and any other state might, by action of the state legislature, take civil and criminal jurisdiction over Indian reservations with certain limitations. Certain states, among them Washington, were listed by Congress as states which would have to amend their constitutions before acting under Public Law 280. Although the state of Washington has passed legislation assuming jurisdiction as provided by Public Law 280, it has not amended its constitution to date, and so is vulnerable to challenge.

In 1968 the ninetieth Congress enacted Public Law 284, which appears to supersede Public Law 280 of the eighty-third Congress. In Title IV Public Law 90–284 repealed a portion of Public Law 280 and specified, as Public Law 280 did not, that before any state could assert civil or criminal jurisdiction in Indian country it must first obtain the consent of the tribes. Treaty hunting, trapping, and fishing rights still are specifically excluded from any such assumption of jurisdiction by any state. (See Appendix 3 for full text of Title IV of Public Law 90–284.)

INDIAN LEGAL STATUS AND PROPERTY

Several elements are crucial to Indian legal status and property: the reservation, aboriginal title, communal property rights, the existence of the tribe, and membership in it.

The Indian reservation is the land base of the American Indian. A great deal of confusion over the nature of the reservation arises because its external boundaries continue to have legal meaning in spite of the individual sale of land to strangers by Indians. One of the most important of the rights which persist, despite land sale, is the right to fish and hunt. In each of the three tribes there has been rather large-scale alienation of

---

[12] Amending Chapter 53 of Title 18 and Chapter 85 of Title 28 of the United States Code.

reservation lands to non-Indians. Hence the importance of determining the original boundaries of the three reservations in order to establish the rights of on-reservation fishing and other rights owned by members of those communities or tribes.

Following World War II a movement within the federal government and Congress arose to favor termination of federal supervision and relationship to the Indian tribes. The first federal act of termination was that of June 17, 1954, relating to the Menominee Indian tribe of Wisconsin. The termination legislation actually provided for the closing out of Indian reservations and the tribal structure, ostensibly terminating all special Indian rights. But the Menominee termination is a warning to Indian tribes as to fishing rights. No mention was made in the legislation concerning hunting and fishing rights; the Indians were told that they were preserved in accordance with the treaty, without need of specific mention or reservation. Yet the state insisted they were not preserved.

In May 1968 the state's stand was overruled. The U.S. Supreme Court held that Menominee hunting and fishing rights had survived termination, in an opinion written by Justice William O. Douglas (*Menominee Tribe* v. *U.S.*).[13] Public Law 280, the Court found, had provided that termination was only of "federal supervision over property and members" of the tribe. Since the termination statute had made no mention of hunting and fishing rights, they were therefore not extinguished.

A second base of support for the Indian case against eliminating or minimizing rights unique to Indians by the state is the concept of aboriginal rights. It has been the basis for many successful claims by both treaty and nontreaty Indians. The Court of Claims has made awards to Indian tribes in Washington based upon aboriginal rights *not* reserved by treaty, as, for example, hunting and gathering rights in lands ceded to the

[13] 391 U.S. 404 (1968).

United States. As a practical matter, recovery of compensation for the diminution or loss of such nontreaty rights, including rights in land, is based upon recognition by the United States of such rights.[14]

The opinion of the regional solicitor quoted in the Muckleshoot case described later in this chapter is a federal expression of the validity of aboriginal title to fishing rights.

The nature of Indian communal ownership, discussed in *Journeycake* v. *The Cherokee Nation,* holds that communal property is owned by every member of the community. The individual "does not take as heir, or purchaser, or grantee; if he dies, his right of property does not descend; if he wishes to dispose of it, he has nothing which he can convey; and yet he has a right of property . . . his children after him will enjoy all that he enjoyed, not heirs but as communal owners." [15]

This pattern of communal ownership has also been noted, specifically as to hunting and fishing rights, in the 1942 Ninth Circuit federal case of *Montana Power Co.* v. *Rochester.*[16] *Federal Indian Law,* a basic work on this subject, states: "Tribal property may be formally defined as property in which an Indian tribe has a legally enforceable interest." [17]

Can anyone use the fishing rights of Washington Indians? This question, which should be decided in regard to communal property rights, has been left unresolved. Some Indians—for example, those associated with the Survival of American Indians, Inc.—assert that any Indian in Washington may exercise, with permission, special fishing rights anywhere Indians have them in the state. It would seem proper that an even broader

[14] *Hynes* v. *Grimes Packing Co.,* 337 U.S. 86, 104 (1949).
[15] 28 Ct. Cl. 281, 302 (1893), Aff'd, 155 U.S. 196 (1894).
[16] 127 F.2d 189 (9th Cir. 1942).
[17] Felix S. Cohen, ed., *Federal Indian Law,* U.S. Solicitor for the Department of the Interior (Wash., D.C.: Govt. Printing Office, 1958), a revision of the 1941 *Handbook of Federal Indian Law;* n.14 at 583.

rule should obtain: that if a tribe owns fishing rights, it should be able to authorize guests or "licensees," including non-Indians, to fish, commercially or otherwise.

The existence of the tribe itself has been attacked in another effort to destroy the treaty basis for unique Indian fishing rights. In a superior court case for Pierce County (Wash.) in *The Department of Game* v. *The Puyallup Tribe,*[18] Judge Cochran held that there was no longer a Puyallup tribe and no reservation (the decision on appeal discussed later in this chapter). According to the *United States* v. *Felipe Sandoval,* the federal courts would follow executive and political governmental recognition of the existence of a tribe unless such determination were clearly counter to the law.[19] This suggests that federal and state courts should accept the determination of the Department of Interior as to tribal existence, but it leaves a loophole for federal courts to make determinations where the policy of the Department of Interior might be grossly in error.

The question of membership in a tribe is crucial, as membership is the connection to the rights owned by the tribe. Federal law provides:

The secretary of the Interior is authorized, wherever in his discretion such action would be for the best interest of the Indians, to cause a final roll to be made of the membership of any Indian tribe; such rolls shall contain the ages and quantum of Indian blood, and when approved by the said Secretary are declared to constitute the legal membership of the respective tribes for the purpose of segregating the tribal funds as provided in Section 162 of this title, and shall be conclusive both as to ages and quantum of Indian blood.[20]

Each of the three tribes of this study has a roll of members approved by the Department of Interior.

[18] 70 Wn.2d 245, 422 P.2d 754 (1967).
[19] 231 U.S. 28 (1913).
[20] 25 U.S.C. § 163 (1919).

WASHINGTON STATE

The power of this state concerning Indians was limited on February 22, 1889, by the Enabling Act for the state of Washington, passed by the U.S. Congress. The constitution of the state of Washington, ratified and established in 1889, carried the language of the enabling act into Article XXVI, the second part:

Second. That the people inhabiting this state do agree and declare that they forever disclaim all right and title to the unappropriated public lands lying within the boundaries of this state, and to all lands lying within said limits owned or held by any Indian or Indian tribes; and that until the title thereto shall have been extinguished by the United States, the same shall be and remain subject to the disposition of the United States, and said Indian lands shall remain under the absolute jurisdiction and control of the Congress of the United States.

The Washington state legislature in 1957 did consider and adopt legislation based on Public Law 280. It brushed aside the requirement of an amendment of the state constitution and adopted a law which had in it a consent provision. The Indians of the state of Washington had to request the extension of state criminal and civil jurisdiction to their reservations before the legislation would apply.

Not only did Public Law 280 exempt fishing rights from its provisions, but the state of Washington added its own disclaimer in its legislation, that disclaimer being found in R.C.W. (Revised Code of Washington) 37.12.060:

Nothing in this chapter shall authorize the alienation, encumbrance, or taxation of any real or personal property, including water rights and tideland, belonging to any Indian or any Indian Tribe, band or community that is held in trust by the United States or is subject to a restriction against alienation imposed by the United States; or shall authorize regulation of the use of such property in a manner inconsistent with any federal treaty, agree-

ment, or statute or any regulation made pursuant thereto; or shall
confer jurisdiction upon the state to adjudicate in probate proceedings or otherwise, the ownership or right to possession of such
property or any interest therein; or shall *deprive any Indian or
Indian Tribe, band or community of any right, privilege or immunity afforded under Federal treaty, agreement, statute or executive order with respect to Indian land grants, hunting, trapping or
fishing or the control, licensing or regulation thereof.* [Emphasis
added]

In 1963 the legislature removed the requirement of Indian
consent; extended civil jurisdiction in the state of Washington
to Indians and Indian territory; and extended criminal jurisdiction, except as to Indians on "tribal lands or allotted lands
within an established Indian reservation and held in trust by the
United States or subject to a restriction against alienation." A
second qualification was that the territorial limitation would not
apply to eight matters: school attendance, public assistance,
domestic relations, mental illness, juvenile delinquency, adoption, dependent children, and the operation of motor vehicles
on public roadways.

Some Indians and tribes opposed the proposed legislation in
1963 because it violated the idea of Indian consent. At this
point the Washington State American Civil Liberties Union became specifically active in Indian rights. That state branch of
the ACLU now has an active Indian Rights Committee, and a
policy linking the Indian desire for freedom from cultural imposition to Indian rights and to basic human rights.

FISHING RIGHTS

The Washington Indian treaties were made before Washington became a state. Territorial Governor Stevens negotiated
a series of treaties, including the relevant treaties of Medicine
Creek and Point Elliott (see chap. ii). Each treaty has approximately the same language concerning fishing rights:

The right of taking fish at all usual and accustomed grounds and stations is further secured to said Indians in common with all citizens of the Territory, and of erecting temporary houses for the purpose of curing, together with the privilege of hunting, gathering roots and berries, and pasturing their horses on open and unclaimed lands: *Provided, however,* that they shall not take shell fish from any beds staked or cultivated by citizens.[21]

The state of Washington is under pressure to provide a maximum number of salmon for both commercial and sport fishermen and of steelhead for the sportsmen. Indian fishing rights, standing as special rights not available to other citizens, are under attack. The police power of the state to protect natural resources by conservation measures is subject to limitations. For instance, the case of *Graves* v. *Dunlap* states: "The state, through its legislature, has the right to control for the common good the killing, taking and using of game, so long as rights guaranteed either by the state or the Federal Constitution are not encroached upon." [22] The case of *Tulee* v. *Washington* holds: "Treaty takes precedence over state law and state conservation laws are void and ineffective insofar as their application would infringe on rights secured by treaty." [23]

The conflict has escalated specifically over steelhead trout in the Puyallup, Nisqually, and Green rivers in February and March, steelhead and salmon at certain other times. The Washington legislature, stimulated by the sport fishermen of the state and the relevant state departments, passed laws removing the steelhead trout from the commercial fishery.[24] These laws go

[21] Treaty of Medicine Creek, Art. 3.
[22] 87 Wash. 648 at 651, 152 P.532 (1915).
[23] 315 U.S. 681 (1942). See also *State* v. *Quigley,* 52 Wn.2d 234, 324 P.2d 827 (1958).
[24] R.C.W. 77.08.020 defines the steelhead as a "game fish"; R.C.W. 77.16.060 makes it unlawful for any person to use any net to catch game fish; and R.C.W. 77.16.040 makes it unlawful for any person to sell or ship game fish.

far beyond regulation. The statutes and the laws prohibiting net fishing in rivers and establishing closures and limits, together with evidence as to the pattern of fisheries management in Washington, demonstrate that the state is engaged not primarily in conservation of fish, but rather in the *allocation* of fish to sportsmen and commercial fishermen. There appears a pattern of legislation and administration to eliminate the Indian stream fishermen except as individual Indians might become sport fishermen.

Washington has elaborate sets of laws regulating fisheries (Title 75 of the Code) and game and game fish (Title 77), while at the same time the legislature has completely ignored Indian treaty rights. Even those rights usually recognized, such as on-reservation fishing, are not mentioned. The absence of such considerations appears to be in violation of federal law, the treaties, and the decisions of the federal courts. By not making regulations recognizing any Indian rights the state administration appears to be "forebearing" and "making an exception" in the case of the Indian fishing and hunting rights which it does recognize.

Washington does not attempt to regulate fishing on reservation by treaty and nontreaty Indians, since the right to hunt and fish on reservation without state regulation is generally considered to be implied by the treaties which distinguish reservation territory from ceded lands.[25] In a supportive case, *Pioneer Packing Co.* v. *Winslow*,[26] the Washington court held that the Quinaults could sell fish from reservation streams for transportation to another state. Under their treaty, they could catch fish on reservation and they had title to such fish:

After considering the provisions of the treaty and the cases cited,

---

[25] See Charles A. Hobbs, "Indian Hunting and Fishing Rights," 32 *Geo. Wash. L. Rev.* 504, notes 37–41 (1964) and *Mason* v. *Sams,* 5 F.2d 255 (D.C.W.D. Wash. S.D. 1925), regarding the Quinaults.
[26] 159 Wash. 655, 294 P. 557 (1930).

we are of the opinion that in the present case the Quinault Indians own the fish in the Quinault River by the same title and in the same right as they owned them prior to the time of the making of the treaty, and that the state has no right to interfere with or control their right to take fish from a stream which crosses the reservation.[27]

The state of Washington has argued in previous cases that the language "in common with all citizens of the Territory" means that Indians have a right the same as all others and are therefore subject to the same regulations. This argument, at root, is based upon the idea that the Indians actually had, in law, nothing; that they could only receive property and rights from the government. It therefore assumes that the treaty-making was a sham procedure.

This argument ignores a fact given recognition throughout federal cases that the Indians who made treaties with the United States owned property and rights. They gave property in exchange for money or benefits, and they could, in their treaties, *retain* certain property and rights. In this case the Indian signatories *retained* the right to fish, absolutely basic to their livelihood. The Indian has exemption from state law regulating fisheries under the treaty, whereas the non-Indian, receiving from the Indians a right to share fishing in the same places, has not.

In 1905 the Supreme Court of the United States, in *U.S. v. Winans*,[28] interpreting a similar provision in the Yakima treaty, sustained this view:

The right to resort to the fishing places in controversy was a part of the larger rights possessed by the Indians, upon which there was not a shadow of impediment and which were not much less necessary to the existence of the Indians than the atmosphere they breathed. New conditions came into existence, to which these rights

---

[27] *Id.* at 662.
[28] 198 U.S. 271 (1905).

had to be accommodated. Only a limitation of them, however, was necessary and intended, not a taking away. In other words, the treaty was not a granting of rights to them but a grant of right from them—a reservation of those not granted. Citizens might share it, but the Indians were secured in its enjoyment by special provisions of means for its exercise.[29]

In the *Tulee* case the court confirmed it again:

In determining the scope of the reserved rights of hunting and fishing, we must not give the treaty the narrowest construction it will bear. . . . It is our responsibility to see that the terms of the treaty are carried out, so far as possible, in accordance with the meaning they were understood to have by the tribal representatives at the council and in a spirit which generously recognizes the full obligation of this nation to protect the interest of a dependent people.[30]

FEDERAL AID IN COURT

The Department of Justice at first declined to enter the fishing rights cases. In February 1965 a private group of Nisquallys and Puyallups sent a "Petition for Action" to the U.S. Attorney General, asking for aid in the *State* v. *Kautz et al.* case. They cited, among other points, the federal statute that holds: "In all States and Territories where there are reservations or allotted Indians the United States attorney shall represent them in all suits of law and in equity" (25 U.S.C. 175). Yet, although the suit in question was a civil suit, the statute stating that it applies to civil cases, the Department of Justice refused to help. Cases interpreting the above statute had stated that it was not mandatory.

But by the spring of 1966 the Department of Justice moved to participate in the fishing cases. The study group does not know the reason for this change of policy. The assistant attorney general, Edwin L. Weisl, Jr., prepared a brief for the United

[29] See also *Senfert Bros. Co.* v. *U.S.*, 249 U.S. 194 (1918).
[30] *Tulee* at 684.

States as *amicus curiae* in *The Department of Game* v. *The Puyallup Tribe.*[31] That brief recognizes an additional possible action by Indians, which had been mentioned in the "Petition for Action," that "the possibility exists, if Indian rights are lost, of assertion of claims against the United States for failure to prevent such loss." [32] A clause in both the treaties with which we are concerned, in which the Indians "acknowledge their dependence on the Government" of the United States,[33] is now considered as a source of such an obligation.

FISHING RIGHTS CASES

The court decisions on Indian fishing rights are a complex of contradiction. The courts of Washington state have readily taken on Indian fishing cases, and rendered opinions which may conflict with federal decisions and with other state decisions.

From 1942 to 1968, the basic United States Supreme Court case on fishing rights has been *Tulee* v. *Washington.* Further basic interpretation was made in 1968, in *Department of Game* v. *Puyallup Tribe,* discussed in more detail later in this chapter.

Both cases are inadequate guides to Indian, federal, and state conduct. In *Tulee,* the question was limited to whether the Indian defendant was required to pay for and secure a Washington license in order to fish for salmon with a net off reservation. The Court held that he was not required to secure the license; other opinions in the case not in direct support of this holding are "dicta," meaning that they are not binding.

The basis for the Court decision was Article 3 of the 1855 treaty between the Yakima Indian Nation and the United

[31] 70 Wn.2d 245, 422 P.2d 754 (1967); 391 U.S. 392, 20 L Ed 689 (1968).

[32] Brief for U.S. as Amicus Curiae at 4, *Id.*

[33] Article 8, Treaty of Medicine Creek, Act of Dec. 26, 1854, 10 Stat. 1132; Article 9, Treaty of Point Elliott, Act of Jan. 22, 1855, 12 Stat. 927.

States, which secured to the Yakimas the right to take fish not only on reservation but also at usual and accustomed places off reservation, and also that the treaty "forecloses the state from charging the Indians a fee of the kind in question here." [34]

The license fees prescribed are regulatory as well as revenue producing. But it is clear that their regulatory purpose could be accomplished otherwise, that the imposition of licenses is not indispensable to the effectiveness of a state program. Even though this method may be both convenient and, in its general impact fair, it acts upon the Indians as a charge for exercising the very right their ancestors intended to reserve.[35]

Ignoring the different theories of title and land ownership and acquisition held by the Supreme Court of the United States since the formation of this country, the Court in this case simply stated: "In 1855, the Yakimas and other Indians owned and occupied certain lands in the Territory of Washington, which the United States wished to open up for settlers." [36] The important dictum of the *Tulee* case was:

We think the state's construction of the treaty is too narrow and the appellant's too broad; that while the treaty leaves the state with power to impose on Indians equally with others, such restrictions of a purely regulatory nature concerning the time, manner of fishing outside the reservation as are necessary for the conservation of fish, it forecloses the state from charging the Indians a fee of the kind in question here.[37]

Much later, in another decision which restricted state power, the federal court for the Ninth Circuit, in *Makah* v. *Schoettler* (1951), held that Washington could not limit Indian fishing on the Hoko River to hook and line because it had not sustained its

---

[34] *Tulee* at 684.
[35] *Id.* at 685.
[36] *Id.* at 682.
[37] *Id.* at 684.

burden of proving that such regulation was necessary for the conservation of fish.[38]

However, the idea of the validity of state regulation for conservation was followed by the Ninth Circuit Court in 1963 in an Oregon case, *Maison* v. *Confederated Tribes of the Umatilla Indian Reservation*.[39] The Supreme Court declined to review the case, stating criteria based on the *Tulee* case:

1. The state can regulate Indian fishing only to the extent the regulation is necessary to conservation.

2. "Necessary" means that the particular regulation is "indispensable" to the limitation of fishing in the interest of conservation.

3. The limitation of Indian fishing is not indispensable if a restriction on non-Indian fishing alone would accomplish the conservation purpose. In the words of the court, "restriction of the fishing of Indians is justifiable only if necessary conservation cannot be accomplished by a restriction of fishing of others."

4. Fishing by non-Indians can be restricted if the restriction is reasonable, which is the requirement of the 14th amendment, but fishing by Indians can be restricted only if the restriction is indispensable, which is the requirement of the treaty.

5. The State failed to show in this instance that its conservation objective could not be obtained by restricting the fishing rights of non-Indians only, and the state law therefore could not be enforced against Indians.[40]

The *Umatilla* holding appears to represent the view of the Department of the Interior, at least as expressed by the Department of Justice giving legal representation to Interior. It also represents the view of the American Civil Liberties Union (ACLU), which is relevant, as the Washington State ACLU has assumed the defense of four Muckleshoot fishermen and is involved in ways which relate to public education. Nisqually River Indian fishermen have argued most vocally the common

[38] 192 F.2d 224 (9th Cir. 1951).
[39] 314 F.2d 169 (9th Cir. 1963).
[40] Summary quoted from 1964 *Hearings* at 4.

Indian view that the state has no right to regulate, either on or off reservation.

The Supreme Court of the state of Washington is divided on fishing rights, as shown by its 1957 *Satiacum* and 1963 *McCoy* decisions. The argument that the federal courts have exclusive or primary jurisdiction to determine Indian rights has not deterred it from making judgments, although its 4 to 4 split in *State* v. *Satiacum* weakens its pro-Indian decision to the vanishing point.[41] Judge Charles T. Donworth declared:

> The courts have generally recognized that the treaty right of fishing at "usual and accustomed places" was given to the Indians to provide for their subsistence and as a means for them to earn a livelihood. *United States v. Winans,* supra (198 U.S. 3717); *Makah Indian Tribe v. Schoettler,* supra (192 F 2d 224); *State v. McClure,* supra (127 Mont. 534). Applying a liberal—and not a strained—construction to the treaty of Medicine Creek as a whole, it is our opinion that the Puyallup Indians so understood Article III of the treaty, and that neither the Indians nor the United States intended that the states would or could enforce general regulations against the Indians "equally with others" or "in common with all citizens of the Territory" and thereby deprive them of their right to hunt and fish in accordance with the immemorial customs of their tribes. As we interpret the treaty, we believe that the phrase "in common with all citizens of the Territory" merely granted the white settlers and their heirs and/or grantees a right to fish at these places with the Indians, but that the Indians thereby reserved their right to fish at these places irrespective of state regulation, so long as the right shall not have been abrogated by the United States.
>
> No other conclusion would give effect to the treaty, since to hold that their right was *equal* to that of the citizens of the territory would be to say that they were given no right at all, except that which any citizen subject to state statutes and regulations may enjoy to fish at the "usual and accustomed grounds and stations." This interpretation would permit the state to abrogate their treaty rights at will.

[41] 50 Wn.2d 513, 314 P.2d 400 (1957).

We are convinced that, under the applicable decisions of the Supreme Court of the United States referred to herein, the statutes and regulations in the case at bar are in conflict with the treaty provisions, constitute an interference with matters that are within the exclusive scope of Federal power and, therefore, cannot be held valid as to the Puyallup Indians, in relation to their rights to fish "at all usual and accustomed fishing grounds and stations."

To summarize, the treaty of Medicine Creek of 1855 is the supreme law of the land and, as such, is binding upon this court, *notwithstanding any statute of this state to the contrary, and its provisions will continue to be superior to the exercise of the state's police power* respecting the regulating of fishing at the places where the treaty is applicable until:

(1) the treaty is modified or abrogated by act of Congress, or (2) the treaty is voluntarily abandoned by the Puyallup tribe, or (3) the Supreme Court of the United States reverses or modifies our decision in this case. [Emphasis added] [42]

In the 1963 case, *State* v. *McCoy,* the court dismissed the *Satiacum* case with a footnote and proceeded to hold against a Swinomish Indian who was gillnetting off the mouth of the Skagit River, and who claimed rights under the Treaty of Point Elliott.[43] The court did not adopt the *Umatilla* standard of indispensable regulation, accompanied by first limiting non-Indian fishing, but upheld a right of the state to subject Indians to "reasonable and necessary regulations" for conservation. The court held that the treaty gave Indians an easement to go upon the land of others at usual and accustomed places and that the treaty was in the nature of a real estate transaction; and also held that the treaties do not impair the police power of the state.

The holding clearly contradicts the *Umatilla* decision, is contrary to the United States Constitution, and to decisions concerning the nature of Indian treaties in relation to state power. Although the majority pointed out that they were simply upholding a ten-day closure of the Skagit, dissenting Justice Don-

---

[42] *Id.* at 523.
[43] 63 Wn. 2d 421, 387 P.2d 942 (1963).

worth pointed out that if the state could enforce the closure for ten days against Indians presumably it could prevent Indian fishing permanently.

In the *McCoy* case the court accepted state evidence relating regulations to conservation needs, which has also been observed by Washington justice and superior courts in the Indian fishing cases. Under the federal cases, however, it would seem that the state would have to *recognize Indian rights in its legislation and regulations on fishing.* Such observance would mean legislative hearings and findings concerning conservation and fishing on particular streams, followed by laws and regulations in line with such findings and the special Indian rights. This has not been done, and gives reason to argue that the state fails to meet even the "minimum and necessary" standard of the *McCoy* case in its relationship to Indians.

In January 1967 the Supreme Court of Washington issued its decisions in the trio of cases concerning the tribes of this study. In the *Puyallup* and *Nisqually* cases it adhered to the *McCoy* standard, declaring that Indian fishing off reservation at usual and accustomed places is subject to laws and regulations which are "reasonable and necessary to conserve the fishery." [44] The court specifically disagreed with the federal court holding in *Umatilla.*

As the conflict continues, Indian bitterness is extended not only to the state, its enforcers, and its courts, but also to the federal government for federal inaction. The creation of federal regulations for Indian fishing would fill the vacuum of weak Indian enforcement and demonstrate federal belief in the primacy of federal jurisdiction over Indian affairs. Such regulations could provide the link in the chain of right for the Indian fishermen: identification, permissible gear, appropriate times

[44] *Dept. of Game* v. *The Puyallup Tribe,* 70 Wn.2d 245, 422 P.2d 754 (1967).

for fishing, specification of places, and recognition of treaty right in the tribe.

In July 1967 the Bureau of Indian Affairs published in the *Federal Register* a set of rules and regulations for "off-reservation treaty fishing" (25 ESC Sec. 256.1–256.7). Under these rules, the Secretary of the Interior, "upon request of an Indian tribe, a State Governor, or upon his own motion," when necessary for conservation purposes, may regulate off-reservation Indian fishing. The regulation will apply only to members of tribes that are on reservations (not to tribes located on public domain land). Language of the regulation refers, interestingly, to the "non-exclusive fishing right." The statement reads: "Before promulgating such regulations the Secretary of the Interior will seek the views of the affected Indian tribes, of the fish or game management agency or agencies of any affected State, and of other interested parties" (Sec. 256.2 [c]). Except in emergency situations when time does not allow, the proposed rules will be published in the *Federal Register* to allow for comments and discussion before they are imposed. The authority, however, resides fully in the Secretary of the Interior, not at all in the tribes.

Identification cards will be issued to applicants whose names appear on the tribal rolls approved by the Secretary of the Interior; or until January 1, 1970 (presumably to allow time for updating tribal rolls that need it), temporary cards may be issued on the tribal chairman's certification of the applicant's eligibility for formal tribal membership. Fishing gear is to be marked for identification as Indian gear.

Jurisdiction will be in the tribal courts, in a federal Court of Indian Offenses, or in a specially created federal Court of Indian Fishing Offenses. The regulation does not specify how enforcement of the conservation rules will be carried out but does say that the identification cards may be taken from any unauthorized holder by any federal, state, or tribal enforcement officer (Sec. 256.3 [f]).

The intent of the Department of the Interior in this regulation is to support the right to "off-reservation treaty fishing and at the same time serve conservation." Initial reactions of some of the western Washington tribes have been to welcome it as reinforcement of their assertion of this right. Others have questioned its failure to place in the tribes the authority for formulation of rules, and see this as weakening tribal authority. Tribes whose land base does not derive from the treaties, either by definition in the treaty or by executive order, presumably will not be affected by the regulations.

STATUS OF THE TRIBES

The status, even existence, of the tribes has been challenged. The Puyallup, Nisqually, and Muckleshoot tribal cases provide excellent examples of the courts' vacillations.

The Puyallups, signatories of the Treaty of Medicine Creek, have been actively and continuously recognized as a tribe since the treaty-signing by both Congress and the Department of Interior. The Puyallup constitution, approved in 1936, defines the territory of the tribe as the "restricted land" (land in Indian ownership subject to holding in trust by the federal government and not subject to state taxes) within the original confines of the reservation. Unallotted Indian land is omitted from this definition, but is referred to in Article IX. The constitution defines membership by referring to the 1929 approved roll, and children born to any member who resides within a certain area on and around the reservation. It provides that the tribal council should have power to act on membership.

The Washington Department of Game and Department of Fisheries are now seeking to enjoin all Puyallups from exercising any special Indian fishing rights, and specifically from using gillnets, on and off reservation. The case is *The Depart-*

ment of Game v. *The Puyallup Tribe,* cited previously. In 1964, Judge Cochran of the Pierce County Superior Court found for the state in a far-reaching decision: that there is no Puyallup tribe which succeeds in interest to the rights of the signers of Medicine Creek; that there is no Puyallup reservation; and that the fisheries regulations of Washington are reasonably necessary for the conservation of fish. He enjoined the tribe permanently from fishing in violation of any state regulation.

Judge Cochran stated in his memorandum opinion: ". . . the Puyallup Allotment Act of 1893 (22 Stat. 633) and the Cushman Act of 1904 (33 Stat. 565) in effect, abolished the reservation and any fishing rights attached thereto as to any land sold subsequent to the allotment to individual Indians" (p. 10). Cochran issued an injunction against all net fishing by the Puyallups.

The decision of the Washington State Supreme Court on the appeal of the *Puyallup* case was handed down on January 12, 1967 (70 Wn.2d 245), together with decisions in the companion Nisqually and Muckleshoot cases. The court first held that the remedy of determining rights through a declaratory judgment action was proper. It then slapped down the extreme position taken by the state that the Indians are a conquered people with no special rights to anything, by holding that "regardless of whether treaties with Indian tribes were necessary, they were deemed desirable by the United States and those entered into by it cannot be repudiated by this state or its courts" (p. 244).

The court reversed the lower court's finding that there was no Puyallup tribe, holding that the tribe exists "so long as the United States government, through its appropriate agencies, continues to recognize the existence of the Puyallup Tribe of Indians and its tribal roll" (p. 247).

The court held that there is no longer a Puyallup reservation and that all the land except the cemetery could be taxed. It held that the treaty fishing rights "are not absolute; they do not extend to the right to take fish with such gear and at such times as would destroy the fishery" (p. 250), proceeding to declare that they thought the judges of the Federal Ninth Circuit wrong in setting up the indispensability standard in the *Umatilla* case.

The Puyallups were held to have no "on-reservation" rights; and their "usual and accustomed" rights were to be subject to laws and regulations which are "reasonable and necessary to conserve the fishery" (p. 257).

In contrast, the Washington Supreme Court in *State* v. *Satiacum* seemed to hold that the Puyallups have the special right to fish on the river within the original boundaries of the reservation regardless of alienation of land.[45] The opinion as a whole indicates considerable disagreement among the judges, ending with the comment of Chief Justice Matthew Hill: ". . . nothing is decided except that the order dismissing the charges against the defendants is affirmed" (p. 538).

The *Puyallup* and *Nisqually* cases were considered together by the Supreme Court of the United States in *Department of Game* v. *Puyallup Tribe,* the decision dated May 27, 1968.[46] The opinion was written for a unanimous court, all judges participating, by Justice Douglas, who ruled in favor of state jurisdiction of off-reservation fishing, saying that it was analogous to prosecution of individual Indians for crimes committed off reservation.

Douglas states in a footnote that the Puyallup reservation had passed to private ownership except for two small tracts used as a cemetery, and that the Court does not decide whether "the reservation has been extinguished." He points out that the Washington State Supreme Court "seems to hold that the right to fish on streams once within the old reservation is protected."

[45] 50 Wn.2d 513, 314 P.2d 400 (1957).
[46] 391 U.S. 392 (1968).

The Court thus recognized the Puyallups as a tribe, and the state definitely lost its contention that the tribe has been extinguished.

The heart of the decision relates to both the Puyallups and the Nisquallys. The Court states:

> The treaty right is in terms the right to fish "at all usual and accustomed places." We assume that fishing by nets was customary at the time of the Treaty; and wc also assume that there were commercial aspects to that fishing as there are at present. But the *manner* in which the fishing may be done and its purpose, whether or not commercial, are not mentioned in the Treaty. We would have quite a different case if the Treaty had preserved the right to fish at the "usual and accustomed places" *in the "usual and accustomed"* manner. But the Treaty is silent as to the mode or modes of fishing that are guaranteed. Moreover, the right to fish at those respective places is not an exclusive one. Rather, it is one "in common with all citizens of the Territory." Certainly the right of the latter may be regulated. And we see no reason why the right of the Indians may not also be regulated by an appropriate exercise of the police power of the State [p. 693].

Astonishingly, the Court deals with the *Umatilla* case in a footnote, appearing to regard the "indispensable" criterion as either an error or a word used as a poor substitute for "necessary." The crucial concept of the *Umatilla* case that Indians should only be limited *after* limitation or prohibition on non-Indian fishing was ignored.

The Supreme Court appears to reject the Cochran ruling against Puyallup fishing, but this is accomplished indirectly and by returning the issue of actual conservation decisions to the state courts, which are directed to act according to the U.S. Supreme Court's criteria.

The decision is unsatisfactory. Here is a climactic determination which does not determine; a decision by the highest Court of the nation which is indecisive! This is a decision cognizable only by the initiate, the lawyers, not by laymen, not by the

Indian most concerned. Here is more language, crucially important as to basic rights, identity, self-respect, livelihood, and money value, which does not inform and which throws back to the lower courts and to further argument several basic questions:

1. Do the Indians have *any* off-reservation rights not shared by the non-Indian, beyond the naked right "to fish"?

2. What regulations are "reasonable and necessary"?

3. How was the determination of "reasonable and necessary" to be made—by legislative finding, by decisions of regulatory bodies, by the Washington state courts?

4. The Washington legislature *allocates* salmon and steelhead to different groups, by political action. Why should such political decisions not be related to and be made in recognition of Indian treaty rights, the protection of which is an obligation of the federal government?

The Nisquallys also were signatories of the Treaty of Medicine Creek in 1854, and were listed first in the preamble of the treaty. They adopted a "Constitution and Bylaws of the Nisqually Indian Community" under the Indian Reorganization Act in 1946. It defines the territory of the tribe as the "Nisqually Reservation" as established by the treaty and by executive order of January 20, 1857.

Membership is defined by reference to the "official census roll" of July 1, 1945, as corrected, and as including all children of at least one-quarter Indian blood born to members *resident* at the community. Power is given "the governing body" to rule, subject to federal review, on membership and "the adoption of new members when the resources of the Community make such adoptions feasible." The Nisquallys presently have a community council organized according to the constitution.

As with the Puyallups, the state sued civilly through its Department of Game and Department of Fisheries for an injunction restraining defendants from using nets or otherwise violating Washington fishing laws. In this case the tribe was omitted, the defendants being twelve named men, *Nugent Kautz, Jack McCloud, et al.*[47] On January 29, 1964, Judge Robert H. Jaques issued a temporary injunction on motion of the state prohibiting the defendants from net fishing "except that any . . . who are members of the Nisqually Tribe . . . may fish within . . . the . . . Reservation." Following a hearing in Pierce County, the case was appealed to the State Supreme Court.

In January 1967 the Supreme Court of Washington gave its opinion, holding that the case was properly in state courts as it was an attempt by the state to enforce its laws and regulations under state police power. The holding against the Nisqually fishermen referred to the decision in the *Puyallup* case handed down at the same time. This case was consolidated with the *Puyallup* case and considered by the Supreme Court of the United States.

The Muckleshoots, having their reservation southeast of Auburn, Washington, are not named as such in any treaty. Under the Indian Reorganization Act of 1934[48] the Muckleshoot Reservation Indians, with the cooperation of the Bureau of Indian Affairs of the U.S. Department of the Interior, adopted a constitution and bylaws, which were approved by the Secretary of the Interior May 13, 1936. It begins:

We, the Indians of the Muckleshoot Indian Tribes of the Muckleshoot Reservation, Wash., pursuant to the Act of Congress of June 18, 1934, do hereby establish this constitution for the Muckleshoot Indian Tribe. The purpose of this organization shall be the economic, educational, social, and moral rehabilitation of the Indians of the Muckleshoot Tribe, the conservation and development of their resources for the common welfare, the ultimate attainment of self-support and political independence, and the furnishing of a responsible organized body through which government subsidy and control may be exercised so long as necessary.

[47] Pierce County No. 158824. On appeal entitled *Dept. of Game* v. *Nugent Kautz,* 70 Wn.2d 275, 422 P.2d 771 (1967).
[48] Act of June 18, 1934, Ch. 576, 48 Stat. 984.

The constitution provides that the name of the organized body would be the Muckleshoot Indian Tribe, and that membership of the tribe shall consist of: (1) all persons of Indian blood whose names appear on the official census roll of Muckleshoot Indians, and who were residents on the Muckleshoot reservation on June 1, 1934; (2) all children born to any member of the tribe who is a resident of the reservation at the time of the birth of said children.

The constitution also gives power to the Tribal Council to pass ordinances, subject to review by the Secretary of the Interior, on "future membership and the adoption of new members." Washington state attorneys have cited the adoption provision as an argument against off-reservation fishing rights, suggesting that the tribe could thereby confer important rights, violating state responsibilities and laws, on any number of Indians or non-Indians.

The tribe insists that the Muckleshoots are treaty Indians under the treaty with the Duwamish, Suquamish, and other Indians, signed January 22, 1855, proclaimed April 11, 1859 (12 Stat. 927), usually known as the Treaty of Point Elliott. The fishing rights, basic to the livelihood of the Indian bands, were reserved:

ART. V. The right of taking fish at usual and accustomed grounds and stations is further secured to said Indians in common with all citizens of the Territory, and of erecting temporary houses for the purpose of curing, together with the privilege of hunting and gathering roots and berries on open and unclaimed lands; provided, however, that they shall not take shell fish from any beds staked or cultivated by citizens.

Since the state of Washington was not yet in existence, the United States was the signatory for the non-Indians. The treaty makes no restraint on the Indian fishing right as to time, gear, regulations, or existing or potential conservation needs. It lists twenty-two bands by name in its preamble, and bears the

signature, by mark, of eighty-two "chiefs, headmen, and dele-
gates of the aforesaid tribes and bands of Indians." No Muckleshoot band is named as such.

The United States Court of Claims, in *Duwamish et al.* v.
U.S., began in great earnest the game of "Find the Muckleshoot." [49] It made extensive findings without sufficient facts,
and concluded: "From contemporaneous records, official in
character, it indisputably appears that several tribes of Indians
other than the so-called 'Muckleshoots' inhabited what was
known as the Muckleshoot Reservation, and that all of those
placed upon the same were parties to the treaty of 1855"
(p. 604).

Many bands were named by the Court of Claims, and more
recently the Muckleshoots have identified themselves with the
former Skopamish or Skopabsh, Smulkamish, and Stakamish.
The state has argued that even if the present Muckleshoots are
composed of those bands, no one signed for them and therefore they are not "signatories" and have no treaty rights.

The first Indian signature is that of "Seattle, Chief of the
Duwamish and Suquamish tribes." The Muckleshoots argue
that Chief Sealth signed for them: "The next morning the
Indians all assembled; the four headchiefs—Seattle, Chief of
the Duwamish and other bands on White River and the Sound
within twenty miles of Seattle." [50] As proof they cite an arc
twenty miles from old Seattle intersecting the Muckleshoot
reservation at the area where the present channels of the Green
and White rivers come closest together.

In the 1934 *Duwamish* case quoted above, the U.S. Court of
Claims acted under a 1925 act of Congress, which is quoted as
finding that the "Muckleshoot" was not a treaty band.[51] In
this case the idea of a Muckleshoot band of 1855, which was

[49] 79 Ct. Cl. 530 (1934), cert. denied, 295 U.S. 755 (1934).
[50] Stevens, *Life of Isaac Ingalls Stevens,* p. 463.
[51] Act of Feb. 12, 1925, Ch. 214, 43 Stat. 886.

not under the treaty, is perpetuated even though the opinion quoted above states that "all bands placed on the reservation . . . were parties to the treaty of 1855." Thus, the ironic conclusion for the Muckleshoots!

Thinking they were a nontreaty tribe under the Congressional declaration of 1925, the Muckleshoots alleged nontreaty status and claimed for the taking by the United States. But the Court of Claims found they *were* a treaty tribe and had no claim because they had been compensated!

The tribe again sued the United States in *The Muckleshoot Tribe of Indians* v. *U.S.*, again alleging nontreaty status, on the grounds that they had not signed the treaty.[52] The tribe claims aboriginal title to a huge tract of land reaching to the crest of the Cascades and the peak of Mount Rainier, asking $3,500,000 compensation for the taking. The 1955 decision of the Claims Commission drops the old mystic idea of an 1855 Muckleshoot band, saying: "It wasn't until approximately 1868 that these Indians were referred to as Muckleshoots, and not until 1870 that the first designation as Muckleshoot Tribe was used" (p. 3 674). The opinion also states: "Admittedly the ancestors of the Muckleshoot Indians did not sign the Point Elliott Treaty" (p. 3 678), and proceeds to find the Muckleshoots entitled to compensation "for the deprivation by defendant of their ancestors' interest in the above area as of March 8, 1859." On appeal to the U.S. Court of Claims, the decision was affirmed, *except* as to the finding that the tribe was not a party to the treaty: "The court vacates the finding and statement without passing in any way on their correctness."

At least into 1967 the Department of the Interior used as its opinion on the treaty status of the Muckleshoots a memorandum from the office of the regional solicitor in Portland, dated October 16, 1961. That memorandum perpetuated the idea of

___

[52] 12 Ind. Cl. Comm. 743, Docket No. 98 (1963) Ct. Cl. Docket No. App. 3–64.

an aboriginal, nontreaty Muckleshoot band, citing *both* claims cases discussed above. However, there is a strange omission in the memorandum, which says: "We do not have the commission's decision of August 25, 1955." That opinion is important, since (at p. 3 674) as quoted above, the decision appears to abandon the idea of an aboriginal Muckleshoot tribe. Hence the solicitor's memorandum concludes:

Based on the above, we would conclude that the Muckleshoot Tribe of Indians are not treaty Indians, but that many of the Indians who now reside on the Muckleshoot Reservation are Treaty Indians.

It does not necessarily follow from the above, however, that the Muckleshoot Tribe and the Nooksack Tribe of Indians do not have federally recognized rights to fish and hunt equal with the rights accorded to the Treaty Indians under the treaties of Medicine Creek and Point Elliott. It seems clear from the Treaty of Point Elliott that the United States was purporting to acquire through cession from the Indians who were parties to that Treaty, all the lands in a substantial area of western Washington which embraced, among others the lands claimed by the Muckleshoot and Nooksack Tribes. It is also evident from those treaties and from subsequent dealings of the Government that the Government sought to impose certain obligations on the Muckleshoot Tribe and the Nooksack Tribe with respect to removal to reservations, which obligations were in the nature of the obligations imposed upon the Treaty Indians. It does not seem improper to conclude that the hunting and fishing rights granted by the Government under the Treaty of Point Elliott were intended for the benefit of all the Indians within the ceded area and that it was felt that the tribal representatives who signed the Treaty were qualified to speak for all such Indians. In other words, what we are saying is that even though the Indian Claims Commission may have subsequently found that the Muckleshoot Tribe and the Nooksack Tribe were in fact not represented at the Treaty by tribal leaders qualified to bind the Tribes and that they were, therefore, not signatories to the Treaty; nevertheless, the United States Senate in ratifying the Treaty, were speaking with reference to all of the Indians who inhabited the ceded area and were at least at that time under the impression that they were acquiring all of the lands within the delineation of the ceded area as described in the Treaty.

At some time after the Indian Claims Commission was established, the Muckleshoot Tribal Council printed identification cards which state:

This is to certify that the bearer _____ is an enrolled member of the Scopabsh-Muckleshoot Tribe and is entitled to the fishing rights granted by the Treaty of 1855 and confirmed by the courts and Indian Claims Commission _____ Tribal Officer.

In 1962 three Muckleshoot Indians were prosecuted for gillnet fishing on the Green River. They were acquitted, the King County Superior Court (Judge James W. Hodson) then finding that they were fishing in accordance with treaty rights. The court in that opinion used a most unusual phrase to describe one of the defendants who was not an enrolled member of the tribe, calling him a "constructive Muckleshoot."

In 1963 the state sued civilly to restrain the Muckleshoot tribe and certain members from gillnetting. In Superior Court the state's view prevailed, and the suit was appealed to the State Supreme Court. That court handed down its opinion on January 12, 1967 (*State* v. *Moses*, 70 Wash. 2d 282 [1967]). The court would not permit a belated correction in the appeal procedure, so the findings of fact of the King County Superior Court were accepted as the facts of the case and no appeal was allowed as to those findings. Thus the court affirmed the decision against the Muckleshoot and would not even go into the matter of treaty rights, accepting the lower court's finding that the Muckleshoot did not have any such rights.

Justices Robert T. Hunter and Frank Hale dissented: "The issue of recognizing the 'Muckleshoots' as descendants of the signatories of the treaties of 1854 and 1855 is necessarily a federal question. This court is acting without jurisdiction in making that determination" (p. 284).

On March 1, 1966, four Muckleshoots gillnetted in the Green

River in the vicinity of Neeley's Bridge, in a deliberate fish-in, with minuted approval of the Tribal Council. They were arrested and convicted in justice court. Muckleshoot Tribal Council members and the defendants, in the justice court, were not able to articulate in the idiom of the non-Indian their connection to the treaty, and uniformly professed ignorance of the tribe's having claimed nontreaty status in the two claims cases.

In this case the Washington state chapter of ACLU secured a volunteer attorney; the United States supplied two attorneys (although in April 1969 the Department of Justice withdrew), one through the Legal Services Program of the Office of Economic Opportunity, and the other an assistant United States attorney with the Department of Justice. Retrial on appeal to the Superior Court for King County took place in January 1968. The United States paid for the research services of an anthropologist, Dr. Barbara Lane of Victoria, B.C. She did extensive research, discovering new materials in government archives as well as performing research in the field. Testimony based on her research into the Muckleshoots occupied several days of the trial, and persuaded the judge that the Muckleshoots indeed owned rights as party to the Treaty of Point Elliott. However, Judge Lloyd Shorett ruled against the Indians on the gillnetting issue. Thus both issues were appealed to the State Supreme Court which, as of this writing, has not acted.

CONCLUSIONS REGARDING JUSTICE FOR INDIANS

It is clear that nonlegal factors determine and further complicate a complex legal situation: the small number of any tribes willing and able to put energy into the effort; the inability to communicate; lack of education leading to minimal historical knowledge; lack of funds for a legal effort competitive with the state; the inability of Washington tribes to unite to save fishing rights; and the massive passiveness of the United

States, with its large professional staff and huge repository of information.

There is also woven into the tattered web of Indian law the thread of the struggle between state and national power in our federal system. Washington's Supreme Court in its *McCoy* decision as well as in the three cases decided in January 1967 violates the supremacy clause of the Constitution relating to treaties and violates the holdings of the federal cases. Washington state appears to want: (1) uniformity of administration of fish and game laws; (2) allocation of anadromous fish to commercial and sport fishermen with exclusion of Indians as such; (3) approval of commercial and sport fishermen; (4) the elimination or minimization of enclaves of Indian power; and (5) decrease of federal power and increase of state power. The state courts have given scant attention to the Indian contention that only they and the federal government have jurisdiction over their exercise of fishing rights.

The state of Washington is not left without a remedy in its desire to make uniform conservation and allocation of fish. If the state believes that Indians at certain times and places threaten the runs, then it may seek to reach agreement with the Indians and the Department of the Interior as to regulations; or enact legislation which takes into account both the differing conservation needs of particular rivers and the rights of Indians on certain rivers.

Instead of doing the above, the state permits and directs its game and fisheries regulatory personnel, and its other police, to enforce the laws regulating fisheries in a way which almost totally ignores the off-reservation rights of Indians.

The Supreme Court of the United States in the consolidated *Puyallup* and *Nisqually* cases, decided in 1968, failed to resolve the basic issues and questions. Thus further cases must be brought to the Supreme Court if the recognition and preservation of basic Indian rights are to be secured.

V | The Controversy Today

The current controversy over Indian fishing rights began in the mid-1950's when the state attempted to control Indian fishing on the Puyallup River. The right to fish at "usual and accustomed" places was upheld at this time,[1] but in the early sixties the state began to arrest Indians fishing off reservation. The disposition of these cases in the state courts has not been consistent, but has tended toward increasingly narrow interpretation of treaty-protected off-reservation fishing rights.

The long years of nonunderstanding of Indian life by whites has made it nearly impossible for either side to talk to the other. The tension has sometimes led to violent confrontations on the rivers. The Indians often feel that the state is not willing even to listen to them and that their only recourse is simply to continue fishing. Harassment by state enforcement officers and reportedly by irate sport fishermen has occurred. Nets have been cut and other gear destroyed. The state has confiscated expensive gear at the time of arrests, according to some of the fishermen involved, and has not returned it even when charges were later dropped or the defendant acquitted. Indian fishermen

---

[1] *State* v. *Satiacum,* 50 Wn.2d 513 (1957). See chap. iv for discussion of this and other court decisions.

say that pressure from the state has kept fish buyers from buying fish caught off reservation.

THE EVENTS

In spite of the United States Court of Appeals decision in 1963 (*Maison* v. *Confederated Tribes of the Umatilla Indian Reservation*) supporting the earlier state supreme court decision in *State* v. *Satiacum,* arrests of Indian fishermen continued. In October 1963 the state obtained an injunction in the King County Superior Court closing the entire Green River to Indian net fishing. The following January, responding to another suit action by the state, Pierce County Superior Court issued an injunction closing the Nisqually River below the Nisqually reservation.

At that time the Survival of American Indians Association was founded, dedicated to the assertion and preservation of off-reservation fishing rights. Members of the Survival Association participated in a series of demonstrations to dramatize their situation. Early in 1964 protest fish-ins were staged on the Nisqually River at Frank's Landing.[2] In March the National Indian Youth Council organized a demonstration in Olympia. Actor Marlon Brando, who came to lend his support to the Indians, was arrested for net fishing in the Puyallup River, but was released on a technicality and not tried. Later he and a number of Indians participated in a conference with Governor Albert Rosellini. Billy Frank, Sr., the elderly Nisqually man on whose land some of the demonstrations had occurred, filed a petition in federal court for investigation of alleged brutality by state enforcement officers.

As the dispute continued, Senator Warren G. Magnuson in-

[2] Frank's Landing is located on the land belonging to Billy Frank, Sr., which he acquired in exchange for his allotment on the Nisqually reservation east of the river when that part of the reservation was taken for Fort Lewis. See chap. iii.

troduced two measures in Congress in an effort to come to a solution. Senate Joint Resolution 170 would have recognized treaty rights but provided that state regulation would apply off reservation. Senate Joint Resolution 171 would have extinguished by purchase the off-reservation fishing right. Neither was acceptable to Indians. The state of Washington supported both, while the Fish Commission of Oregon and the Idaho Fish and Game Department favored S.J.R. 171.[3] Hearings were held in August 1964, and the proposals were allowed to die in committee.

In September in the Pierce County Superior Court, Judge John D. Cochran (who the next year held that there is no Puyallup tribe) ruled in another case against Satiacum that net fishing is legal as on reservation within the boundaries of the original Puyallup reservation.[4] However, that same fall Judge F. A. Walterskirchen of the King County Superior Court made permanent the injunction against the Muckleshoots on the Green River on the ground that the Muckleshoots are not a treaty tribe.

Another demonstration took place in Olympia in February 1965, but did not attract as much participation as the one the previous year. In May, in the previously quoted case of *Department of Game* v. *Puyallup Tribe,* Judge Cochran ruled that the Puyallup tribe no longer exists, and issued a permanent injunction against their fishing in the Puyallup River. In the summer, in another effort to resolve the controversy, the Department of Interior proposed federal regulation of off-reservation fishing. Because the proposal provided for possible delegation of regu-

[3] Passage of S.J.R. 171 would have made S.J.R. 170 irrelevant. Washington officials regarded S.J.R. 170 as confirming what they considered the situation to be already, but believed Indians should be compensated for the abrogation of treaty rights, whatever they were. Robert W. Schoning, director of the Fish Commission of Oregon, was not opposed to S.J.R. 170 but believed S.J.R. 171 to be better. See 1964 *Hearings,* pp. 25–49.

[4] See chap. ii for discussion of reservation boundaries.

latory authority to the state, the tribes feared this would lead to state control. The state, on the other hand, viewed the suggestion that a federal agency assume the function as a usurpation of state authority.

In October 1965 violent confrontations broke out on the Nisqually River, which had become a center for the controversy. An Indian boat was spilled by state officers, and several nights later a force of officers attempted a raid at Frank's Landing. The Indians resisted, and state patrol officers were called in. On October 13, in a well-publicized protest at the same spot, Indians put a canoe into the water. Officers attempted arrests for alleged illegal fishing, and an emotion-charged battle of paddles, sticks, and stones ensued.[5] On the twenty-sixth the Survival of American Indians Association marched in protest at the federal court house in Seattle.

In the spring of 1966, Dick Gregory, national entertainment and civil rights figure, participated in a series of fish-ins on behalf of the Survival of American Indians Association. He was arrested and convicted, and subsequently served a sentence in the Thurston County jail.[6]

---

[5] Two observers from the American Friends Service Committee arrived after the main battle. The scene was still tense and confused. One AFSC observer was threatened with arrest as he asked what was happening. Both reported that they smelled liquor on the breath of two state officials. Unknown to the AFSC beforehand, this report was carried by a radio news broadcast. It is symptomatic of the situation that this incidental information received attention from the media and state officials far out of proportion to its importance, obscuring the more important question of whether undue force was used by the state officers in dealing with the fish-in. The seven Indians arrested for interfering with the officers were brought to trial more than three years later, in February 1969, and were acquitted. Their defense was based on the assertion that their own intent at the demonstration had been peaceful, and that an extensive and unnecessary show of force by the state officers had constituted a threat to their safety, producing the defensive reaction on their part.

[6] Gregory was convicted in the Thurston County Superior Court of Judge Hewitt Henry on three counts of illegal net fishing, and was sentenced to serve ninety days on each charge, to run concurrently. The

Members of the Muckleshoot tribe demonstrated on the Green River in March to dramatize their situation.[7] The Washington state chapter of the American Civil Liberties Union undertook to defend the Muckleshoot fishermen arrested, thus for the first time entering a case specifically on the fishing right.

On May 31, 1966, the Department of Justice, having announced that on request of a tribe it would defend Indian fishermen who were fishing off reservation in accordance with tribal regulations, entered the *Puyallup* case before the Washington Supreme Court as *amicus curiae*.[8]

In the fall of 1967 Judge Lloyd Shorett of the King County Superior Court ruled, on the basis of anthropological testimony, that the Muckleshoots are a treaty tribe.[9] However, the decision upheld the state's right to regulate Muckleshoot fishing off reservation.

On May 27, 1968, the United States Supreme Court handed down its decision on the Nisqually and Puyallup cases it had agreed to hear. The decision confirmed the treaty-protected right of Indians to fish off reservation, but declared the state had the right to regulate "provided the regulation meets appropriate standards and does not discriminate against In-

---

conviction was upheld on appeal to the State Supreme Court in March 1968. Gregory returned to the state of Washington to serve the sentence. He was in jail forty of the ninety days, and was then released as a "trusty at large." He fasted while in jail. On his release he said to newsmen: "If more people went to jail for rights, fewer would go for wrongs."

[7] Also in the spring of 1966, conflict occurred on the Columbia River. Some Yakima Indians, not supported by the Tribal Council, took up arms to defend themselves against the Washington state enforcement officers, and made a citizen's arrest of an officer, claiming he was trespassing. The state of Oregon, which had had a cooperative agreement with the Yakimas, arrested several fishermen who were fishing in accordance with tribal regulations.

[8] *Department of Game* v. *The Puyallup Tribe*, 70 Wash. 241, Dec.2d, 1966.

[9] *State* v. *Robert Moses et al.*, King County Superior Court, No. 44836.

dians." [10] The question of what is "reasonable and necessary" regulation was remanded to the state courts for further clarification. A revised injunction subsequently obtained by the state for the Puyallup River is essentially the same as the old. A new injunction was not obtained for the Nisqually.

The fall of 1968 brought renewed demonstrations on the lower Nisqually, this time with support from numerous students and out-of-state Indians. Certain Indians announced that they were arming themselves to prevent what they considered to be trespass by state enforcement authorities. [11] The Bureau of Indian Affairs now made a statement supporting the Nisqually right to an off-reservation fishery and questioning the necessity of the state regulation which outlawed the Indian net fishery there. The Governor's Advisory Committee on Indian Affairs investigated the problem and made recommendations to the governor. Lower Nisqually River fishermen continued to fish in the Frank's Landing area. The end of the season brought an end to the immediate tensions but not to the controversy. In the fall of 1969 the Department of Fisheries allowed an off-reservation Nisqually fishery but excluded the part of the river customarily fished by those involved in the Frank's Landing actions.

An intense partisanship has developed from the disputes on the several rivers. It has obscured obvious areas of common interest and made it next to impossible for either side to see the viewpoints of the other. The reactions of the antagonists, in part the product of the differences in the cultural backgrounds, have exacerbated the already existing problems of communica-

---

[10] *Puyallup Tribe* v. *Department of Game et al.,* 391 U.S. 392 at 398.
[11] Understandably this move attracted much attention from the public. See Appendix 1 for "A Citizen's Letter to His Governor," dated Oct. 17/28, 1968, by Hank Adams of the Survival of American Indians Association, in which he expressed the seriousness of purpose and sense of responsibility of the people at Frank's Landing. The letter specified conditions and limits for the use of arms.

tion which are rooted in those same cultural backgrounds. A look at the various interpretations of the issues is needed.

To the American Indian, the treaty is a living document. Though often ignored, circumvented and trampled upon, the treaty continues to occupy a position of prime importance to the Indian. It is difficult to convey the depth of feeling of the American Indian on this subject. It is indeed unfortunate that once again in our history, our non-Indian neighbors have found it so difficult sharing, even in the most unequal proportions, the natural bounty of this country. It is sad indeed that the Indian is again called upon to defend against another onslaught, one of the remaining precious assets left to him under his treaty.[12]

Concern for the preservation of the salmon is implicit in the Indian heritage. In our extensive contact with Puget Sound and other Northwest Indians, we have found the fishermen to have a strong sense of responsibility for the welfare of the fish. Conservation is essential to the economic and social well-being of the tribes, which depend to a large extent on fishing for their livelihood, and which hold to their fishing rights as one of the remaining expressions of their Indian identity. The Western Washington Indian Fisheries Association, active during the early sixties, was a significant expression of Indian outlook.[13] The preface of their constitution read:

We the Indians of Western Washington, recognize that our fisheries are a basic and important natural resource and of vital concern to the Indians of this state and that the conservation of this resource is dependent upon effective and progressive management thereof. We further believe that by unity of action we can best accomplish these things, not only for the benefit of our own people, but for all of the people of the Pacific Northwest.[14]

[12] 1964 *Hearings,* p. 84.
[13] The organization was founded in 1962 and was active for two or three years.
[14] Constitution of Western Washington Indian Fisheries Association.

The need for accurate and detailed knowledge of present conditions of the fish runs and the factors which affect them, a prerequisite to an effective and equitable program for redevelopment of the fish runs, has been a long-standing concern of western Washington Indians. In 1964 a petition was presented to Governor Rosellini requesting that an impartial study, involving federal and state agencies, be made of all salmon and steelhead fishing in the state as a basis for determining the best methods of managing the runs. No such move has been undertaken.

The same year the Intertribal Council of Western Washington Indians adopted a resolution giving qualified support to Senator Magnuson's Senate Joint Resolution 174 calling for a comprehensive study of the country's commercial fishery resources:

> Whereas the tribes of the Pacific Northwest desire that the fish runs be increased so that there are more fish available for all parties: commercial fishermen, Indian fishermen, and sportsmen, and are desirous of engaging actively and constructively in any program to insure that the fish runs do increase; and
>
> Whereas it is the opinion of the Indians of the Pacific Northwest that there is no definitive study . . . which covers the salmon resources, and it is the belief of the Indians that the statistics and data introduced at prior hearings by representatives of the Washington State Departments of Fish and Game and by sportsmen are unreliable and should not be used as a basis for abrogating or limiting treaty rights; and
>
> Whereas it is to the interest of all that the cause or causes of depletion of salmon runs be accurately determined . . .
>
> The intertribal council supports the proposed legislation of Senator Magnuson calling for such survey, provided the same be enlarged to include the study of Indian fishing as above requested; . . .[15]

The National Congress of American Indians at its twenty-

[15] 1964 *Hearings,* p. 215.

first Annual Convention on July 31, 1964, adopted a similar resolution urging "that Congress be urged to enact legislation for a comprehensive study and survey of the fishing industry from the time of spawning to the catching, processing, and distribution, including a detailed study of the extent of Indian fisheries, the percentage of the Indian catch in relation to the catch of commercial and sportsmen fishing [*sic*], and the effect of Indian fishing on the fish resources"; and that action on proposed legislation regarding Indian fishing rights (S.J.R. 170 and S.J.R. 171), be withheld pending completion of the study, in order to avoid violation of the Indian treaty rights.[16]

Differences among Indians have been cited as reason for not recognizing off-reservation rights, on the ground that Indians themselves do not agree on their continuation or even on what they are. Walter Neubrech, chief of the Enforcement Division of the Department of Game, said he believed not over 1 percent of the Indians were involved in off-reservation net fishing, and that many had expressed concern to him that conservation practices be enforced.[17] The implication is that the "good Indians" are on "our side," and that that includes most Indians. An interpretation of the differing opinions is needed.

Some tribal leaders in the past have said privately they did not realistically believe that off-reservation sites would be recognized. The Survival of American Indians Association, on the other hand, argues that by making their stand they are preventing the take-over of all Indian fishing by the state.[18]

Some Indians have taken the position that it was not the intent of the treaty-makers that any governmental regulation be exercised over Indians fishing and therefore that no agency, not even the Tribal Council, has the authority to regulate. No

[16] *Ibid.*, pp. 24, 25.
[17] *Ibid.*, p. 31.
[18] The U.S. Supreme Court ruling in 1968 in the *Puyallup* decision now affirms the existence of off-reservation rights.

tribal government supports this view. At the other extreme are a few Indians who believe assimilation is inevitable, and that hunting and fishing rights are no longer relevant.

Some hold that members of any tribe within a particular treaty area are entitled to fish at any of the accustomed sites there, or even in any of the treaty areas. At least within the area covered by the Treaty of Medicine Creek this is reasonable, as it is consistent with pretreaty practice. Moreover, such a view lends itself to the development of a more rational and effective program in Indian fisheries in the area than has yet occurred.

Many Indians believe they have a poor public image in the controversy, and act according to their assessment of what the effects on that image are likely to be. Consequently, support given by tribal officials to off-reservation fishermen varies. The Muckleshoot Council is united with the Indians who fish off reservation. The Puyallup Tribal Council also is actively engaged in fighting for the off-reservation fishing right, but has taken issue with the Survival of American Indians Association and with some individual Puyallups over tactics.

The Nisquallys, Puyallups, and Muckleshoots, small tribes with few resources and having some of the factional divisions common in small communities, have been particularly exposed to outside criticism. Their internal disagreements have been publicized, and in the nature of a self-fulfilling prophecy the publicity has sometimes aggravated the differences. Publicity heightened a rift between the Nisqually Community Council and off-reservation fishermen on the Nisqually River. Some council chairmen reacted against the demonstrations on the lower Nisqually, whose participants have included Puyallups, other non-Nisquallys, and on occasion non-Indians. The chairman of the Nisqually Community Council in 1965 is said to have publicly characterized as renegades those taking part in the demonstrations on the lower Nisqually River.

However, the present Fish Committee of the Council includes members from both the active fishermen on the lower river and the on-reservation fishermen. The Nisqually fishing regulations clearly assert off-reservation rights. During the demonstrations in the fall of 1968 at Frank's Landing, some council members privately expressed discomfort with the participation of the non-Indians, but there was no public rejection of the effort.

The principal differences are not disagreements about the importance of fishing, treaty rights, or conservation, but are over questions of proper strategy and tactics for defending those values. The hearings in 1964 on S.J.R. 170 and S.J.R. 171 gave Indians an opportunity to present their views. Testimony and exhibits were presented by the Yakima, Makah, Puyallup, Quinault, and Tulalip tribes from Washington; the Confederated Tribes of Warm Springs from Oregon; the Intertribal Council of Western Washington Indians; and the National Congress of American Indians. Basic agreement in outlook and position runs through their testimony.[19] The Yakimas declared that Indian fishing was not endangering the fish, but that other fishermen were encroaching on the Indian fishing right. Along with the Makahs, they emphasized the dependence of many Indian people on fishing as a livelihood.[20] The Puyallup tribe entered into the record their fishing regulations together with a resolution requesting the Bureau of Indian Affairs to provide enforcement assistance.

The Puyallup vice-chairman, Silas Cross, declared: "During the fishing seasons, the Indians dare not leave the river because the sportsmen smash our boats and rip our nets, steal our motors, in order to get revenge on the Indians." Chairman Frank Wright of the Puyallup Tribal Council testified that because of intimidation the Puyallups fish "less than 10 percent

---

[19] See 1964 *Hearings.*
[20] See 1964 *Hearings,* "Statement of the Yakima Indian Nation," pp. 50–61; and "Statement of Makah Indian Nation," pp. 76–84.

of the area they had reserved for themselves in the treaty of
1855." [21] Wright emphasized the tribe's desire for a positive
approach as he continued:

> We request this committee and Congress to uphold our treaty
> rights . . . and we request assistance to develop our fishing in-
> dustry and their sanctioning of our authority to police our own
> fishing areas for which we have been seeking from all branches of
> the Indian Bureau since 1954.[22]

Whatever else one may think of the matter, on reading the
pages of the testimony one can hardly doubt the seriousness
with which Indians regard fishing, the maintenance of the rights
guaranteed by treaty, and conservation practices. In the Indian
view the fishing right is something which cannot properly be
bought or sold. A monetary value is artificial and sale would
be immoral. It would detach the people from the world in
which they live and sever the continuity from the past to the
future, and deprive their descendants of an important element
of life's meaning.

SPORT FISHERMEN

The number of sport fishermen, as shown by the number of
licenses issued, has increased consistently over the years.[23] The
Washington State Sportsmen's Council, Inc., gives voice to the
opinion of sport fishermen. It counted twenty thousand members in member clubs two or three years ago, but the number
has now dropped to nine thousand (March 1969).[24] Officials
of the Department of Game attend all meetings of the council
and often participate in the business of the organization. The
council also influences the composition of the Game Commis-

---

[21] *Ibid.,* pp. 100, 104
[22] *Ibid.,* p. 105.
[23] See *Biennial Reports* of the Department of Game.
[24] Information from Howard Nelson, Jr., Secretary of the Washington
State Sportsmen's Council, Inc., in early 1969.

sion, whose six members serve six-year overlapping terms with two being appointed every other year.

The organization of the Department of Game lends itself to influence by the Sportsmen's Council.

> The director of the Department of Game . . . is one of the few department heads who is not appointed directly by the Governor. Instead, the Governor appoints the State Game Commission, consisting of six qualified voters, who, in turn, appoint the director. The director is the ex officio secretary of the commission, which decides on the regulations to be enforced by the director and his employees.[25]

Although it is not required legally, since the mid-thirties all appointees to the commission have been from slates recommended to the governor by the Sportsmen's Council except during one term when the council was at odds with the governor, and in the fall of 1968 when Governor Dan Evans appointed one commissioner not from among those recommended by the council.

For many years the council has had an Indian Committee. A former chairman was sympathetically interested in Indian views and tried to develop relationships between Indians and the organization. He was unsuccessful except with the Yakimas, who regularly sent observers to meetings of the council. Many members of the Steelhead Club tried to have him removed, but the board of the council upheld his right to the position. When he resigned, however, a member of the Steelhead Club took his place.

The Sportsmen's Council, apparently speaking for the majority of sport fishermen, has made clear its position of opposition at all points to off-reservation Indian net fishing. It is especially disturbed by Indians netting steelhead, which the state has endeavored to reserve for sport fishermen. The council is

---

[25] Mary W. Avery, *Government of Washington State* (Seattle: University of Washington Press, 1966), pp. 102–3.

opposed to any net fishing in the rivers, contending that it is impossible to take salmon and not steelhead, and pointing out that the state has closed the rivers to net fishing. They assert that Indians are subject to all state regulations except on the reservation. They interpret the treaty phrase "in common with all citizens of the Territory" to mean that Indians have the same, not a superior, right to the fish. They voice the fear that Indian net fishing will endanger the state program of stocking the rivers. The council is particularly sensitive about the steelhead stocking program, since it is financed principally by license and other fees paid by sportsmen.[26]

Sport salmon fishing, mostly offshore either in the ocean or inland bodies like Puget Sound, attracts increasing numbers of fishermen. In 1963 the Department of Fisheries said:

Washington salmon anglers had a big year in 1963, with the estimated catch exceeding one million for the first time. . . . Fishing effort, which obviously has a profound effect on catch, also took a considerable jump during the year to 1,467,000, an increase in angler trips of 337,000 over the previous high of 1962.[27]

In 1966 the report was: "Although salmon angling effort (number of angler trips) and catches were down from the near record 1965 figures, the largest *even* year . . . harvest occurred in 1966." [28]

COMMERCIAL FISHERMEN

Commerical fishermen do not have a well-organized lobby and exert only small pressure on the state. The Department of Fisheries exercises tight control over commercial fishermen, imposing restrictions on certain kinds of fishing at very short

[26] See chap. iii, section on Development of Fisheries in Washington State.
[27] Washington State Department of Fisheries, *Annual Report*, 1963, p. 42 (hereafter cited as *Annual Report*).
[28] *Annual Report*, 1966, p. 121. The significance of the even year is that pink salmon run only in odd-numbered years. See chap. vi.

notice in response to specific variations in the runs and conditions. Groups representing commercial fishermen presented
statements in the hearings on S.J.R. 170 and S.J.R. 171 in
1964, indicating opposition to Indian fishing, especially on the
Columbia.[29] However, there is little evidence that commercial
fishermen generally feel themselves in direct competition with
Indian fishermen. State officials often point out that many
Indian people are in commercial fishing, mostly as employees,
and follow the same rules and regulations as other commercial
fishermen.

THE NUMBERS GAME

The 1960 U.S. census showed slightly more than 21,000
Indians in the state of Washington, including those both on and
off the reservations. The same census recorded a total state
population of 2,853,000.

Available statistics do not present a precise and adequate
picture of the fishing effort of the fisheries based on these
populations.[30] However, some figures, as shown on the following pages, will serve to give an impression of the comparative
status of the fisheries.

In 1963 the Department of Fisheries estimated that 2,750
Indians fished "commercially" in the state, on reservations and
at the usual and accustomed stations.[31] Our own observation
suggests that this would include even the most casual fishermen, and that those who fish with any regularity would total

[29] See testimony of Theodore T. Bugas, executive secretary of Columbia River Salmon and Tuna Packers Association, 1964 *Hearings,* pp.
122–30, and some included letters.
[30] For detailed discussion of the fisheries statistics see Mary B. Isely, "A
Look at the Washington State Indian Fisheries, As Shown in State
Department of Fisheries Statistics," mimeographed (Seattle, Wash.:
American Friends Service Committee, 1969).
[31] 1963 *Annual Report,* p. 195. There is no source of accurate information as to the number of Indian fishermen in the state.

between one third and one half of that number. The number of salmon sport fishermen is not known, since no license is required for salmon sport fishing. However, Washington marine salmon sport "angler trips" in 1965 totaled 1,270,000.[32] Non-Indian commerical salmon fishermen in 1966 can be roughly estimated as between 4,000 and 4,500, based on the state licenses issued.[33]

As to steelhead fishing, 187,525 steelhead permit cards were issued in 1966 and 140,375 fishermen actually fished for steelhead, according to Department of Game data.[34]

Because of the history of nonrecognition of the Indian fisheries by almost everybody but the Indians themselves, information regarding them is less precise than for the other fisheries. Nevertheless a rough idea of the proportional relationships of the numbers of salmon caught by the three fisheries—the *de facto* allocations—can be obtained. Figure 1 shows, in total numbers of salmon of all five species, the catches for Puget Sound (all Washington waters inside Cape Flattery) of each of the three fisheries year by year since 1950. Figure 2 shows the same information for Washington state.[35] These two graphs picture the gross changes that have occurred for each fishery, with all of the yearly fluctuations. The changes depicted must not, however, be taken as accurate for any particular species or for any particular fishing area—the variations are great.

For summary proportional figures which are sufficiently current to have meaning in the present controversy but still will avoid a generalized picture based on just one or two years, we show each fishery's proportion of the ten-year total catch for

[32] See 1965 *Annual Report*, p. 16A.

[33] This does not allow for duplication if some of the same fishermen get more than one license.

[34] *Summary of 1966 Steelhead Catch,* State Game Department, Olympia, Wash.

[35] Information based on data in *1966 Fisheries Statistical Report,* State of Washington Department of Fisheries, and from 1967 Department of Fisheries statistics not yet published.

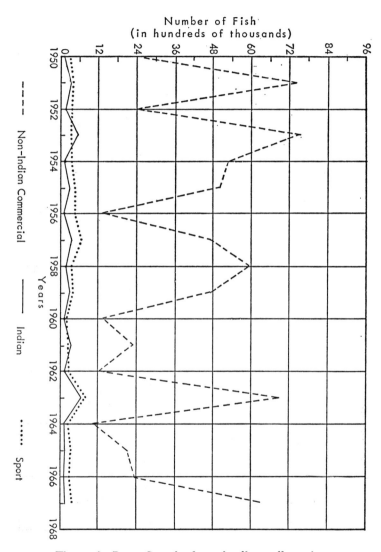

Figure 1. *Puget Sound salmon landings, all species,
in numbers of fish yearly, 1950–67*

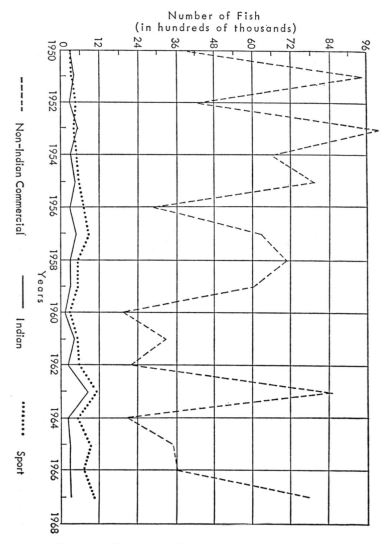

Figure 2. *Washington State salmon landings, all species,
in numbers of fish yearly, 1950–67*

1958–67. Figures 3 and 4 are computed on the total catch of all species of salmon for Puget Sound and for Washington state, respectively. Figure 5 shows the proportions by individual species for Puget Sound, and Figure 6 shows the proportions by individual species for all of Washington.[36]

The steelhead catch by Indians goes unreported as far as the state of Washington is concerned. A total sportsmen's catch of 347,100 steelhead in 1966 is shown by the Department of Game. The 1965–66 winter season catch was 4.9 percent greater than the previous record high in 1963–64; and the 1966 summer-run catch was 51.7 percent greater than the previous summer-run high in 1965.[37]

THE POSITION OF THE STATE

The Department of Fisheries and the Department of Game, separate agencies which were originally one, carry the state's responsibility for its fish resources and in practice are the state's spokesmen on the subject. They speak with one voice on the matter of Indian fishing. While in actual approach the Department of Fisheries has been more flexible than the sport-oriented Department of Game, the testimony of Joseph L. Coniff, assistant attorney general speaking for the Department of Fisheries in the 1964 Indian fishing rights hearings on S.J.R. 170 and S.J.R. 171, expressed the overall state view of its proper position with respect to off-reservation fishing by Indians:

The State has to operate on a system of equality of all its citizens, and in order to have an effective management program under our State police power it is essential that we have a system of regulation. . . .

. . . the State of Washington is unalterably opposed to Federal regulation of off-reservation fisheries. . . . Historically the State

[36] *Ibid.*
[37] *Summary of 1966 Steelhead Catch,* State Game Department.

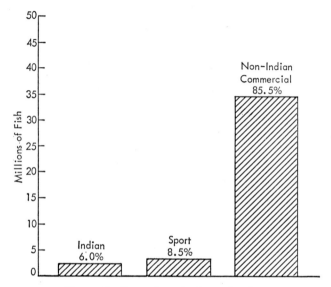

Figure 3. *Puget Sound salmon landings,*
all species, 1958–67, by fishery

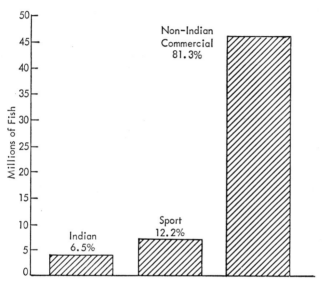

Figure 4. *Washington State salmon landings,
all species, 1958–67, by fishery*

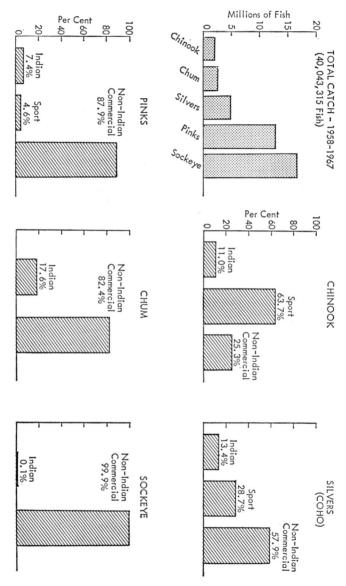

Figure 5. *Puget Sound salmon landings, by species, 1958–67.*
Percentage of catch, by fishery

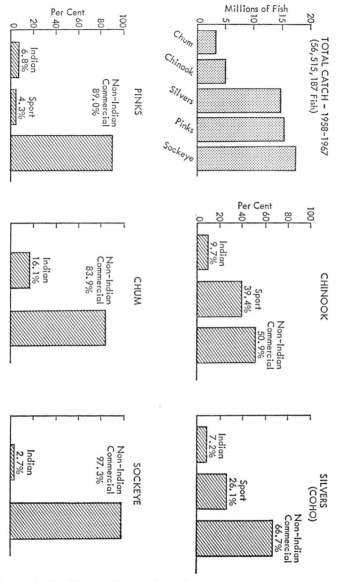

Figure 6. *Washington State salmon landings, by species, 1958–67.*
Percentage of catch, by fishery

has been the proper party, the proper managing party, and has been attempting to the extent that we have been able to fulfill our obligations insofar as conservation of its resources are concerned. . . . I feel that it is essentially an unworkable program, that is, to divide the management power for each run of fish. In other words, in order to have an intelligent management program, it should be unified. . . .[38]

Early *Reports* of the Department of Fisheries indicate that the state's view of its authority over off-reservation fishing has been basically the same for many years. The *Report* for 1899–1900 included a discussion entitled "Trouble with Indians on Our Hatchery Streams," in which the following appears:

The general fisheries law passed by the last Legislature provides that any Indian residing in this state may take salmon or other fish by any means and at any time for the use of himself and family. The Attorney General has advised us that . . . this clause . . . does not allow the Indians to violate the general fishing laws.[39]

While the state's view that it has the same authority over off-reservation Indian fishing as over any other is apparently of long standing, the state has not acted uniformly with respect to Indian fishing. The state has also been much more inclined at some periods than at others to see a unique Indian right to fish as valid. As was noted in Chapter III, some state officials in the years around 1915 attempted to control certain Indian fishing on the reservation. In contrast, during the 1940's and 1950's the Department of Fisheries entered into a number of agreements with various tribes, under which the Indians agreed to certain limitations in the interest of adequate "escapement." [40]

[38] 1964 *Hearings,* p. 27.
[39] *Annual Report* for 1899–1900, p. 21.
[40] For some discussion of the agreements, see *Annual Reports* of the years mentioned. "Escapement" is a somewhat imprecise term used to describe the fishes' passing by—escaping—all the dangers, including

In 1958 Milo Moore, at that time director of the Department of Fisheries, wrote:

If any man or race of people merit consideration in a fishery beyond that of all others, the American Indians claim that right. . . . Recognizing whatever rights the Indian people have reserved to them, and the desire of most tribes people to establish methods of improving their fisheries, the matter rests with the Federal Government to seek the understanding necessary to establish their right.[41]

Six years later Coniff's testimony in the hearings on S.J.R. 170 and S.J.R. 171 seemed to reflect quite a different view:

The facts and figures which the department has developed indicate . . . that unregulated Indian net fishery of the nature which has been described is totally incompatible with any intelligent management program designed to conserve this great natural resource. . . .[42]

Moore's statement also reflects another aspect of the state's view of Indian fishing—that it is not clear what the Indian fishing right is, and that it is the responsibility of the federal government to clarify and "establish" it. Coniff expressed it thus: "We do not take a position regarding what is the quantum of treaty rights. We frankly do not know." [43] Similarly, a working paper prepared by the Department of Fisheries for the 1965 legislature stated: "The guarantee of the Indian right must be determined and defined. Once their rights and responsibilities

---

all the fisheries, along the way as they travel from the ocean and up the rivers to the gravel beds to spawn. A principal task of "fisheries management" is to plan for sufficient escapement to maintain or enhance the runs, at the same time allowing for maximum use of the resource consistent with such maintenance or enhancement. If the fish pass more than one fishery, escapement past the first must be great enough to allow for the catch of the fisheries further along as well as for spawning.

[41] Milo Moore, Ken McLeod, and Don Reed, *Fisheries,* III (Olympia: Washington State Department of Fisheries, 1960), 26–27.

[42] *1964 Hearings,* p. 25

[43] *Ibid.,* p. 27.

are determined, the state agencies involved will manage accordingly." [44]

The agreements made by the tribes and the Department of Fisheries were generally a limited and one-sided type of cooperation, however sound they may have been for conservation. They were to a large extent a matter of the Indians' acceding to limitations determined by the state to be necessary to maintain the fish. Nevertheless, since interest evidently existed on both sides, the agreements might have led to more extensive communication and cooperation.[45]

That did not happen. The Department of Fisheries and Department of Game moved instead toward more stringent interpretation of their authority over off-reservation Indian fishing. By 1963 the state's public position was that cooperation with tribes on matters of off-reservation fishing is impossible, and the state must have full control. It withdrew from certain agreements regarding off-reservation sites.[46] In discussion with study group members in January 1966, an assistant attorney general of the state voiced the opinion that while the state might have been willing to negotiate with the tribes three or four years previously, at the time of speaking it was impossible.

Since that time, and following the *Puyallup* decision of 1968, the Department of Fisheries and the Squaxin Indians near the southern end of Puget Sound signed an agreement regard-

[44] Washington State Department of Fisheries, "The Off-Reservation Indian Fishery," in *Working Draft: The Ingredients of a Ten-Year Plan* (Olympia, Wash., 1965?).
[45] Indian interest shows in the fact that they entered into the agreements; state interest is evident in comments in some of the *Annual Reports*. However, see also testimony of Robert Jim for the Yakima tribe in 1964 *Hearings,* pp. 62–68.
[46] An agreement regarding the Columbia with the Confederated Tribes of the Warm Springs Reservation and the Confederated Tribes of the Umatilla Reservation, both of Oregon, and the Fish Commission of Oregon; and an agreement with the Yakima tribe regarding the Klickitat River. For Yakima comments on the Klickitat agreement, see 1964 *Hearings,* p. 64.

ing off-reservation gillnet fishing.[47] However, continuing actions against Nisqually and Puyallup fishermen, as well as official statements at the time of the Squaxin agreement (see Appendix 2), suggest that the state's basic view has not changed.[48]

The state agencies have maintained that agreements are unsatisfactory because their experience proves Indian regulation to be ineffective, even though some were acknowledged to be effective and some working arrangements have continued. The effectiveness and appropriateness of various tribes' regulation of their fisheries both on and off reservation have unquestionably varied.[49] In some instances the state contention that tribes have no authority off reservation has been a factor in tribal regulatory difficulties.[50] So far as the agreements are concerned, their having originated with the state's view of what was needed has not contributed to Indian satisfaction with them, which may be part of the difficulty in their working.[51] Again non-Indian inability or unwillingness to take into account Indian viewpoints and the need for Indian participation, even when recognizing Indian interest, has been exhibited.[52]

[47] The Squaxins were also party to the Treaty of Medicine Creek. Squaxin Island is their reservation, but they live either on the nearby mainland or in other communities.

[48] The *Puyallup* decision upheld the state's authority to regulate under certain conditions if required for conservation, without spelling out how the necessity would be proven. State actions have been continued on this basis without, in the view of some, providing proof of the conservation need. See Epilogue for discussion of subsequent U.S. District Court decision (*Sohappy* v. *Smith* and *U.S.* v. *Oregon*) and recent state actions.

[49] See 1964 *Hearings,* pp. 81, 85.

[50] For example, the Nisqually; see chap. iii.

[51] See testimony of James Hovis, attorney for the Yakimas, in 1964 *Hearings,* pp. 68–75; Alvin J. Ziontz, attorney for the Makahs, pp. 84–88; and Charles Hobbs, attorney for the Quinaults, p. 146.

[52] The state's interest in the agreements with Indian tribes as being a matter of protecting the non-Indian fisheries is not unnoticed by the Indians. It called forth several comments in the 1964 *Hearings.* Ziontz put it: ". . . since State officials have never acceded to the idea that the Indian is entitled to a fair share of the salmon, it is difficult for the Indian to escape the feeling that the restrictions requested by the

The Department of Fisheries and Department of Game also point to an increase in "fishing effort" by Indians beginning in the 1950's. "The effort on most Indian fishing streams has increased tremendously over the past several years and the results of many a protective regulation on commercial and sport fishing has served merely to fill an Indian net." [53]

The increase in sport fishing was noted in a previous section. The simple fact of competition between the two has undoubtedly been an important factor in precipitating the present controversy, but Indians and sportsmen have not been looked upon by the state as two groups of competing fishermen. They have received totally different publicity, Indians depicted as a threat and sportsmen presented as examples of progress.

During the years that the Department of Fisheries worked on agreements with Indian tribes, the Bureau of Indian Affairs showed little interest in the matter. Neither the tribes nor the state received encouragement from the bureau to develop this rudimentary cooperation further, or even to continue with it. In the 1959 *Annual Report,* the Department of Fisheries, in discussing difficulties it had encountered in trying to secure agreements from some tribes, sharply criticized the Department of Interior. "Little or no interest in balancing these problems has been shown by Indian agents of the Interior Department, who are rightfully in this case responsible for the general overall welfare of the tribal people." [54]

The state's increased effort to bring off-reservation fishing under its control followed the increased efforts by the federal government to bring Indians "into the mainstream" (see chap. iii). The repeatedly stated idea that modern conditions have invalidated the terms of "hundred-year-old treaties" also ex-

---

State are imposed merely to provide more fish for sports and commercial fishermen with no allowance for the Indian economy" (p. 81).

[53] *Annual Report,* 1959, p. 221.

[54] *Ibid.,* p. 222. Another view was expressed by James Hovis, attorney for the Yakimas, in the 1964 *Hearings,* p. 69.

presses the now really timeworn idea that it is high time for Indians to start doing things the way other people do.

The state has not thought of the Indian fisheries as a segment entitled to a continuing existence which would need to be taken into account in overall fisheries planning. The agreements may to some extent have been regarded as temporary or stopgap measures. At the time of the hearings in 1964 on S.J.R. 170 and 171, the state of Oregon apparently had a much more positive opinion of agreements than the state of Washington, yet the following appears in the testimony of Robert W. Schoning, director of the Fish Commission of Oregon:

> We have attempted to establish and maintain a reasonable management program under voluntary tribal regulations which vary considerably among tribes and which differ markedly from those imposed by the agencies on non-Indians. . . . This is "a heck of a way to run a railroad," particularly when it belongs to all the people—Indians and non-Indians alike—and is threatened with elimination ultimately.
>
> We in Oregon have attempted to make the very best of this very difficult situation. It is obvious that it will not be an acceptable permanent solution.[55]

Some Indians express fear that the state's ultimate goal is to bring all Indian fishing under its authority. In spite of explicit disclaimers of jurisdiction, in discussing the subject of Indian fishing the state does not always distinguish clearly between on- and off-reservation fishing. Since the state's view, like that of non-Indians generally, appears to be that assimilation is the only appropriate goal for Indians, and since the logic of conservation does not end with the reservation boundaries, the next step would be to move to control all fishing, on the reservation as well as off.[56]

[55] *Ibid.*, p. 47

[56] The apprehension may be well founded. Persons living on the Quinault reservation report that the Department of Fisheries has sent

The position of the state as shown in statements and actions over the last few years has four principal points:

1. Fishing by Indians on reservations is a right protected by treaty and does not fall under state jurisdiction.[57]

2. Uncontrolled off-reservation net fishing by Indians would constitute a major threat to the salmon and steelhead runs and cannot be allowed, and such fishing cannot be controlled or regulated by the tribes because they have neither the ability nor the authority to do so.

3. The federal government has no authority to regulate Indian fishing off the reservations.

4. The Department of Fisheries and Department of Game are the only appropriate agencies to control off-reservation Indian fishing, and except in the matter of licenses (see preceding chapter) Indians fishing off reservation are or should be subject to the same laws and regulations as others.

What has changed basically in seventy years is neither the state's view nor the Indian fisheries, but the pressure of people and industry on the fish and the conditions which support the fish. The state has shown varying degrees of tolerance toward the Indian fisheries, from being "very lenient" to harassment, from disclaiming jurisdiction (on reservation) to endeavoring to secure agreements to carry out what it sees as conservation needs. But it has never seen the Indian fisheries as part of the

planes up and down the river to observe the fishing activities there, the purpose being, these persons believe, to discover violations of the tribal regulations in order to claim that the tribe cannot enforce its own. The Quinault River runs entirely through areas under federal jurisdiction. Both forks rise in the Olympic National Park. For a few miles between their juncture and the head of Lake Quinault, the Olympic National Park is on the north and the Olympic National Forest is on the south. From the head of the lake to the ocean, the river's course, including the lake, is entirely within the boundaries of the Quinault Indian reservation.

[57] Even this is complicated. As already noted, Indians and the state disagree over the matter of reservation status of Frank's Landing on the Nisqually River, and over the actual existing boundaries of the Puyallup reservation.

total fisheries of the state except as a threat to commerical and sport fishing. In the state's view the non-Indian commercial and sport fisheries are the real fisheries. Their protection has been the purpose of the agreements with the tribes. Any recognation of Indian interest has been incidental.

However, the new agreement with the Squaxin Island tribe which has just been made, together with some working arrangements which have survived through the years, may yet be useful in opening the way to improved communications between Indians and the state. Limited as they are, they have a foundation in common interests of the parties involved.

THE BUREAU OF INDIAN AFFAIRS

Because the Bureau of Indian Affairs is the trustee of Indian lands and is publicly regarded as the official guardian of Indian rights, its position is important both as a shaper of opinion and as a mediator of relationships between Indian tribes and state and other federal agencies.

A major part of the task of the bureau is the management of Indian land resources. Many aspects of Indians' property use, resource use, and tribal functioning are supervised by the bureau or strongly influenced by its services. Formal recognition of a tribe's constitution and bylaws requires bureau approval; and tribal membership rolls, though based on regulations developed by the individual tribe as to blood quantum, lineage, residence, and other factors, are subject to review and approval by the Commissioner of Indian Affairs. The bureau also has responsibility for Indian rights based in treaties and federal statutes. So far as off-reservation fishing is concerned, until very recently the bureau's position has not been clearly stated, and over the years its actions have not been consistent. Like the state, the bureau seems to have found it difficult to accept the actual legitimacy of the Indian fisheries even when recognizing their legality.

Two functions of the bureau have been particularly important for fishing: (1) its supervision over the activities of tribes in organizing themselves and regulating their members; and (2) its supervisory and approbatory authority over the preparation and maintenance by the tribes of their membership rolls. In effect the bureau participates in the decisions as to who has the right to fish and how the fishing will be done.

A common misconception among the general public is that the Bureau of Indian Affairs is the spokesman for Indian tribes. The bureau is the administrator of trust property and of certain services, and it has certain supervisory functions with respect to tribal government, but it is not the tribal government. Important differences of opinion exist between Indians and the bureau. Examples already discussed are the quarrels between some of the Nisquallys and the bureau over the reservation status of fishing at Frank's Landing, and between the Puyallups and the bureau over the location of their reservation boundaries.

However, because many non-Indians tend to regard the point of view which the bureau supports, either explicitly or by implication, as the official one, its failure to take a clear position on a particular question has sometimes been regarded as evidence that there is none to be taken. Until July 1965, when the Department of Interior proposed itself to regulate the off-reservation fisheries (see earlier discussion in this chapter), and thus recognized their right to existence, the bureau's silence had lent credence to the state's contention that no such rights exist. Indians have found it difficult to understand the bureau's apparent unwillingness to speak in support of the off-reservation fishing rights, or to see the bureau as a beneficial guardian when it does not move vigorously to oppose attempts to eliminate the Indian fisherman.

Other aspects of bureau activity have added to the Indians' feeling of incomplete bureau support. Generally it has advised

Indians to observe the injunctions against off-reservation fishing on certain rivers even though they believe the injunctions violate treaty provisions. In the past it has not approved codes proposed by some tribes (for example, as previously mentioned, the Puyallup) to regulate their off-reservation fishing.

Developmental programs of the Bureau of Indian Affairs have not included fisheries, until the appointment in 1962 of one fish biologist in the Portland area office. This is in contrast to the position taken toward certain other resources, including agricultural land, livestock, and timber, in other parts of the country.[58]

Today the bureau's one fisheries expert serves a three-state area which includes thirty-four reservations, on almost all of which fishing is important. The U.S. Fish and Wildlife Service cooperates with the bureau, but its staff for services to Indian fisheries is essentially limited (see discussion in the following section). No attention has been given to the Puyallups or Nisquallys; limited activity with the Muckleshoots was begun in 1966. The obvious limitations on the services one fish biologist can provide are doubly unfortunate, when on one hand tribes are seeking fisheries assistance, and on the other are being labeled as unconcerned about conservation and fisheries management.

As noted above, the Bureau of Indian Affairs has been slow to move in active defense of fishing rights. In general this has been characteristic of it in relation to Indian treaty rights over the country. The bureau becomes more vigorous in helping to obtain monetary payment for treaty rights when they are abrogated. The inference can be drawn that in the bureau's

---

[58] It should be noted, however, that with the exception of some of the cattle and sheep-raising programs, the bureau's principal attention has been directed toward development of the resource, not toward Indian activities to develop the resource. The result has been that most of the development or exploitation has been carried on by non-Indians.

frame of reference the value placed by Indians in the treaty rights is less significant, and therefore less readily asserted, than the value in the monetary sense which the wider society applies—a part of the view that money can appropriately and adequately compensate for any loss.

Since 1965 the bureau, in public actions and statements, has presented an increasingly clear position in support of the tribes' rights both to fish off reservation at "usual and accustomed" places and to regulate such fishing. As discussed earlier in this chapter, the Department of Justice, which serves the bureau in legal actions, in March 1966 announced that if asked it would support any Indian arrested by the state while fishing in accordance with approved tribal fishing regulations. (However, in April 1969 the Department of Justice withdrew from the Muckleshoot case, *State of Washington* v. *Moses,* now on appeal to the U.S. Supreme Court.) Bureau personnel have cooperated with attorneys for the Indians in fishing rights cases and have testified on request. They have not taken initiative in the court fights over fishing rights. In July 1967 the Department of Interior, having in 1965 proposed federal off-reservation regulation, again published in the *Federal Register* assertion of authority over the regulation of off-reservation treaty fishing.[59] In 1968 it approved Nisqually regulations applying to off-reservation fishing, and questioned the necessity for the state injunction imposing total closure of the river outside the reservation.

As for Frank's Landing, however, the bureau made the following statement: "Frank's Landing on the Nisqually River is not under Federal jurisdiction. The State has full law enforce-

---

[59] The *Federal Register* is the publication in which all official rules and regulations and orders of any department are published. It is placed in a limited number of repository libraries throughout the country, of which the Seattle Public Library is one.

ment jurisdiction there as elsewhere outside an Indian Reservation. Of course, it must respect legitimate treaty fishing rights there as elsewhere, but it does not lack any jurisdiction over that area." [60]

The present stated position of the Bureau of Indian Affairs is that treaty-protected fishing rights exist off reservation, and that under the 1968 United States Supreme Court decision in the *Puyallup* case the state may regulate if it recognizes the Indian right and does not require Indians to conform to the same rules as other citizens. At the same time it is encouraging tribes to develop their own regulations and to argue, with bureau support, for state recognition of them. As reported in the press:

> The bureau, which is not always viewed with benevolence by the Indians, "expressly refuses to sustain the validity of the application of the state's present set net prohibition to Indian treaty fishing." . . . The bureau's position, based on earlier court decisions as well as the one in May, is that off-reservation fishing is a tribal right—that the tribes may set up regulations, including who may fish. . . . "If an Indian is fishing in his usual and accustomed place (on the Nisqually River) under tribal rules and regulations and he is arrested by the state, the Department of Justice will defend the Indian person," Balsiger says.
>
> . . . the state must do three things. . . . The first is that it must deal with the matter of Indian treaty fishing rights "as a subject separate and distinct from that of fishing by others." . . . Secondly, the BIA says the state must "so regulate the taking of fish that the tribe and its members will be accorded an opportunity to take at their usual and accustomed places by reasonable means, feasible to them, a fair and equitable share of all fish which the state permits to be taken from any given run." . . . The third "must" applies to conservation and apparently puts the burden of proof on the state. The state must "establish that it is necessary for

[60] Press release, Oct. 23, 1968, Bureau of Indian Affairs, Portland Area Office.

conservation to impose the specifically described restrictions on the exercise of treaty rights." [61]

The Fishery Services Division of the Bureau of Sport Fisheries and Wildlife of the U.S. Fish and Wildlife Service might well play a major role in Indian fisheries development. In 1963 it established a field office with a staff of one in Olympia, "to work closely with fishery projects in Western Washington, with primary emphasis placed on assistance to Indian Tribes in cooperation with the Bureau of Indian Affairs." [62] The responsibilities of the division are many:

> The Division has the responsibility of providing technical assistance in the management of fishery resources in waters which are owned, controlled or in trust of the Federal Government in addition to a number of State-Federal cooperative projects. . . . Basically, our responsibilities are to evaluate fishery problems and needs. . . . We may recommend and participate in such things as habitat protective measures, fish stocking, ecological controls, harvest methods, etc. Extension services include addressing public schools, Indian groups, business and conservation organizations. . . .
> In addition to Indian Fisheries, this office is active in management on the military installations, both Mt. Rainier and Olympic National Parks, on numerous smaller Federal areas such as McNeil Island Penitentiary, and in the State-Federal cooperative projects in Western Washington. . . . The various areas referred to above contain over 685 miles of streams, 108 lakes totalling 16,300 surface acres, and 105 miles of marine shoreline. [63]

The extent of the responsibilities obviously limits the amount of service the office can provide to Indian groups. Programs,

[61] *The Daily Olympian* (Olympia, Wash.), Oct. 22, 1968. The headline, "Confrontation on the Nisqually: Indian Bureau to Back Fishermen," was not accurate if it implied, as might have been thought, that the bureau backed the Indians protesting at Frank's Landing.

[62] Letter from James L. Heckman to Charles L. McEvers, Feb. 16, 1966.

[63] *Ibid.*

some limited, have been developed on three reservations— Makah, Quinault, and Muckleshoot—but requests from tribes for assistance have far exceeded the ability of the agency to respond.

The work until recently has been concentrated on a model program of stream improvement, planting, and hatchery development on the Quinault reservation. The importance of the Quinault program is its position as a tribal program—a program carried out by the tribe with technical assistance from the Fishery Services Division, not a program of the Fishery Services Division to develop a tribal resource. It has been related to the citizenry of the reservation in several significant ways— conservation study in the Taholah Elementary School, for example, and some employment, including the use of technically trained members of the reservation community.[64]

The Olympia staff was increased to four in 1968—an expansion which Indian tribes had wanted for a long time. With the additional staff, the office was able to assist in forming the White (Stuck) River Fishery Improvement Committee, a cooperative endeavor involving the Muckleshoot tribe, the Bureau of Indian Affairs, and some of the industries which affect the river. Its purpose is to study the conditions and needs of the river in order to develop a fisheries program there. Work for a survey was getting under way in the late fall of 1968.

The basis for the operation of the Olympia office is a "Memorandum of Understanding," made in 1941 between two agencies of the Department of Interior—the U.S. Fish and Wildlife Service and the Bureau of Indian Affairs—further implemented by administrative provisions set forth in 1963 within the Department of Interior. Primary responsibility remains with the

---

[64] Construction of the fish hatchery on the Quinault reservation is going forward, bringing closer to realization a long-held dream of the Quinault people. Taholah is the larger of two villages on the reservation and the seat of tribal government.

Bureau of Indian Affairs, with the Bureau of Sport Fisheries and Wildlife the fact-finding and scientific arm or technical adviser. The undertaking of cooperative enterprises is stated in the departmental manual to depend upon the availability of funds and personnel.[65]

The administrative provisions state: "Wildlife (including fisheries) is an integral factor in the social and economic life of the Indians, and must always be so managed as to furnish a maximum contribution to their welfare consistent with a continuance of such benefits to future generations." [66] This is public policy, buried in a departmental manual and further limited by express dependency on money and staff resources available, at the same time that various public and private actions contravene. On its premise, however, a most promising approach to the problems of Indian fisheries has been built, and at least one sound program developed—a program which takes into account, draws upon, and enhances the Indians' traditional sense of the direct relationship between personal and community well-being and the well-being of the salmon.

FACTORS IN COMMUNICATION

Any serious attempt either to understand or to resolve with equity the fishing rights dispute must take into account dif-

[65] Correspondence with Washington senators Magnuson and Jackson, and with three congressmen from western Washington, Brock Adams, Julia Butler Hansen, and Lloyd Meeds, indicates that all these legislators gave their endorsement and some their active support to proposals to enlarge the Olympia office of the Fishery Services Division. However, such proposals do not have a priority, and no increase was made until 1968. Clarence F. Pautzke, Commissioner of the U.S. Fish and Wildlife Service, wrote in a letter to the study group on March 4, 1966: "The Bureau of Sport Fisheries and Wildlife has sought to expand its program with the Indian tribes and the Bureau of Indian Affairs on numerous occasions but Federal budget policy limitations on funds and the high priority requirements facing the Bureau have prevented achieving this objective. The budget now being considered by the Congress for fiscal year 1967 does not contain funds for an expanded program with the Indian tribes."

[66] Department of the Interior Departmental Manual 501.2.

ferences between Indian and non-Indian styles of thinking. These are differences which have resulted in problems for Indians in communicating their points of view, and problems for non-Indians in understanding what is being said by Indians. Communication in our society has been developed primarily by non-Indians, based on their view of what is good, their decision-making processes, and their pragmatic experiences. Theoretically, in a democracy this serves all members equally well. However, those who differ significantly from the norms find that respect, opportunity for responsible participation, and equitable treatment are available largely in proportion to readiness to conform, and that unwillingness or inability to do so is viewed as incompetence or bad intent. The Indian, to the extent that his Indian-ness involves significant differences from the majority society, has become an alien, a stranger in his own land.

The principal surviving part of the traditional inheritance—the invisible, attitudinal part—has much to do with how the Indian views himself and the world and how he relates himself to his environment. It largely determines both what he feels is important and how he will try to communicate about it. Language itself is a more significant factor than may at first appear. Although English is the first language in virtually all Indian homes in western Washington today, the constructs of the Indian tongues still affect the understandings and thought styles, even of many persons who have no actual knowledge of any Indian language.

As a consequence, Indian and non-Indian do not always mean the same thing when they say the same thing, and do not understand the same thing from the same words. An Indian attempting to convey his feeling and knowledge about fishing rights in a non-Indian setting such as a court of law is at a tremendous disadvantage, and stands in danger of being not only misunderstood, but rejected as incomprehensible. The state official, the sportsman, the fisheries expert, on the other hand, knows the language of the setting and how to speak within the rules of the institution.[67] Again, in the matter of court cases, the mere lack of funds for hiring expert witnesses— such as biologists who know Indian fisheries or anthropologists who understand Indian points of view—weights the processes of the courts against Indians, whether defendants, plaintiffs, or appellants.

Theoretically, too, the mass media are channels for communication open to all groups. However, they also are products of the non-Indian culture, and access to them is in proportion to the ability to operate within that framework. This involves not only language and styles of communication, but also money and technical knowledge. The state Department of Game could afford to hire people to make an effective film depicting Indian fishing as universally detrimental to salmon and steelhead, and threatening to sportsmen.[68] To date no Indian group has had the funds, the skills, or the compulsion for "public relations" to put together a film presenting another side of the story. Media reporters, even in attempting to get facts, often come to the fishing rights question armed with the misconceptions common in the non-Indian society.

Indians are at a disadvantage in the effort to communicate, and non-Indians in the effort to understand, so long as it is insisted that the Indians perform according to standards not their own. If democracy actually means the protection of minority views and rights, special effort must be made both to hear what Indians are saying and to incorporate their views and knowledge into the overall decisions.

---

[67] See chap. iv, pp. 105–6.
[68] "Indian Fishery Report," a fifteen-minute news documentary filmed in 1963 and released in 1964, available for viewing by any organized group.

VI | The Fish and Their Environment

The fish which are the subject of the controversy and the ancient center of Pacific Northwest Indian life are five species of Pacific salmon (*genus Oncorhynchus*). Included with these in the present disputes is the steelhead trout (*Salmo gairdnerii*), a sea-run rainbow trout.[1] Like almost all others of the family *Salmonidae,* these six are anadromous fish—they hatch in fresh water, go down to the ocean as young fish and live most of their lives there, and return to the fresh-water streams to deposit their eggs. The steelhead, like the related Atlantic salmon (*Salmo salar*), may return to the ocean after spawning and come back to lay eggs again; but all species of Pacific salmon spawn once and then die. Each species has a particular season for the spawning migration, but overlapping by the various species is considerable. The eggs are deposited in the gravel

[1] Principal sources for this discussion and the section on environmental factors are: J. F. Andrew and C. H. Geen, *Sockeye and Pink Salmon Production in Relation to Proposed Dams in the Fraser River System,* International Pacific Salmon Fisheries Commission, Bulletin XI (New Westminster, B.C., 1960); Milo Moore *et al., Fisheries,* Vol. III; Milo Moore, *Salmon of the Pacific,* Washington State Department of Fisheries (Olympia, 1960?); Department of Fisheries *Annual Reports.*

in shallow water, usually in small streams. The newly hatched fish, called alevins, also spend their earliest life in the gravel, emerging only after the yolk-sac is absorbed. These fish are all carnivorous, living on smaller fish, shrimp, and various other small aquatic animals. However, the adults for the most part do not eat after re-entering the rivers.

One of the well-known characteristics of the Pacific salmon is their "homing instinct," which brings the adult fish back to spawn in the river in which it was born—many times even to the same small tributary creek. The salmon from a short coastal stream like the Quinault return there, and those fish from the upper reaches of a sub-watershed of a great system like the Fraser return there. Salmon even of the same species therefore vary greatly in the distances they travel to spawn, depending on the river or part of the river which was their birthplace. The homing tendency also varies somewhat with the species. Sockeye and chinook possess it to a remarkable degree, while chum and silvers sometimes "wander," returning not to the natal stream but to a nearby similar one. The fact that salmon are specialized to their rivers in this way is a complicating factor in their conservation. If the environment is destroyed in a particular river, they cannot simply shift to another river. Furthermore, if suitable conditions are later restored in that river, it does not necessarily follow that salmon will come into it again.

The largest of the salmon is the chinook (*O. tshawytshca*), also called king, tyee, spring, or quinnat salmon. Those caught average from twelve to twenty-five pounds, but there are records of specimens over one hundred pounds. The Columbia River system has been the great breeding ground of this species. The chinook's average age for spawning is four or five years. They show considerable variation in their patterns of return to the spawning areas. Some enter the rivers in the spring and remain until fall, when they spawn. The fry then tend to remain in their fresh-water home for a year before going to sea. Others run in the fall and spawn immediately, and the fry descend to the ocean on hatching. Chinook travel enormous distances, both to and from their spawning grounds and in the ocean itself. The chinook is commercially one of the most important salmon, and it is also one of the three which are important in the sport fishery. It is one of the two species most amenable to artificial propagation.

The silver salmon or coho (*O. kisutch*) is another which is important to both commercial and sport fishermen. Silvers reach maturity at three years, with an average weight of ten pounds. The young fish spend their first twelve or fourteen months in the rivers. Although all salmon are travelers, the silvers do not cover the distances chinook or sockeye do in their ocean life. Silver salmon also respond well to artificial rearing.

The sockeye (*O. nerka*), also known as blueback, quinault, or red salmon, is one of the smaller species but is considered by many to be the choicest of all. It is rarely taken by sportsmen, but has long been of the greatest importance commercially. At four years, the usual age of maturity, the average weight is four to seven pounds, varying from one river system to another. Sockeye run only in streams where there are lakes, which serve as rearing areas for the young fish during their first one to three years.[2] Spawning occurs at the edges of the lakes or near them in the streams, both above and below. The Fraser River system of Canada is the great producer of sockeye. Like chinook, sockeye travel tremendous distances both in the rivers and ocean; and although they may have to go hundreds of miles to reach their spawning grounds, they do not eat after they re-enter the rivers. No great success has been achieved in attempting to rear sockeye artificially.

The smallest of the five is the pink salmon (*O. gorbuscha*),

[2] Small landlocked sockeye, called konakee or silver trout (*O. nerka Kennerlii*), are found in some lakes. Apparently they, too, tend to become anadromous if given the opportunity

also called humpy or humpback because of the pronounced hump which the adult males develop. It matures in two years, when it weighs four or five pounds. In Washington streams, pinks run only in odd-numbered years. The young fish move toward the ocean as soon as they hatch. Their ocean travels are incompletely understood, though it is known that they spend some time in favorable areas near the shoreline when they first enter the sea. The pink salmon is the third species important to both sportsmen and commercial fishermen. Pinks are not artificially reared as extensively as chinooks and silvers.

The chum or dog salmon (*O. keta*) is the last species to return to the rivers in the fall, and frequently they go only short distances upstream to spawn. Those caught average eight to twelve pounds. Like the pinks, they enter salt water shortly after hatching. Marking studies have produced a considerable body of knowledge about the ocean movements of the other species of salmon, but so far almost nothing is known of where chum go. They simply disappear for the three to five years which elapse between the time they enter the sea and their return to spawn. To date chum have not responded well to efforts at artificial propagation.

Steelhead trout spend their first two years of life in the rivers before descending to the ocean, where they remain another two years. They are four years old when they first return to their natal rivers to spawn, for they also have the homing characteristic. They occasionally make the spawning migration as many as three or even four times. Mature steelhead weigh about ten pounds, but a few attain a weight of up to thirty pounds.[3] Steelhead, which are rarely caught in the ocean, are perhaps the most highly prized of game fish. This species is artificially propagated with great success.

All of these species are important to Washington Indians.

[3] 1964 *Hearings*, p. 28.

However, the Indians on Puget Sound take almost no sockeye, which require a river system that contains a lake for the rearing of the juveniles. Among the Muckleshoots, Puyallups, and Nisquallys the chinook, silvers, and steelhead are important in the waters of all three tribes. Pinks as well are important to the Puyallups, who also take some chum.

ENVIRONMENTAL REQUIREMENTS

Salmon rivers vary from the great systems of the Columbia and the Fraser, which flow through many kinds of topography and climate, to the short streams of the moist, forested Pacific coast.[4] Some include lakes in their courses. Some enter salt water through extensive estuaries, some quite abruptly. Some flow into inland waterways like Puget Sound, and some reach the ocean directly. The four rivers in which the Nisqually, Puyallup, and Muckleshoot people fish all rise high in the Cascades, three of them—the Nisqually, the Puyallup, and the White—in the glaciers of Mount Rainier. All flow in comparatively short courses from the western Cascades to Puget Sound, which the Nisqually and the Puyallup enter through their own estuaries. The White and the Green rivers enter, respectively, through the Puyallup and the Duwamish rivers.[5]

Whatever the variations, all salmon rivers are alike in certain respects. When Robert J. Schoettler, then Washington State Director of Fisheries, wrote in 1953 that the requirements of salmon are simple—they need only that their streams remain cool and pure and their spawning grounds accessible—he was describing the important characteristics of salmon rivers.[6] The events of these rivers set in motion responsive mechanisms in the salmon and steelhead. It is through the fitting together of

[4] The discussion is in terms of salmon, but the requirements of steelhead are essentially similar.
[5] See also chap. ii for discussion of the rivers.
[6] *Annual Report,* 1953, p. 2.

those responses with the normal occurrences in the rivers—
freshets, temperature changes, and so on—that the fish are able
to accomplish their life activities. Let us therefore look in some
detail at the needs of salmon, and at what changes in the environment may imply.

A number of characteristics of the water itself are important
—purity, current, turbidity, volume, temperature, dissolved
oxygen content—and there are, besides, the factors of food
supply, gravel bars, and unimpeded movement in the river.

Water pure enough for some fish may not be so for salmon.
It must, of course, be free of noxious substances directly harmful to the salmon and to the life forms on which they depend.
Equally important are substances which, though not in themselves harmful, induce detrimental changes, such as reduction of
the amount of oxygen dissolved in the water. In general, the
tolerance of salmon to any kind of pollution is low, with the fry
more vulnerable than the adults.

Current also influences the salmon. A stream normally does
not proceed over its course at a uniform rate, but is deflected
and obstructed by the unevenness of its bed, and thereby over
short distances is alternately retarded and accelerated. The
adult salmon moving up the river have a chance to rest in the
quieter water, and the young fish coming down can both rest and
feed there. The pools afford hiding places. At the same time, response to current seems to be part of the set of mechanisms
which enable the salmon, both young fish and adults, to get
where they must go. Changes in current connected with the increased runoff of rainfall or melting snow appear to be among
the factors which induce the returning salmon to move up the
streams.

Ordinarily optimum conditions for salmon mean that the
water is clear. Highly turbid water may afford protection from
predators to young fish, but it may also inhibit the growth of
their food. Turbidity associated with runoff, perhaps along with

the increased volume of water, appears to stimulate the movements of the fish; and the increased volume of fresh water coming from a river may be a stimulant inducing the fish waiting at the mouth to enter it.

The thermal tolerance of salmon and steelhead is exceedingly low—they thrive and even survive only within narrow ranges of temperature. For the developing eggs, the difference of a degree or two changes the required incubation time (usually about two months) by several days. For both young fish and adults, too high a temperature can impair vitality or cause death. Responses to temperature variations associated with seasonal changes, rain, or snow melt also appear to be part of the mechanisms inducing the salmon to move as required; slight changes accelerate or delay the movements of the fish.

Oxygen is another primary factor. Many kinds of fish can thrive in water with a lower dissolved oxygen content than can salmon and steelhead. Oxygen is especially needed in the water passing through the gravel in which the fry are developing. Oxygen content and the amount of oxygen required by the fish are both affected by temperature, and also by the movement of water. Standing or lake-bottom water tends to lose its dissolved oxygen. Substances in the water also affect it—large amounts of decaying organic material, for example, use up the oxygen.

Food is principally a need of the young fish so far as salmon in the rivers are concerned. In general, good environment for the salmon is also best for the tiny animals on which the salmon live. Changes which inhibit their growth or stimulate competing species not useful to salmon are detrimental to the fish even when there are no directly adverse effects.

Gravel bars are as essential as the right conditions of water, for they are the nurseries of the salmon and steelhead. While eggs are developing in it, the gravel must remain covered by shallow water, it must remain permeable so that water can percolate through it and around the eggs, and it must be free from disturbance until the fry have emerged.

Finally, the fish must get from the gravel bars where they are born down to the ocean, and then as adults back up the rivers to the gravel. Either way, it must be possible for them to travel at the rate required by their development. Salmon and steelhead need to be able to move unimpeded the whole length of their rivers.

In fact, salmon seem in many respects to be among the most specialized of fish, and their "simple requirements" actually to be quite complex. The nuances of the river are built into their movements. The rivers and the land have a set of relationships with each other, a series of delicate balances, each river with its own watershed; and the salmon, over thousands and thousands of fish generations, have become interwoven into those relationships. Small changes and adjustments occur constantly, but what happens when the changes are drastic and fundamental?

ENVIRONMENTAL CHANGES AND THEIR EFFECTS

The most dramatic change in the salmon environment in Washington and other western states and provinces is the series of great dams which have been built in the last thirty-five years. So far as salmon are concerned, the obvious effect is to block the rivers—to cut off the spawning migrations. Much effort has been expended to enable the fish to get around some of these. "Fish ladders" have been built at Bonneville and many other dams on the Columbia. At Mud Mountain Dam on the White River, too high for a fish ladder, the fish are trapped and carried by truck around the dam. The new Mayfield Dam on the Cowlitz River has a complex combination of fish ladder, elevator, and trucking, as well as a pipeline suspension bridge to convey the young fish down past the dam. At best, however, the dams delay the fish, both adults and ocean-bound young—

fish whose built-in timing demands that they reach a certain place by a certain time. Important as all the helping devices are, they do not make up for the difficulties caused by the dams, and they are subject to failure as well—disrepair or human error.

In the opinion of some, the great dams present the greatest of all the environmental threats to the fish. Anthony Wayne Smith, president and general counsel of the National Parks Association, wrote in a personal letter:

> The great threat to all the anadromous fish in the Northwest is the big dams, which cut off the runs. Nothing else has anything like such importance, whether over-fishing, pollution, or other causes. Every one of the big dams which is built, regardless of efforts to get the fish over by fish ladders, delays the migration and reduces the number reaching spawning grounds.[7]

No way has been provided around some dams, and above them there are no more salmon. Grand Coulee is one of these. It was too high for a fish ladder, and no other way was provided for the fish to pass it to continue to the upper Columbia in Washington and Canada, and the runs were destroyed. Great areas of this watershed, part of the greatest chinook-producing river in the world, no longer produce salmon.

Excerpts from the introductory discussion of a 1938 report by the Washington State Department of Fisheries on a cooperative study for the U.S. Bureau of Reclamation done by the State Department of Game and the U.S. Bureau of Fisheries illustrate recognition, albeit fruitless, of the problem:

> In the first burst of enthusiasm that the whole Northwest felt at the culmination of its plans [for construction of Grand Coulee Dam], the fact that the construction of this dam would strike a serious blow to the Columbia River fishery was overlooked by the general public. When the plans for the high dam were finally approved, it became apparent . . . that salmon could not be put over a dam of

[7] Letter to Walter Taylor, Jan. 13, 1966.

this height. . . . The stock of salmon spawning in some 1,100 miles of river and tributaries was to be permanently destroyed. Further study revealed that the alternative methods for preserving these runs would be expensive, if they were possible. There was a feeling that the vast economic gains to be derived from this project should not be endangered by consideration of the fish. It was even felt in some quarters that the fish were not worth the money that it would take to preserve them.

That this last statement was erroneous is at once apparent from a glance at the facts . . . the expenditure of a sizeable sum of money to preserve the salmon runs of the upper Columbia is justified purely from a financial viewpoint. There is a further consideration from the national viewpoint; that is, that a necessary basic protein food resource should not be destroyed. . . . Food resources must be preserved for the future. There is no reason why agriculture and aquiculture cannot exist side by side.[8]

However, as noted above, no provision was made for passage of the fish, and the spawning beds on 1,100 miles of river and tributaries were thus eliminated.

Besides the big dams, a great number of small dams, often hardly noticed, close off the upper reaches of many small streams, causing tremendous aggregate loss of spawning areas. Recently small dams have been constructed to form lakes for waterfront property in new subdivisions—a growing trend capable of appreciable damage.[9]

Dams have been built on each of the four rivers of this study —Alder Dam on the Nisqually; a power dam at Electron on the Puyallup; Mud Mountain Dam and a water diversion dam of Tacoma City Light on the White; and Howard Hanson Dam on the Green.

Because of the river changes they bring about, dams affect salmon in other ways than interfering with their movements.

[8] Washington State Department of Fisheries, "Report of Preliminary Investigations into the Possible Methods of Preserving the Columbia River Salmon and Steelhead at the Grand Coulee Dam" (Seattle [?], 1938, mimeo), p. 2.

[9] See *Annual Report,* 1963, p. 65, and later *Annual Reports.*

The fry journeying downstream encounter new dangers in passing through turbines or over spillways. Although more and more effort is being made to provide fishways and other aids, often there is still no way for the young fish to pass the dam except by going over it or through the penstocks; injury and mortality rates are high in spite of continuing work to improve design to reduce the dangers.

Inducing the fish to enter the fishways remains a problem. Because of their natural responses to current, the adults are reluctant to move out of the fast water at the foot of the dam to the slower water of the fishway; adults or young may become confused when they find themselves in the quiet water above the dam, with detrimental delays resulting. Juveniles may be prevented from moving in accordance with their optimum development—some species, like the silvers, have only a short time to get down to salt water. The adult salmon, if too long delayed, may die before reaching the spawning grounds or be too spent to spawn after arriving. Where they must be trapped and actually transported past the dam, as at Mud Mountain, some delay and injury are unavoidable.

Water current below a dam may also be modified to the detriment of spawning. For power generation, the current may be maintained at a constant rate, with a constant volume of water, which, because it never slackens and the water never lowers, can make spawning impossible.

The water which backs up behind the dam, called the forebay, inundates the gravel bars in the stream above, and so further constricts natural breeding areas. This process has gone so far on the Columbia that if the presently proposed Ben Franklin Dam is built, there will be no natural spawning grounds left in the main river.

Sockeye, which frequently spawn at the edges of lakes, find a special danger in the reservoir. They have sometimes adjusted to change by laying their eggs at the edges of the artificial lake behind a dam. If the water level is lowered the developing fish are destroyed.[10]

One purpose of dams is to modify runoff in order both to store water and to prevent floods.[11] This means that natural changes associated with runoff—changes in temperature, turbidity, volume of water—to which the salmon are geared to respond, are also modified. These changes in turn set off others —temperature affects dissolved oxygen, both affect food supply, all three affect the movements of the fish as well as their general well-being.

Several changes occur in the water of the lake behind a dam. Its basin, sometimes described as a half lake, is quite unlike that of a natural lake, and the movements of water in it consequently are also different. Water at the top becomes warm; cold water sinks to the bottom, accumulating in the deepest part, and remains there undisturbed; and, because it is undisturbed, it loses its dissolved oxygen. Water released from either the top or the bottom brings a sudden change to the river below, and either the warm water of the top or the dead water of the bottom, if let out in volume, can bring disaster to migrating salmon.

Dams for water diversion drastically affect the stream environment below. At times so little water is left in the White River below the Tacoma City Light dam (which is above the Muckleshoot reservation) that the temperature rises to a point unsuitable for salmon, and the habitat is further impaired by the changes brought about in the other life forms in the water.

Rivers are also changed by events other than dams. Especially in populous areas, they are frequently diked and straightened as a matter of flood control. These changes obliterate the

[10] See "A Nursery in No Man's Land," *Annual Report,* 1962, pp. 53–54.
[11] Rivers may be more subject to flooding now than in aboriginal times, and the need for flood control greater, because of the destruction of the natural vegetative cover. The primary reason for flood control, however, is the existence of expensive structures beside the rivers.

characteristic of alternating pool and gravel bar, slow water and fast water, and so eliminate the natural resting, feeding, and hiding places, besides destroying spawning places. Diking and channeling have been carried out on many Puget Sound rivers, including the Green, the White, the Puyallup, and to a lesser extent the Nisqually.

Diversion of water from a stream, as for irrigation, can also be dangerous for the fish. If it is done without proper screening, the fish can get lost in the irrigation ditches.

Road building and logging operations, as well as other construction and land clearing, also change rivers. Slides and the rapid pile-up of eroded material, frequent by-products of these activities, create obstructions, some small, some sizable, but all serious when added together.[12] Construction in which small streams are filled over without proper culverts also block out the fish.

The gravel of the river bars and small streams, the indispensable salmon nursery, is also damaged by erosion which these activities set off. The erosion brings into the water excessive amounts of fine silt, which acts as a cement to the gravel.

---

[12] Such incidental effects of other activities are unintended. However, that they are allowed to occur is often due to indifference which verges on irresponsibility. A spectacular example was the blockage of the Fraser River, which, while fortunately not irreversible, went unremedied for 32 years. In 1913 the Canadian Pacific Railway, constructing a route down the Fraser, blasted off an overhanging cliff in the Hell's Gate Gorge about 120 miles up the river and below the main spawning grounds of this great system, all but completely obstructing the stream. The sockeye run dropped from millions in 1913 to 4,000 fish in 1945. In that year a fishway was opened, constructed by the International Pacific Salmon Fisheries Commission, an agency set up for that and other purposes concerned with the conservation of Fraser River salmon, and for the allocation of the catch of Fraser River sockeye between Canadian and American fishermen. The sockeye have come back, though not to their former numbers.

In discussing declines in salmon runs in its 1950 *Annual Report,* the Department of Fisheries said of the blockage of the Hell's Gate Gorge that it "caused a loss of nearly one billion dollars in canned salmon potential from 1913 through 1950" (p. 5).

Though the gravel may look normal, the fish cannot deposit their eggs in it, water cannot get into it to the developing eggs which may already be there, and it may become a sealed prison to fry ready to emerge.

In addition, rivers often are easily accessible sources of gravel for roads and other construction. Taking gravel at a given point causes shifts in the river bed which may extend as much as a mile in either direction. If improperly timed, therefore, it can destroy the eggs not only at the particular site but at many more besides. The White River is extensively used as a source of gravel.

Logging, a major economic activity throughout the Northwest, including the areas drained by the four rivers, is an important influence on salmon and steelhead habitat. Logging is frequently carried on in the upper parts of a watershed, in places which include many of the remaining suitable spawning areas. Logging causes sudden and drastic changes in the land and in the streams which drain it. Besides the slides and erosion, logging activities have frequently left streams blocked by debris.

Many of the river changes already discussed are in some degree associated with logging, including changes in rate and amount of runoff, temperature, silt content, and sometimes chemical content of the water as well, especially if there is fire. The decomposing debris in the streams—a form of pollution—exhausts the dissolved oxygen. The need for great quantities of gravel for logging road construction, together with its accessibility in the streams in logging areas, can lead to destruction of eggs and young fish. The cementing action of silt on the gravel is almost unavoidable with the erosion which follows destruction of the forest cover. These changes are not necessarily permanent, and more and more attention is being paid to stream clearance and tree planting. However, a great deal of deterioration has already occurred because of past neglect, neglect which has by no means entirely ceased; and as with the dams, some destruction is inevitable.

Finally, there are changes caused by pollution, which is perhaps what most people think of first in connection with damage to the fish environment. Pollution is also often thought of as causing direct harm. This sometimes happens—the newspapers from time to time carry stories of specific fish kills.[13] However, much greater damage is often less apparent. A U.S. Public Health Service bulletin notes the following: "Water pollution exerts its greatest toll on the fishery not because of individual kills but by destroying habitat. Serious fish kills seldom occur in badly polluted water because there are usually few or no fish left in the stream to die." [14]

Many pollutants are not directly harmful, but they exhaust the oxygen in the water—for example, sewage and other organic substances, including the debris of logging. The decomposition (oxidation) of these materials is more than the waters can carry out unaided. Certain other substances are themselves harmful. These include the traces of agricultural sprays which eventually reach the rivers, some wastes from the Hanford atomic plant on the Columbia, and most pulp mill waste. However, any kind of pollution sets in motion other changes detrimental to the fish and, usually without killing them directly, makes the water unlivable. The greater part of present-day

[13] An unusual kind of pollution caused a fish kill in the White River in November 1965. It was brought about by flushing operations at the Mud Mountain Dam, which carried such a great amount of silt into the river that the gills of the fish were filled and they died. The newspapers reported that the Muckleshoot tribe formally protested this kill, as did Thor Tollefson, present director of the Department of Fisheries, in a sharp exchange with the Army Corps of Engineers. According to the news report, however, the corps said the operation would continue because of flood control needs.

[14] *Pollution Caused Fish Kills*, U.S. Public Health Service, Bulletin No. 847 (Wash., D.C.: Govt. Printing Office, 1964), p. iii.

pollution is of industrial origin. In the Puget Sound region a principal source is the wastes of one of its most important industries, the pulp and paper mills. Since many of these are located at the lower ends of rivers, they especially affect the young fish during the time they are entering and adjusting to salt water.

At the present time, of the four rivers of this study only the Nisqually flows through comparatively undisturbed rural land as it reaches its mouth. Its future is uncertain—the Port of Tacoma Authority plans industrial development there.[15] The waters of the other three rivers reach Puget Sound through highly industrialized areas in Seattle and Tacoma.

Since 1900 the Puget Sound region has changed from a thinly populated region with much wilderness still intact to one of reasonably dense population, with two large cities, both growing, and many small ones; intensive agriculture; and increasing industrialization, particularly pulp and paper and wood products manufacturing. Indians had nothing to do with any of this change. That it has affected the salmon and steelhead, however, is beyond doubt. Puget Sound salmon landings for a period of years as reported by the Washington Department of Fisheries confirm the change. (See Figure 7.) There are ups and downs and there are certainly other factors affecting catch, such as changes in gear regulations. However, if numbers taken are any indication of the numbers present, the overall trend since 1913 has been downward.

CONTROL OF ENVIRONMENT

Although they are reduced, the Pacific salmon and the steelhead have not, as yet, joined their cousin the Atlantic salmon

---

[15] Gordon D. Alcorn, *Shadow on the Land,* John Dickinson Lecture (Tacoma, Wash.: University of Puget Sound, 1968), p. 2.

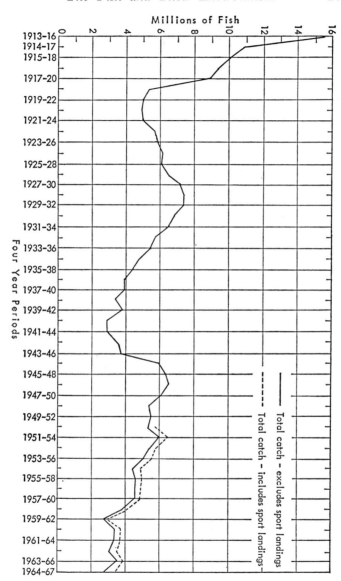

Figure 7. *Puget Sound salmon landings, all species, by four-year running averages, in numbers of fish, 1913–67*

among the "vanishing animals." [16] They continue to reach Mud Mountain Dam and the state fish hatchery at Voights Creek in spite of the wastes coming into the lower Puyallup; they continue to get through Elliott Bay and up the Duwamish and Green to the hatchery at Soos Creek. The Green River remains one of the best steelhead streams, its banks lined with sport fishermen during the season, including those parts which look more like a canal than a river. Several reasons can be listed. (1) The fish themselves, in spite of their sensitivity and specialization, are somewhat tolerant of change. (2) Fishing is regulated. There is almost none which is not regulated by some agency—the state, the federal government, an international commission, an Indian tribe. (3) Extensive artificial propagation and stream planting are carried on. (4) The environment, however disturbed, has not, as yet, been destroyed entirely or in all parts of the region. (5) Effort is directed toward controlling adverse environmental changes.

It cannot be assumed from their present survival, however, that the salmon will be able indefinitely to keep coming into the rivers if changes continue against them. Let us therefore look at some of the aspects of controlling the anadromous fish environment.

Concern about the condition of the salmon runs is not new. The first attention was to overfishing, which came with commercial civilization. Traditionally the Indians stopped fishing when they had enough, and removed the traps, weirs, and nets and let the fish go by. In later days, however, there is hardly such a thing as a sufficiency of anything. In 1893, R. D. Hume, an Oregon writer, advocated a fish commission and the regulation of gear, as well as hatcheries. His remarks referred to the Columbia, and had nothing to do with Indians. "I will add that unless some such steps are taken, in less than ten years

[16] See *Encyclopedia Britannica,* Vol. XIX (Chicago, 1960), s.v. "Salmon."

the packing of salmon on the Columbia river will have become impossible as a business proposition, and in much less time the truth of this proposition will be apparent." [17]

The critical importance of environment became obvious as time went on.[18] In 1953, in a small pamphlet entitled *The Salmon Crisis,* the Department of Fisheries stated: "The main cause of salmon depletion can be traced directly to the environmental changes that have taken place since the advent of civilization in the Pacific Northwest." [19] In 1958 Clarence F. Pautzke, then assistant director of the Department of Fisheries, wrote: "What has then reduced these runs so drastically and in many areas caused a complete loss of certain races? I believe the answer can be stated simply—the loss of environment to the fish." [20] In its *Ten-Year Plan* prepared for the 1965 legislature the Department of Fisheries said:

The term "stream loss" . . . pertains to the loss of salmon-production potential through the destruction or drastic alteration of the fish's natural spawning and rearing habitat. . . . Stream losses . . . have been occurring since man began utilizing the water resources and developing the land associated with it. . . . Now, with the rapidly increasing population making more and more demands on this resource, this loss is taking place at an alarmingly rapid pace.[21]

[17] R. D. Hume, "The Salmon of the Pacific Coast," published 1893, reprinted in Washington State Department of Fisheries, *Annual Report* (Olympia, Wash., 1958), p. 125. Hume, with whom Crawford, Washington's first commissioner of fisheries, carried on correspondence, put into practice his belief in the need for artificial propagation of salmon. At his own expense he built and operated a hatchery on the Rogue River in southwestern Oregon, where he lived.

[18] The *First Report* of the commissioner of fisheries in 1890 discussed the harmful effect on salmon of sawdust dumped from sawmills into the rivers.

[19] Washington State Department of Fisheries, *The Salmon Crisis* (pamphlet), 1953.

[20] Moore *et al., Fisheries,* III, 100.

[21] Washington State Department of Fisheries, "Natural Rearing of Salmon," in *A Ten-Year Plan.*

At the present time a number of laws, state and federal, are directed toward maintaining the salmon and steelhead. Some are written expressly for federal-state cooperation. Within the state of Washington an appreciable amount of land, such as national parks and national forests, is under federal jurisdiction. In these areas the responsibility for fish conservation activities rests with the federal government, and the work is carried on by the Bureau of Sport Fisheries and Wildlife.

The principal agencies of the state which work directly with such problems are the Department of Fisheries and the Department of Game, which operate together in a number of functions besides law enforcement. Under the law, "The Department of Fisheries is charged with the maintenance, preservation and enhancement of the commercial fisheries of the State." [22] Its job is "fisheries management"—an integrated program of regulation, propagation, control of environment, and use of the resource. In carrying out those duties which relate to the environment, it issues permits for various kinds of construction, oversees construction of fishways, carries out stream clearance operations, carries on research, and cooperates formally and informally with many other agencies, governmental and private. It has cooperative agreements or programs with the State Highway Department, the U.S. Fish and Wildlife Service, the Army Corps of Engineers, the Bureau of Indian Affairs, the U.S. Geological Survey, the National Forest Service, and others.

Part of environment control is "watershed management." State law declares that it is "the policy of this state that a flow of water sufficient to support game fish and food fish population be maintained at all times in the streams of this state." [23] When an application is made to the state for water rights in-

[22] *Annual Report,* 1963, p. 51. Discussion in this section of activities of the Department of Fisheries is based on information in the *Annual Reports,* especially 1963, 1964, and 1965-66. Discussion of pollution control activities is based principally on the statute.

[23] *Annual Report,* 1964, p. 95.

volving any surface water area, the departments of game and fisheries jointly investigate and make a recommendation to the Department of Water Resources. Applications are made "for almost every imaginable purpose," domestic, agricultural, municipal, and industrial. They have averaged five hundred to six hundred a year in recent years, and they relate to almost every surface water area in the state.

The law also requires "that any individual, group, or agency wishing to accomplish work within, or affecting streams or other surface waters of the state must first submit full plans and specifications to the Department of Fisheries and Department of Game and receive approval from both agencies." [24] Approvals given have risen from approximately four hundred in 1960 to more than eighteen hundred in 1965, and about two thirds of them involve streams in which active salmon runs exist. Projects covered include flood control, road and bridge or culvert construction, channel changes, gravel removal, dredging, small dam construction, land beautification, pipeline crossings, and logging operations. Continuing population growth, together with increasing awareness of the requirements of law, will undoubtedly keep the trend upward.

The following suggests some of the complexity of the task of maintaining the environment of the anadromous fish:

A single pipeline project, completed during 1965, extended from Ferndale in Whatcom County to a Columbia river crossing at Vancouver, Washington. This pipeline crossed 172 streams or other bodies of water and required the constant attention of two Department of Fisheries inspectors over a 3½ month period. Additional man months went into pre-planning, preliminary on-site investigations and reviewing plans and engineering specifications. Aircraft was utilized to keep abreast of activity by the 8 to 12 crews engaged at clearing, ditching, pipe laying and backfilling at water crossings. A consulting firm of soil engineers was required to solve problems of earth movement triggered by ditching opera-

[24] *Annual Report,* 1965, p. 59.

tions at two locations. . . . Totally, an excess of one man year was required for this single project.[25]

There are few projects of such size, but there are hundreds of small ones. Every culvert on a salmon stream, every embankment, every removal of gravel, every small logging operation on adjacent ground, every little blockage or diversion of water, threatens that much of the salmon world.

The control of pollution in the water, a particular aspect of the control of environment, is the responsibility of the Washington State Water Pollution Control Commission, established by act of the legislature in 1945, with subsequent amendments. It is composed of the directors of the departments of water resources, fisheries, game, health, and agriculture. A director carries out many of its functions. Amendments passed in 1967 strengthened the commission's authority and expanded the scope of its activities.

Public policy of the state as declared by the law is

. . . to maintain the highest possible standards to insure the purity of all waters of the state consistent with public health and public enjoyment thereof, the propagation and protection of wild life, birds, game, fish and other aquatic life, and the industrial development of the state, and to that end require the use of all known available and reasonable methods by industries and others to prevent and control the pollution of the waters of the state of Washington.[26]

Any industrial operation which discharges any kind of waste into the waters of the state through any channels, including the sewage system of a city, is required to have a permit from the commission.

The commission shall issue a permit unless it finds that the disposal of waste material as proposed in the application will pollute

[25] *Ibid.*, p. 60.
[26] R.C.W. 90.48.010. One of the problems is to determine what is reasonable.

the waters of the state. . . . The commission shall have authority to specify conditions necessary to avoid such pollution in each permit.[27]

No permit is valid for more than five years—at the end of that time the operator must secure a new one. Temporary permits may be issued on condition that certain requirements are met. Permits may be canceled for cause, and the commission may specify additional requirements for permits already issued if conditions change. The commission can also take emergency action to order the closing of an operation where serious pollution exists.

Before 1967 a contested order of the commission did not go into effect until the question was settled, and many delays often occurred before an improvement could be effected. The 1967 amendments provide that an order which has been issued must be complied with regardless of whether it is being appealed. Federal law provides for federal participation, on the request of a state, in the state agency's effort to obtain compliance with its orders.

The commission works cooperatively with numerous other agencies. It participates in research. Its approval is required for construction or improvement of any sewage disposal system. It is the state agency designated to cooperate with the U.S. Public Health Service under the Federal Water Pollution Control Act.

The commission is empowered to take action through the courts to enforce its regulations and orders. The courts can issue injunctions against detrimental activities or citations for contempt for failure to comply with commission orders. Violators of the provision of the law forbidding the discharge of polluting matter into the waters "shall incur, in addition to any other penalty as provided by law, a penalty in the amount of

[27] R.C.W. 90.48.180.

one hundred dollars a day for every such violation." [28] However, the law allows wide discretion to the commission's director in carrying out this provision. "The director may, . . . when deemed in the best interest to carry out the purposes of this chapter, remit or mitigate any penalty provided for in this section . . . upon such terms as he in his discretion shall deem proper." [29]

The enforcement remedies are all civil actions. The law contains no criminal sanctions.

What are the prospects?

In January 1962 the Pollution Control Commission jointly with the U.S. Public Health Service held hearings in the matter of certain pulp mill operations in Puget Sound. The following statement was made on behalf of the U.S. Fish and Wildlife Service:

Recognition of polluted waters in Puget Sound is not of recent origin . . . but little progress has been made toward adopting proper abatement measures. Polluted waters have resulted in no less than sixty-three recorded fish kills in Puget Sound in the last ten years. On four separate occasions in the same area on the Duwamish River, thousands of salmon, steelhead and other game fish perished from pollutants. Each incidence [sic] resulted in an unproductive investigation. . . .[30]

The Pollution Control Commission testified as follows:

. . . acting under 1955 permit law, the Commission issued certain waste discharge permits. The permits to our large sulfite mills specify reduction of approximately 85% of sulfite waste liquor solids discharged to state waters, the Commission has been unable to obtain compliance from the pulp mills. . . . There is no indication of early resolution of these pollution problems.

[28] R.C.W. 90.48.144 (3).
[29] Ibid.
[30] Washington State Pollution Control Commission, *Transcript of Conference in the Matter of Pollution of Interstate Waters*, 1st sess., Jan. 16–17, 1962, p. 173. These hearings deal with Puget Sound, Strait of Juan de Fuca, and their tributaries and estuaries.

. . . The pulp mills have repeatedly expressed themselves in favor of pollution control. Regular reports on research being conducted have been submitted, but no action taken to reduce pollution from sulfite waste liquor. During this time [1955–62] sulfite pulp production has materially increased with a consequent increase in pollution.[31]

A report published in 1967 of studies made since those hearings showed that in the same areas sulfite wastes were still being discharged in amounts at times sufficient to be detrimental or lethal to juvenile salmon.[32]

Because of the strengthening of the law in 1967, such conditions will probably improve to some extent. However, some agencies which use the streams are in positions of sufficient power to be able to disregard not only other segments of public interest such as wildlife or fisheries, but also at least the intent of the law. It is difficult for an agency like the Water Pollution Control Commission to affect the destructive actions of large industrial enterprise regardless of what harm is being done. Neither is the part of the public which is economically dependent upon such enterprise likely actively to support actions which the enterprise says hamper it.[33] These factors, together with the discretionary provisions in the law, may indeed mean that no early resolution is in sight for some of the problems of pollution.

The environmental changes brought about by the many small operations also continue. The 1966 *Annual Report* of the Department of Fisheries notes problems and projected difficulties "not experienced heretofore." Urban sprawl, "enveloping many

[31] *Ibid.,* pp. 123–24.

[32] See Washington State Pollution Control Commission, *Pollution Effects of Pulp and Paper Industrial Wastes in Puget Sound* (Olympia, Wash., 1967). Because dead juvenile salmon sink to the bottom, it is hard to discover a kill of them.

[33] Labor unions, for example, are not usually active spokesmen for "conservation."

once highly productive [salmon] streams," [34] more people, more industry, and more recreation, all mean more uses for the water, and increasing conflicts of interest.

Real estate development continues to contribute an increasing number of hydraulic project proposals. . . . Solutions to these problems can usually be worked out, but protection to the fishery is not always easily attained as fishway construction and alteration of plans may be costly to the developer.[35]

This kind of work, the importance of which is repeatedly pointed out in the material included in the Department of Fisheries *Annual Reports,* holds no great priority in the distribution of public funds. In 1965 coverage for the pipeline project described above "was attained at the expense of other activities . . . as budgetary limitations precluded accomplishing both responsibilities." [36] In 1966: "Stream improvement projects and stream maintenance work were somewhat limited during 1966 due to lack of funds and personnel required to pursue both functions effectively." [37]

New dams are projected or under way. The dams are not natural phenomena. They are built. Federal agencies are involved—the Federal Bureau of Reclamation and the powerful Army Corps of Engineers. Federal money comes into an area with the construction, at least for the period of building—the so-called pork barrel. The dams are identified as progress, and it is hard for the public to examine even some of their obvious implications.[38]

[34] *Annual Report,* 1966, p. 176.
[35] *Annual Report,* 1965, p. 61.
[36] *Ibid.,* p. 60.
[37] *Annual Report,* 1966, p. 176.
[38] Two of the newest are a high dam on the Wynooche River at the southern edge of the Olympic Mountains, on which work has begun; and the proposed Ben Franklin Dam on the Columbia mentioned earlier. The Sierra Club says of Ben Franklin Dam and the Army Corps of Engineers: "Between Priest Rapids and North Richland is the last 57 miles of free-flowing Columbia River in the United States. The Army Corps of

Mayfield and Mossyrock are two recently constructed dams on the Cowlitz River, a western Washington tributary of the Columbia, built by the city of Tacoma to meet its growing public power needs. The Department of Fisheries included in its 1949 *Annual Report* a statement of opposition to dams on the Cowlitz, and discussion of dangers they would present to the important Cowlitz River salmon runs.[39] In 1950 it said, "The Cowlitz program is opposed by the department without reservation." [40] The department suggested a site in the Columbia system above Grand Coulee.[41] In the fall of 1950 the Federal Power Commission held hearings in Washington, D.C., on the matter of the Cowlitz project. The Department of Fisheries appeared to oppose construction of the two dams, along with the Department of Game, the U.S. Fish and Wildlife Service, the Alaska Department of Fisheries, the Fish Commission of Oregon, the California Fish and Game Commission, the University of Washington School of Fisheries, and the Fisheries Research Institute.[42] Five years later the *Annual Report* said, "Maintaining fish runs at their existing level will present a difficult if not impossible problem if Mayfield and Mossyrock dams are built." [43] In 1963 it reported, "The down-

---

Engineers proposes to tame this stretch. . . . The Corps of Engineers has followed its usual *modus operandi:* line up the commercial interests beforehand and then push the politicians into the position of being obligated to support the project. . . . There is considerable public opposition in the Tri-Cities to the proposed dam, much to the surprise of the Corps and local politicians, who aren't saying much, don't seem too happy about the dam either. . . . This is a reach of the Columbia River where the chinook salmon and steelhead still use their natural spawning grounds." John C. Sheppard, "Ben Franklin Dam: Last Stand on the Columbia," *Northwest Conifer* (March 1969), p. 9.

[39] *Annual Report,* 1949, pp. 2–4.
[40] *Annual Report,* 1950, p. 3.
[41] See *ibid.;* discussion on pp. 10–19, map on p. 11, diagram on p. 19.
[42] The interest of Oregon, California, and Alaska lay in the fact that damage to the runs in any river increases the pressure on remaining runs in other rivers.
[43] *Annual Report,* 1955, p. 18.

stream migrant fish facilities at Mayfield Dam were placed in operation in April, 1963 when power generation commenced. . . . Adult fish have been transported past Mayfield Dam since July, 1961 when the fishway was first placed in operation. . . . Preliminary meetings have been held with the City of Tacoma concerning the fish facilities to be located at Mossyrock Dam immediately above the Mayfield reservoir." [44] Work and study go on as to how best to get the fish, both the upstream and the downstream migrants, around the two dams.

The city of Tacoma has built or has supplied the funds for the fishway facilities at Mayfield and Mossyrock dams, and it is also funding the construction of the huge new Cowlitz hatchery, the largest ever to be built, "as part of the mitigative facilities required by the construction of Mayfield and Mossyrock Dams." [45] A large proportion of the "reimbursable projects" (see chap. iii) which are part of the work of the Department of Fisheries fall into the category of mitigative work.

As an aid to the Department, certain statutes in the fisheries code require that any governmental agency or individual responsible for obstructions to fish runs or other activities harmful to fish life shall make provision to compensate for or mitigate damage caused, or provide other suitable alternative. . . . Items . . . include the provision of fish passage over dams or other obstruction. . . . Alternatively, such obstructions may be compensated for by the construction and operation of hatcheries, spawning channels, spawning beaches, etc., where the provision of fish passage is impracticable or will not fully mitigate damages.[46]

The value of having such requirements in law is apparent. A strenuous effort is being made to maintain the runs of the Cowlitz, and up to now it is not, like the upper Columbia, without salmon. Yet the fish were the losers. Even the implications of compensation as described above make this clear.

[44] *Annual Report,* 1963, p. 26.
[45] *Annual Report,* 1966, p. 163.
[46] *Ibid.,* p. 168.

Moreover, in their few years of operation the Cowlitz facilities have been repeatedly troubled by slides and floods; they will always be dependent upon manpower and appropriations.

In its *Ten-Year Plan*, the Washington State Department of Fisheries stated:

If no more stream losses were to occur, natural production of salmon would probably be maintained at a relatively high level. . . . There is every reason to believe that *this situation will not continue* with stream losses occurring at their present rate. . . . The future outlook for our Puget Sound and Washington rivers and streams for salmon use appears rather bleak if we allow the present trend of hydraulic changes and encroachment to persist. [Emphasis in original] [47]

A legal and organizational framework exists for maintaining the fish environment, and technical knowledge and skill have greatly increased. There are genuine conflicts of interest, but a reasonable possibility exists that they can be negotiated.

Far more serious are the conflicts of values. The salmon are not looked upon as important—not important compared to "development" or "progress." Progress means conquest of nature, industry, highways, suburbs, bulldozing, dams. The extinction of beautiful or valuable species is regrettable, but secondary and incidental. Interrelationships and the pervading character of responsibility are lost to sight. Few in this society regard the destruction of the upper Columbia River salmon— a great natural supply of protein food and a beautiful and fascinating phenomenon, as well as a great recreational resource—as a crime against the future. The river is seen as an object for development, not as a part of a balanced, functioning whole, in which disruption in one part will set off repercussions the extent and nature of which really are not known. Ecology is a word in the dictionary, not a description of the interrelationships upon which the continued survival of all

[47] "Natural Rearing of Salmon," in *A Ten-Year Plan.*

species, all varieties of man as well as of salmon, may depend.

The attitude which is needed was expressed at the dedication of one of Seattle's recently completed Metro treatment plants, which Chief Sealth might have approved: "Ten years is a short day in the life of a great city. We are transients on these hills and shores, and the waters are not ours to spend." [48]

WHOSE FISH? CONSERVATION AND JURISDICTION

Traditional Indian fishing practices seem to have allowed deliberately for adequate escapement. Swindell reports testimony by Sextas Ward, a Quileute Indian who was about three years old when the treaty was signed in 1855:

. . . ordinarily each village would have at least one trap and that in addition to the traps the Indians caught fish with spears and nets; that when the Indians had obtained enough fish they would remove the wiers [sic] from the river in order that the fish they did not need could go upstream and lay their eggs so that there would be a supply of fish for future years; that the fish traps or wiers were made of fine maple boughs laced together with spruce limbs and they stretched entirely across the stream in which they were built; that the nets used by the Indians were made out of twine which the Indians manufactured from maple vines. . . .[49]

Swindell also reports from James Kash Kash, a Umatilla Indian who was born about 1863:

. . . it was customary for the Indians not to catch the salmon in the tributaries until after they had spawned for the reason that they knew there would be no salmon in the future if they did not permit the females to lay their eggs to be hatched . . . there are so few fish now as compared to what there were when he was a boy.[50]

Indians have had very little to do with the changes which

[48] Quoted from the speech of James R. Ellis in "Northwest Today," *Seattle Post-Intelligencer,* Nov. 13, 1966, p. 3.
[49] Swindell, pp. 221–22.
[50] *Ibid.,* p. 305.

have so seriously affected the salmon environment. They did not build Grand Coulee, which at one stroke destroyed all the salmon of the upper Columbia, nor any of the other great dams. They have not dumped sewage into the rivers, and they have not polluted the streams and bays with sawdust, sulfite, or atomic wastes. They have not cut down the forests nor destroyed the vegetative cover of the land with real estate sub-divisions. If the repeated statement is true that loss of environment is the cause of the decline of the salmon, the responsibility does not rest with the Indians.

Yet it is in the name of conservation that the Indian fisheries have been attacked—the Indian off-reservation fisheries, though the distinction has not always been carefully maintained. The Indian fisheries constitute a special threat to the salmon and steelhead runs, in the opinion of the state—the Department of Game and the Department of Fisheries—because by fishing in the rivers they catch the fish which are returning to spawn, returning as into a funnel.[51] This position has been repeatedly implied or stated, in Department of Fisheries *Annual Reports,* in the 1964 *Hearings,* in news stories.

While percentagewise the Indian catch in the Pacific Northwest is not of major significance, the locations where the Indian fishery is carried on make it of extreme importance insofar as the proper management of the anadromous fish is concerned . . . the Indian catch usually takes a disproportionately high percentage of the spawning runs. . . .[52]

What is a "disproportionately high percentage" of the spawning population? Are the Indian fisheries a unique danger to the runs because they "work on the seed stock for the fu-

[51] See 1964 *Hearings,* p. 29.
[52] Memorandum from Clarence F. Pautzke, Commissioner of Fish and Wildlife, to the Assistant Legislative Counsel, Office of the Solicitor, Sept. 3, 1964. Pautzke was formerly assistant director of the Washington State Department of Fisheries.

ture"? [53] All salmon, whatever their location at a given time, are potential spawners. As a fish biologist put it, "Whoever *fishes* works on the seed stock for the future." The crucial question is whether enough fish get to the spawning grounds and spawn, not where the fish which are caught are taken. Enough fish must pass each fishery—all the fisheries in the sea and the Sound, as well as the Indian and the sport fisheries in the rivers.

Not all tribal regulation has always been adequate for the needs of a situation, even for securing compliance with the tribe's own rules. Not all Indian fishing practices have always been sound in relation to the maintenance of a salmon run. These facts, of course, are not unique to Indians. What is more to the point is that adequate assistance has not been available to enable tribes to handle the matters more effectively. Each tribe has been left to cope with its problems as it could, whether or not it had funds for enforcement or access to advice on good codes.

Our tribe has fishing regulations in effect for the purpose of conservation, as do most of the tribes of Washington. But tribal regulation of fishing is not and under present conditions cannot be a satisfactory solution to the problem . . . tribal councils have no way of knowing what regulations are actually necessary for proper conservation. Fisheries management is an uncertain science at best. But certainly no control measures can be established without first having some basic factual information necessary to establish an overall plan.

. . . As much as our fish-producing streams contribute to the overall economy of the State, little has been done by either the State or Federal fisheries agencies to perpetuate the runs of salmon originating on Indian streams and rivers. Few biological studies have been made of Indian streams and rivers. . . . Without this biological information, it is impossible for Indian tribal councils

[53] Expression used in a release by the State Department of Fisheries, "Indian Fisheries Problem," 1964.

to establish regulations with any confidence that they represent valid conservation measures.[54]

Cooperative efforts among tribes, either for regulation of fisheries or their development, have never been promoted by the Bureau of Indian Affairs. The weight of that agency has rather been lent to more and more strict delimitation of fishing rights in terms of particular fishing areas belonging to particular tribes, together with definition of the individual's rights as strictly attached and limited to formal membership in a particular tribe. Considerations related less to community life than to technical questions of genealogy, tribal membership, and tribal legislation have become increasingly demanding because of the dominant society's insistence that they are the rules of the game.[55] The bureau has not attempted to mediate with the state, or to work for a complementary fitting together of tribal and state regulations and plans. It has approved various off-reservation fishing codes, but its principal proposal to help in resolving the controversy between the tribes and the state has been to have the Department of Interior regulate the off-reservation fishing.

No program of assistance to tribal fisheries maintenance and development was ever seriously contemplated by any agency before the limited program begun in 1962 (see chap. v). Neither have Indians been invited by state agencies or others to participate as interested parties in overall conservation plans and projects, except on a nominal basis. To a very considerable extent, Indians have been denied the right of participation in the responsibility for their fisheries.

The departments of fisheries and game work against some

[54] Testimony of Alvin Ziontz, attorney for the Makahs, 1964 *Hearings*, p. 81.

[55] It may be that some modification of this is implied in the position stated since the *Puyallup* decision. See quote from *The Daily Olympian*, Oct. 22, 1968, in chap. v, section on The Bureau of Indian Affairs.

odds in their work of maintaining the anadromous fish. The Department of Fisheries fought the construction of Mayfield and Mossyrock dams, which block the last sizable salmon river in southwest Washington, to the end, even to seeking an injunction against it through the courts. Yet no such publicity campaign was raised against the dams as has been carried on against Indian fishing. The Department of Fisheries does not release statements to the press on the dangers of "urban sprawl" and real estate subdivision. Even pollution does not rate many stories, and these are rarely followed by stories of action being taken or remedies invoked. Loss of environment is not easy to publicize. Neither is it easy to campaign against such an agency as the Army Corps of Engineers, such interests as real estate operations or pulp and paper manufacture, or such an idea as development. Nets and visible persons, comparatively inarticulate and without wealth or influence, are a far simpler target, especially when the thought that they are catching "our fish" is added. The Indians are visible and vulnerable.

It is therefore not surprising that some Indians feel that they are being made the scapegoat for conditions caused by other factors and beyond their control.

At night it looks like a floating city out there; these commercial men, they have nets 1,800 feet long and they go row after row down the straits here by Whidbey Island and whatnot and they take all those salmon before they come to us, and when the salmon reaches the Puyallup River they come to us and they say, "Well, the runs of the Puyallup River is depleted and you will have to let them go by . . ." But then they point to us and that gets me hot under the collar, I get worked up when they talk about it.[56]

And from the Makah Indians:

[56] Testimony of Frank Wright, chairman, Puyallup tribe, in hearings before the Commerce Committee on Northwest Salmon Fishery Resources, Oct. 13, 1961; quoted in 1964 *Hearings,* pp. 116, 117.

. . . there are examples which can be found of Indians in the State of Washington who have refused to exercise self-restraint in their fishing practices. While we may understand the reasons for their behavior, we do not condone it. Nevertheless, we do not believe the Indian citizens of the State of Washington and of the Pacific Northwest generally should be made the scapegoat for the practices of a few. Likewise, we do not believe that the Indian fishermen should be made the scapegoat for salmon depletion, when every reputable study of the problem clearly points to other factors.[57]

The Department of Fisheries, regarding itself, along with the Department of Game, as the "proper managing party" for maintaining the fish resources, has opposed Indian off-reservation regulation, or Department of Interior regulation, or agreements with the tribes, or anything except state control of off-reservation fishing, as unfeasible and improper because of the need for unified control. It has at times given the impression of being more interested in the control than the fish.

Federal plans to build a $1 million hatchery to replenish fish runs on Washington Indian reservations could lead to legal difficulties, partly stemming from the state's battle to control off-reservation Indian fishing. . . . The Federal Bureau of Sports Fisheries is planning to put up a "Quinault national fish hatchery" on the Cook Creek tributary to the Quinault River, about 35 miles north of Aberdeen. . . . The bureau has asked the State Department of Fisheries for permission to stock state rivers with excess fish beyond what is needed for the Indian reservation waters. . . .

. . . The . . . request, says a state attorney, could pose serious legal questions striking at the very heart of the state's fisheries conservation program. Asst. Atty. Gen. Joseph L. Coniff Jr., who represents the Fisheries and Game Departments, says the planting of Indian fish even on the reservations could undermine state legal efforts to regulate the off-reservation fishing . . . the Indians might strengthen their position, said Coniff, if they could claim ownership to some of the fish moving off the reservation waters. . . . The

[57] 1964 *Hearings,* p. 81.

problem, he said, would be how to separate the Indian fish and their offspring from other fish belonging to all citizens.[58]

As a part of the same fisheries development program, the Quinaults were already carrying on a program of planting juvenile silver salmon in their rivers. Study of where these fish, marked before release, were later taken showed that 65 percent or more were caught by sport or commercial fishermen in the open ocean. Tribal officials stated that they were glad to be able, through their fisheries program, to benefit the general public as well as the tribe.

Who owns the salmon and steelhead? They do not stay in one place. They move up some Washington rivers into Oregon, Idaho, and Canada (though not via the upper Columbia), and the young fish move back down those rivers into Washington and to the sea. They range far and wide in the ocean, not always within the three- or twelve-mile limits. Salmon from Washington move down the coast to waters off Oregon and California, and northward along British Columbia and Alaska, and possibly Siberia. Salmon from California, Oregon, Alaska, and British Columbia move along Washington shores; Canadian fish enter Washington waters. For such a river as the Columbia, coordinated "management" can be carried out only through the cooperation of reciprocally independent jurisdictions—no state can impose its program on another.[59] Coordination between federal and state jurisdictions even within a state has to be by agreement—the two are independent of each other.

The same holds, with a great deal more force, between

---

[58] Joe Rigert, "Hatchery Brings Up Legal Difficulties," *Aberdeen Daily World,* Aberdeen, Wash., June 17, 1965.

[59] For example: "In 1957 the sports catch in Idaho nearly equalled the entire spawning escapement. . . . It has been demonstrated that the curtailment of the gillnet fishery in the lower Columbia River to increase upriver escapement has provided more fish for the Idaho sportsmen . . . hence deliberations on management problems must bring all agencies together." Moore *et al., Fisheries,* III, 243.

nations. When Russian fishing boats appeared off the coast of Washington at the three-mile limit in the summer of 1966, the United States acted unilaterally to extend its stated jurisdictional limits from three to twelve miles; but it also moved immediately to enter into discussions with the Russians and to work for agreements, which were subsequently concluded.

The sockeye runs of the Fraser River, no part of which flows within the boundaries of the United States, are the basis of the important Puget Sound sockeye landings. They are under the jurisdiction of the International Pacific Salmon Fisheries Commission, established by convention between Canada and the United States. It built the fishway at the Hell's Gate Gorge (see note 12, above); it monitors the runs; it allocates the catch between American and Canadian fishermen. Americans have supported Canadian conservationists in opposing the construction of dams on the Fraser.

Besides all of these elements, there are many users of the waters, as well as of the lands, which affect the salmon rivers. As previously noted, the Department of Fisheries enters into agreements with many agencies in order to maintain the suitability of the rivers for salmon. Only through such cooperation can the conservation and appropriate utilization of the anadromous fish be carried out. The state's "unified management program" is not unitary, but a complex of cooperative arrangements and agreements.

Even within its own jurisdiction, the Department of Fisheries works with different interests and notes the necessity for negotiation and agreement between them. Referring to conflict between salmon sport fishermen and commercial fishermen, it said in its *Ten-Year Plan*:

Efforts must be increased to bring about greater understanding and unity of effort among the fishing interests. Competition has led to a degree of disunity which prevents their full strength being used to increase and preserve their own resource; i.e., energy spent fighting each other cannot be used to combat pollution or aid in protecting vital spawning grounds.[60]

The same document discussed Indian fisheries as a problem to fisheries management, not as a fishery. Only with respect to the Indian fisheries does the state say that it will "manage accordingly," by implication that it will ignore them. The state's view has been that Indian fisheries as such have no place in fisheries planning. In effect, the state's definition of the problem is that Indians refuse to move into the category of sportsman or conventional commercial fisherman.

. . . the segments of the anadromous fishery are sport fishing, commercial fishing, and Indian fishing. The States' regulations have been designed to accommodate the needs of the first two segments, sport fishing and commercial fishing, but we have not recognized any separate need for the Indian fishing, believing that the Indians should engage in sport and commercial fishing on the same terms that apply to other citizens.[61]

The matter was more emphatically stated by James Hovis, attorney for the Yakimas:

These Washington state departments . . . are joined together . . . only by one common purpose, and that is to stop Indian landings by any means that they can. They do not have any interest in the Indian landings whatsoever . . . they do not want regulation for conservation. They want to stop Indian fishing. . . .[62]

In this context it is impossible to think in terms of what would constitute a suitable or equitable proportion for Indians to take. If legitimacy is not presumed, no basis exists for determining what is equitable. To say that Indians take a "disproportionately high percentage" of the spawning or any other

[60] "Conflict Between Salmon Fishermen," in *A Ten-Year Plan.*
[61] Testimony of John A. Carver, Jr., assistant secretary of the Department of the Interior, 1964 *Hearings,* p. 12.
[62] 1964 *Hearings,* p. 64.

population has no meaning unless it is recognized that they are actually entitled to a share.

The Indian fisheries, off reservation and on, are the fisheries within the state which agencies of the state have been unwilling to recognize as having a valid existence. The *Puyallup* decision, again confirming their legitimacy, pointed to the need for allocation to make recognition effective.

Such allocation would help both Indians and the state. It is doubtful that the state will or can maintain the position that it has no interest in on-reservation fishing, for the fish cannot be separated. Allocation would thus resolve the state's impasse regarding on-reservation fishing. And the tribes are aware that they need to know something of what is going on in related fisheries.

VII | Toward Cooperation and Dignity

CONSERVATION, INDIANS, AND ALLOCATION

Beyond any doubt, continuation of the salmon and steelhead resource requires the vigorous and coordinated application of conservation principles and practice. All share the responsibility—users of the rivers, users of the land through which the rivers flow, all categories of fishermen, the various local, state, federal, and international agencies which are responsible for control of land and river use, and the citizenries to which these agencies are accountable. The mere listing of interests indicates part of the complexity of the task, for no one agency controls more than a comparatively small portion of the total.

Indians share the responsibility as users of the fish—perhaps no group has a greater interest in the outcome. Although the non-Indian community, including both the state and the Bureau of Indian Affairs, has looked upon Indian fishing as something which would soon disappear as Indians became farmers or industrial workers and "entered the mainstream," nothing of the sort has happened. Fishing by Indians of the Pacific Northwest, including the Muckleshoots, Puyallups, and Nisquallys, has continued as one of the most important aspects of their life, important in both economic and nonmaterial ways.

The economic value is obvious—for many Indians fishing is their only effective income-producing skill, whether the fish are caught for personal use or for sale to provide other necessities. A great many people believe that the Indians' only reason for insisting on their treaty rights to fish is the economic advantage. The values, however, are more than economic. People already poor do not deliberately risk expensive equipment and their own imprisonment solely for the hope of financial gain. Fishing is their life in a much more profound sense than simply making a living.

Traditionally, life on the sea and the rivers dominated the economy, art, religion, and social life of the Northwest Coast Indians. Though patterns have changed, to many modern Indians the meaning of the inherited tradition is so strong that their determination to hold it for themselves, to use it, to insist on fishing even in defiance of official interference and legal actions, continues in spite of all the pressures to change. The intensity of feeling has led some Indians to apply the term "cultural genocide" to the attacks on their fishing. Fishing remains the center, in a sense the soul, of the Indian time-continuity and of the feeling of relationship to the environment. The fact of fishing as a fundamental aspect of personal and group relationship to what is important in existence is as real for many Indians today as it was for the treaty signers, and for those before them.

This sense of the spiritual, essential nature of fishing has not been understood by non-Indians, or even perceived by them. It is surely part of the reason that Indian tenacity in insisting on holding to their own fishing, their "treaty rights," has been so perplexing to most outsiders.

Another factor in the perplexity has been the complete confidence of the white people and the white agencies in the superiority of their own outlook and ways. That confidence was also the root of the agencies' inability, from Stevens on, to see what was already at hand—a ready-made fishery, capable of extended development and indefinite continuation for the support of the Indian people, to the benefit of both themselves and others. The same unexamined confidence also brought about the insistence upon imposing inappropriate and irrelevant non-Indian patterns, demanding the remodeling of the Indians. To this day, if an Indian man's occupation is given as "fisherman" it is frequently taken as indicative of backwardness and lesser competence.

Therefore no real planning assistance has ever been given to the Indian fisheries. Except for approving tribal regulatory codes, the federal government has virtually ignored them. Until 1962 it offered no technical advice or assistance to tribes either for setting up suitable regulations or for developmental programs. It did not attempt to obtain, or to make it possible for tribes to obtain, biological and other information about Indian rivers and the runs in them. Only in the last few years has it provided educational assistance for some young Indians to become fish biologists or fisheries technicians.[1]

The state of Washington has never taken Indian fisheries into consideration in fisheries planning, except as they affect other fisheries. In one way or another, by legal definition, licensing, regulation of gear, and agreement, the state has allocated the salmon and steelhead between commercial and sport fishermen and between different types of commercial fishermen. It has accommodated to Indian fisheries from time to time, sometimes with good will and sometimes as a result of court action, and sometimes simply as a *modus vivendi;* but it has never planned for the allocation of salmon or steelhead to the Indian fisheries as a legitimate part of the total fisheries. It has never looked at the Indian fisheries as a component of an integrated fisheries program. The Indian catch has been seen

---

[1] A few Indians have expressed the opinion that these courses were really intended to get the young men into non-Indian fisheries work.

primarily as a nuisance or a threat, and generally as an impingement on those regarded as the appropriate users. The efforts of the state to come to agreements with Indians have been principally designed to assure fish to the sport and commercial fishermen.[2]

The Indian fisheries have in a real sense survived and developed in isolation. Indians have not had access to the growing body of knowledge about the anadromous fish, nor have they had the opportunity to contribute their own knowledge. They have not been brought into any kind of overall decision-making, by either state or federal governments, with respect to managing the fisheries. Their authority to regulate their members' fishing at sites outside reservation boundaries has generally not been supported. They have been expected by state agencies to accept decisions and controls made for the state's view of needs, and based on the attitude that the Indian fishery as a distinct fishery is a troublesome anachronism. Indians have in effect been denied the right of responsible participation.

Their isolation is increasingly less tenable. Whatever the effect of the Indian fisheries on other fisheries or of others on them—and they all reciprocally affect each other—the fisheries of both Indian and non-Indian are inexorably affected by the changes in the physical environment of the region. Before white men came to the Northwest Coast, Indian tradition and practice took into account salmon propagation needs, and the fish continued in ample supply. Today the question of salmon and steelhead survival remains moot. The ending of all Indian fishing, perhaps of all fishing, would not appreciably affect the outcome. The salmon will not survive unless enough of their world survives for them to live.

[2] The new Squaxin agreement seems to be based on the idea that at the present time a separate Indian fishery can be tolerated at that place and still allow adequate escapement.

The environmental changes to which every serious discussion of salmon depletion points as the fundamental cause of the decline, and as the basic continuing threat, were not brought about by Indians. They came with the industrial and commercial activities of white men and with the growth of population. Neither have Indian fishing practices changed as much in kind or degree as those of the non-Indians. Indians have not been in a position to control or remedy the major changes affecting the fish.

The state, attempting to establish its own "unified control," has endeavored to regulate Indian off-reservation fishing. Because a net in a river can block it—though less efficiently than a dam for real estate development or power—the attack has been based on conservation: Indians endanger the "seed stock for the future." The argument ignores the fact that all salmon, including the alevins waiting to emerge from the gravel which may be taken for a logging road, are "seed stock." It ignores the effects of sportsmen's fishing on the same rivers, with different gear but in far greater numbers. It ignores the environmental damage which has destroyed more salmon than the most controversial Indian fishing. It ignores the kind of concern the Muckleshoots, Puyallups, and Nisquallys have expressed about the condition of their rivers, and it ignores the fisheries programs developed by the Quinaults and Makahs. An argument basically so fallacious could not have been used to such effect if the Indian fisheries had not already been regarded as being not actually legitimate fisheries.

Including the Indian fisheries in overall planning, which requires consideration of the share to be allocated to them, would provide a basis for settling the disputes. Allocation of the fish among the various fisheries has been carried out as a function of the state. Allocation to a particular fishery is based on its recognition as legitimate. In the state's general position of antagonism to the Indian fisheries and its attempt to ignore the on-reservation fisheries, it is left without a logical basis for discussion or agreement with the tribes; and any steps it takes from this position the tribes are certain to rebuff. Recognition of the Indian fisheries' place in the total fisheries and their inclusion in allocation would allow consideration of them as distinct fisheries whether on or off reservation.

It would also make active participation by Indians both possible and necessary.

Allocating a share to the Indian fisheries, however, presumes their legitimacy. Legally, legitimacy seems to be well established. The question about it exists in people's minds. What is the reason?

THE ISSUE: DIFFERENCE, NOT CONSERVATION

However real and serious the problems of conservation, they are not the basis of this controversy. The real issue is the attitude of the whole society toward difference.

The Indians look at fishing and fishing rights differently, and they fish in different ways. Difference is nearly intolerable in a society which expects conformity in behavior and outlook— one which tends to equate equal treatment with identical treatment, acceptable behavior with conforming behavior, integration with assimilation. The Indians' right to fish in different ways and under different rules is felt by many non-Indians to be completely inappropriate, and the connection of fishing rights with identity to be nonsense. Hostility rises from the threat presented by the differences, not from danger to the fish. Efforts to control Indian fishing have been rationalized around conservation, but they have recognized neither the pervasive importance of environmental changes nor the questions of humanness.

Indians, on the receiving end, see the matter more clearly than do non-Indians. Although they may not express it in so many words, they are well aware that the aim is to get rid

of them as Indians. The expression "treaty rights" becomes
emotion-laden and, like "conservation" on the other side, may
sometimes arouse feeling more than promote thought. The
terms become shibboleths, and the arguments go past each
other. But the fact remains that for many Indians survival as
Indians requires the survival of Indian fishing; the end of Indian fishing would be a great step toward extinction as Indians.

The problems of conservation have actually been obscured
by the fishing rights controversy. The attention of all—the
public, the conservation agencies, the Indian tribes—has been
diverted from basic problems of environment to the quarrel
over the right of certain Indians to fish at certain places. The
controversy has rendered impossible the orderly regulation of
their own off-reservation fishing by these three small tribes. It
has contributed nothing toward working out a suitable integration of Indian fishing with other fishing. On the contrary,
it has fanned fears and antagonisms which may make this
much more difficult. The state's attack on "Indian fishing" is
viewed by many, Indians and others, as meaning that state
officials desire control of fishing on the reservations as well as
off, and regard such control as the proper ultimate outcome.

The Muckleshoots, Nisquallys, and Puyallups—and most
other Indian groups in the state of Washington—face significant problems in mustering resources for communicating
their views of fishing with those having different styles of thinking, and in resisting the pressures that would submerge them.
None of these groups have adequate funds for legal representation in their disputes with the state agencies. Neither do
they have the political power of the other fishing interests,
especially the sport fishermen. Within Indian groups, differences over strategy in meeting the threats have produced divisions which have impeded efforts at rational fisheries development. Some of the extreme reactions have further hampered
communication both among Indians and between Indians and

others, and have rendered the Indians' planning more difficult. A tremendous amount of the resources and energy which could have been directed toward development of the fish has been spent instead on defense of the very right to an Indian fishery.

News stories in the mass media both illustrate the problem of attitude toward differences and contribute to it through their public impact. The message frequently is: "Indian fishing is destroying the salmon and steelhead." Important distinctions have not been made between off- and on-reservation fishing, different reservations, different practices, and different fishermen. "Hundred-year-old treaties" are described directly or by implication as outdated and inappropriate. The concern of the state and the sportsmen for preservation of the fish runs is emphasized. The massive problems of controlling the fish environment are touched only in passing.

One of the effects of the publicity attending the fishing rights dispute has been to induce a further sense of separation on the part of the Indians. What has been the effect on the attitudes about Indians on the part of others, the largely non-Indian public? The portrayal of Indians as irresponsible and unreasonable in their fishing practices must have strengthened existing stereotypes, without conveying a sense of legitimate disagreement.

What responsibility do public officials and mass media have in presenting complex issues to the public? The information is bound to be equally complex. Sometimes that released to the mass media has been simplified to the point of distortion, and apparently selected to support the view that Indian off-reservation fishing, not very clearly distinguished from on-reservation fishing, is the principal danger to fish runs in many of the rivers. Few readers are likely to question the statements of experts; nor will it even occur to them that there might be a question. Few have knowledge enough to evaluate and put into perspective specific statements made by game and fisheries department representatives about "Indian fishing."

The *Annual Reports* and other papers of the Department of Fisheries show their concern about all the elements of conservation and their continuing efforts to control conditions detrimental to the fish. Their *Ten-Year Plan* (see chap. vi, section on Control of Environment) could not have stated more plainly the seriousness of the threats from the environment. However, the publicity campaign has been directed against Indian fishing. "Conservation," with its connotations of reasonableness, cooperation, and progress, has been given a narrow definition and made the summation of intolerance toward certain differences.

Indians, insisting on their right to unique tribal existence, including fishing, are asserting the right to a freedom of choice —asking to *stay out* of certain aspects of American society. Whether intentionally or not, they are challenging the claim that the society believes in freedom of choice, and are providing the opportunity for the society to conserve, to its own enrichment, a certain human viewpoint and set of values. Both the fish and the particular people are part of the country's patrimony, part of its diverse wealth. The loss of either as a by-product of change would be an irredeemable impoverishment.

AN APPROACH

Diversity, both in outlook and in ways of operating, is a source of strength—this is a fundamental premise of our study. It follows that to eliminate differences because they require special procedures or arouse discomfort undermines the basis of the strength.

The Indian fisheries exist in fact, supported by history and the law. Biologically and environmentally they cannot be separated from others—they are part of the region's total fisheries. They must therefore be included in the allocation of the fish.

The statement of the Bureau of Indian Affairs, based on the *Puyallup* decision, points to the responsibility of the state in the matter. However, it can properly be considered a joint responsibility. Equitable allocation requires the participation of Indians.

Agreement on the legitimacy of the Indian fishery in its own right would make possible its inclusion in planning suitable allotment among the three groups, and would provide a rational basis for genuine cooperation between Indians and others—actual working together. It would allow an integrated and enhanced management program because the parts would no longer be obliged to expend their energies fighting each other, and no part would have to fight for existence.

Devising an operating system for actually bringing about allocation, integrated planning, and coordinated conservation efforts offers an opportunity for experimentation both in ways of getting the job done and in developing communication between people who think somewhat differently. It offers the chance for learning on both sides and for the exchange of information and skill, as well as the chance for reciprocal appreciation—all to the benefit not only of the groups directly participating and of the salmon, but also of the society at large.

Taking a cue from the International Pacific Salmon Fisheries Commission, which allocates the Fraser River sockeye and pinks between American and Canadian fishermen, we suggest the use of a commission composed of representatives of all three groups of fishermen. (Because of the special status of steelhead, two commissions might be necessary.) Its task would be to develop suitable and equitable means for allocating the fish among the three groups, taking the needs of all into consideration. It would undoubtedly need a legislative basis, both in the state and in the Indian tribes, and its tools would probably include extensive use of agreements.

It could also assist in the coordination of such matters as the regulatory codes used by the three groups, both with each other and with other fisheries regulations. Support and respect for the tribes' authority over their members' fishing, off the reservations as well as on, would thereby be incorporated into overall fisheries planning. The separateness, as well as the relatedness, of tribes and states would be maintained. However, their working together would become possible on an accepted and rational basis, far beyond the limited and half-recognized cooperation which presently exists.

Such a commission could also assist in the effective intermeshing of conservation programs carried on by Indians, the state, and the federal government. As has been discussed, much of the state's "management" at the present time is carried out by means of agreements with various agencies and cannot be done in any other way (see chap. vi).

Use of such a commission would mean that Indians are included in their own right, with their own representatives, for their own interest, as active participants in planning the salmon and steelhead programs for all fisheries, not only Indian. They would carry out their own programs in their own waters, though some of these might be joint programs. They could receive the assistance and cooperation of other agencies, federal, state, private, without domination from them. They would also be able to assist others.

The idea of such coordinate working together is not new. Charles Hobbs, attorney for the Quinaults, stated in the 1964 *Hearings:*

In my opinion, based on my knowledge of the needs and desires of the [Quinault] tribe and what would make sense for that situation, I think the solution to the problem which is before this committee is agreements between the Indians and the State. This problem that is here today is probably due as much as any other factor to the factor that the State wants to impose its solution on the

Indians. If the spirit were to consult with the Indians and obtain their agreement, common agreement on what the problem was, there is a reasonable chance that an agreed-upon solution could be reached.[3]

To put such a cooperative agency into operation would not be an easy undertaking, for either the state or the Indians. Hostility, mutual distrust and lack of respect, and intercultural misunderstanding pervade the situation. However, the hostile aspects have received far more attention than the constructive ones which presently exist. We believe that such an effort has enough promise to make it worth trying. From the standpoint of conserving the strength of diversity, it offers more than does repeated confrontation. It would serve much more than the technical requirements of maintaining and allocating the fish. It would serve people.

All of the Indian fishing communities need increased economic activity, and we suggest that tribes consider the establishment of buying, marketing, and processing enterprises. These could be cooperatively owned and controlled by the fishing groups themselves. Special attention could well be given to cooperation between tribes, with several groups joining together in the kinds of associations that make the most sense to them. Such projects might be explored by the intertribal organizations.

Activities of this type are already going on in some Indian communities, as was noted earlier (see chap. v). We recommend that all possible assistance be given to the Indians to develop their own businesses for optimum use of the fish.[4]

The fishermen—Indian, commercial, and sport—have an ob-

[3] 1964 *Hearings,* p. 146; see also statement of John Carver, pp. 12–13.
[4] The Lummi community is developing a tribal program related not to salmon but to use of their tidelands. The Lummi Aquaculture Project was funded initially in March 1969 by the Office of Economic Opportunity with the Lummi Tribal Council as the sponsoring agency.

vious common interest in conserving the fish. All will suffer if the fish are lost, and all will benefit if they can come to terms on allocation and unite to devote their attention to the environmental threats. The remarks quoted in Chapter VI from the Department of Fisheries' *Ten-Year Plan* about the energy lost to conservation because of the disputes between sport and commercial fishermen apply with at least equal force to the disputes between Indian fishermen and others.

Rather less obviously, for each of these three groups there is also a spiritual component in fishing, somewhat different for each but important to all. It is not just to make a living that every year the commercial fisherman incurs the cost and risk of fishing—it is "in his blood." The sport fisherman, of course, goes for "re-creation." The Indian fisherman, as we have tried to show, feels that his fishing and the fishing of his fellow Indians is an essential part of their being as Indians.

Effective participation of Indians in the solutions to overall fisheries problems needs a higher degree of public information and concern for the human element of the controversy. The conditions for finding constructive human answers depend not only on the attitudes of Indians and agency officials, but also on informed and supportive public opinion. We suggest that there are important roles for private organizations, churches, colleges and universities in their research activities, all educational institutions in their curricula at all grade levels, and private citizens, as well as for Indian groups and public agencies. The materials are fascinating, and they lie waiting for the curious and concerned to seek them out.

PHILOSOPHIC RECAPITULATION

In the end we come back to the philosophic questions which led us into this inquiry. Salmon, important in their own right, are important here because people are important. In this uncommon controversy the fish are tied to the questions of how a minority, a minority view, a minority style of life and thinking, are to be treated.

It is not that a people's ways of doing or thinking do not change. It is how the change is brought about which is important. Is it to be by destruction of something present and meaningful, or by development that produces a contribution and enrichment of the whole? Will it be related to what is already there, based on what is needed and appropriate, or will it tear down and leave less than it replaces? If it is to conserve and build upon what is presently valuable—in a sense to be change without change—what are the forces and the planning to be brought into play?

What happens when people think differently? What is the outlook for *any* view if *one* view is treated with contempt, overridden, ignored as valueless? What is the real nature of integration? Does it mean the disappearance of all significant differences, or does it imply accommodation and complemental fitting together? Can we tolerate diversity?

In the Indian fishing rights dispute we have differences in outlook between two groups; we also have conflicts between incompatible values held within the majority society. How the differences are resolved will affect all—not only Indians. Furthermore, the implications go far beyond this particular controversy and these particular people. Both in outlook and in the nature of their experiences with the aggressive, development-oriented Western culture, this group has much in common with many other groups of people over the world. The dispute contains in microcosm the ingredients of many conflicts in which people in many places are now struggling.

Neither the waters, nor the fish, nor the people are ours to spend. More is at stake than the unusual status and the unconforming viewpoint of one small minority. The Indian rivers are a proving ground of our society's substance.

Epilogue

"I can state categorically that the state of Washington will be guided by the wording and spirit of the Belloni decision. Governor Evans, the director of game, and the director of fisheries have met together, and this is to be the policy of the state."

James Dolliver, administrative assistant to Washington's Governor Dan Evans, was speaking to the Governor's Advisory Committee on Indian Affairs, July 10, 1969, requesting Indian participation in the state Fisheries Advisory Committee. The decision referred to was from the U.S. District Court of Oregon, where Judge Robert C. Belloni's opinion had been handed down two days earlier on two concurrent cases dealing with regulation of Indian treaty fishing by the state of Oregon. In the first of the two cases to be filed, *Sohappy* v. *Smith,* fourteen individual members of the Confederated Tribes and Bands of the Yakima Indian Nation filed against the members and director of the Fish Commission of the state of Oregon and the Oregon State Game Commission, seeking definition of their treaty fishing right on the Columbia River and its tributaries and of how and to what extent the state of Oregon may regulate Indian fishing. In the second case, *United States* v. *Oregon,* the United States filed against the state of Oregon for itself and for the Yakima, Umatilla, and Nez Perce tribes; and those three tribes and the Warm Springs tribe later intervened in their own behalf.[1] As an interpretation of the 1968 decision of the U.S. Supreme Court in the *Puyallup* case,[2] Judge Belloni's judgment in *Sohappy* v. *Smith* should be read in its entirety:

The court having filed its opinion dated July 8, 1969, as Findings of Fact and Conclusions of Law in these proceedings,

NOW, THEREFORE, I T IS HEREBY ORDERED, ADJUDGED AND DECREED as follows:

1. Before the State of Oregon may regulate the taking and disposition of fish by members of the Intervenor Tribes herein at usual and accustomed fishing places pursuant to treaties between the respective tribes and the United States:

(a) It must establish by hearings preliminary to regulation that the specific proposed regulation is both reasonable and necessary for the conservation of the fish resource. In order to be necessary, such regulations must be the least restrictive which can be imposed consistent with assuring the necessary escapement of fish for conservation purposes; the burden of establishing such facts is on the state.

(b) Its regulatory agencies must deal with the matter of the Indians' treaty fishing as a subject separate and distinct from that of fishing by others. As one method of accomplishing conservation objectives it may lawfully restrict or prohibit non-Indians fishing at the Indians' usual and accustomed fishing places without imposing similar restrictions on treaty Indians.

(c) It must so regulate the taking of fish that, except for unforeseeable circumstances beyond its control, the treaty tribes and their members will be accorded an opportunity to attempt to take, at their usual and accustomed fishing places, by reasonable means feasible to them, a fair and equitable share of all fish which it permits to be taken from any given run.

2. ORS 511.106(1) may not be applied or relied upon by the State of Oregon or its agents, officers or employees to restrict

---

[1] *Sohappy* v. *Smith,* USDC D. Oregon, No. 68–409, and *U.S.* v. *Oregon,* USDC D. Oregon, No. 68–513 (1969).

[2] *Puyallup Tribe* v. *Department of Game,* 391 U.S. 392, 20 L Ed 689 (1968).

fishing by members of the Intervenor tribes at their usual and accustomed places pursuant to their tribe's treaties with the United States.

3. The State of Oregon, to the extent that it can establish that such regulations are reasonable and necessary for conservation of the fish resources and do not discriminate against the Indians, and in accordance with the other provisions of this decree, may regulate the treaty Indian off-reservation fisheries; provided, that this judgment does not modify or affect in any way the judgment or orders of this court in the case of *Confederated Tribes of the Umatilla Indian Reservation, et al v. Maison, et al,* Civil No. 77–59, or any proceedings therein. In promulgating these regulations the protection of the treaty right to take fish at the usual and accustomed places must be an object of the state's regulatory policy and any restriction on the exercise of the treaty right must be expressed with such particularity that a member of the intervenor tribes can know in advance of their actions precisely the extent of the restrictions which the state has found to be necessary for conservation. In promulgating regulations, the State of Oregon must give the Intervenors and designated representatives of their members whose name and address are on file with the State of Oregon Fish Commission appropriate notice of the hearing and of the proposed restrictions to be considered and accord them an opportunity to be heard and participate meaningfully in the rule-making process.

4. This judgment constitutes a final judgment under Fed. R. Civ. P. 54(b) on the segregated claims above set forth, there being no just reason for delay. The court retains jurisdiction of the matters in suit herein for disposition of the remaining claims of the parties or to grant further or amended relief upon application of any of the parties. Any party at any time may apply to the court for a subsequent modification of any provision of this decree where the continued application of the decree has become inequitable or impracticable, but this right shall not affect the finality of the decree with respect to times prior to any such modification.

5. Each party shall bear its own costs.

Dated this 10 day of October, 1969.

A number of aspects of this decree are particularly noteworthy.

The Indians' treaty-protected right to fish in their usual and accustomed places is clearly upheld. The state is directed that the Indians' treaty fishing must be dealt with "as a subject separate and distinct from that of fishing by others." The July 8, 1969, opinion in this case clarifies the significance of this point:

[Oregon] has divided the regulatory and promotional control between two agencies—one concerned with the protection and promotion of fisheries for sportsmen . . . and the other concerned with protection and promotion of commercial fisheries . . . not just to preserve the fish but to perpetuate and enhance the supply for their respective user interests. . . . There is no evidence in this case that the defendants have given any consideration to the treaty rights of Indians as an interest to be recognized or a fishery to be promoted in the state's regulatory and developmental program. . . . [The state] must manage the over-all fish run in a way that does not discriminate against the treaty Indians as it has heretofore been doing. Oregon recognizes sports fishermen and commercial fishermen and seems to attempt to make an equitable division between the two. . . . If Oregon intends to maintain a separate status of commercial and sports fisheries, it is obvious a third must be added, the Indian fishery. The treaty Indians, having an absolute right to that fishery, are entitled to a fair share of the fish produced by the Columbia River system . . . the state cannot so manage the fishery that little or no harvestable portion of the run remains to reach the upper portions of the stream where the historic Indian places are mostly located. . . . In the case of regulations affecting Indian treaty fishing rights the protection of the treaty right to take fish at the Indians' usual and accustomed places must be an objective of the state's regulatory policy co-equal with the conservation of fish runs for other users.[3]

The state's argument that to allow Indians to fish under special regulations would be discriminatory against non-Indian fishermen is specifically struck down in the judgment: "As one method of accomplishing conservation objectives [the state] may lawfully restrict or prohibit non-Indians fishing at the In-

[3] *Sohappy* v. *Smith,* Opinion.

dians' usual and accustomed fishing places without imposing similar restrictions on treaty Indians."

Under the *Sohappy* decree any state regulation of off-reservation Indian treaty fishing must be the *least restrictive possible* for conservation needs, and the burden of proving the necessity is placed on the state. Further, hearings must be held *prior to regulation,* with the tribes and "designated representatives of their members" given opportunity to be heard and to have a meaningful part in the making of the rules. This would seem to require that the state really seek a meeting of minds with each tribe regarding specific rules and not simply expect rubber-stamped approval of predetermined regulations. The opinion suggests interesting possibilities in this regard:

. . . certainly agreements with the tribes or *deference to tribal preference or regulation* on specific aspects pertaining to the exercise of treaty fishing rights are means which the state may adopt in the exercise of its jurisdiction over such fishing rights. Both the state and the tribes should be encouraged to pursue such a cooperative approach.[4] [Emphasis added]

The possibility of tribal jurisdiction over off-reservation fishing by tribal members does exist; and in fact, the Yakima Tribal Council asserts it by resolution passed February 27, 1968, and subsequently approved by the Commissioner of Indian Affairs.

The issue of state authority over off-reservation treaty fishing was not argued in *Sohappy* v. *Smith.* The argument of the plaintiffs seemed to carefully avoid reference to the states as having exclusive jurisdiction, but rather described them as "one class of agents of the public to determine and administer such regulations—provided they act with due regard to their responsibilities under the laws of this land, including these treaties." [5]

Worthy of note is the specific provision in *Sohappy* v. *Smith*

[4] *Ibid.*
[5] *Ibid.*

that the judgment and orders in *Maison* v. *Umatilla*[6] are not modified or affected in any way by the *Sohappy* judgment. Argument has been made both in Washington and in Oregon that the Umatilla decree is unreasonable—and Washington has chosen not to follow it—in its requirements that all possible restriction of the sport and commercial fisheries be carried out before any restriction of the Indian fishery, and that any restriction of the Indian fishery be shown to be indispensable for conservation of the runs of fish. Under the *Sohappy* interpretation, with these principles of *Umatilla* unaltered and therefore still fully applicable, the Indian fishery's "fair and equitable share" would seem to take precedence over those of the sport and commercial fisheries since fishing of Indians can be restricted "only if necessary conservation cannot be accomplished by restriction of the fishing of others."[7] The Indian catch must be given priority and cannot be defined in terms of a proportional relationship to the other catches. Ambiguity remains, however, as to how the Indians' "fair and equitable share" will be defined.

The tribal interest in the fishery is strongly emphasized in both the opinion and the judgment in *Sohappy* v. *Smith*. No departure is indicated from previous federal rulings that the treaty fishing right is tribal rather than individual and that the right of the individual derives from his membership in the tribe.

In retaining jurisdiction the U.S. District Court provides a means by which the Indians who were plaintiffs in this case may seek redress without instituting new cases if they think any state regulations do not comply with the decree. It should be noted, however, that such continuation of jurisdiction is due to the court's recognition of the existence of unresolved prob-

---

[6] *Maison* v. *Confederated Tribes of the Umatilla Indian Reservation,* 314 F.2d 169 (CA 9, 1963)

[7] *Ibid.,* p. 174.

lems, and it may be terminated at any time solely on the judgment of the court.

For Indians who were not plaintiffs in this case the only legal recourse will be the initiation of further court cases. Setting up test cases still will mean, as in the past, subjection to arrest, confiscation of gear, and loss of fishing time; and the process will require again entering the arena of the court with financial, technical, and legal resources far less than those of the state.

Since only Oregon was named in this suit, the practical responses of other states who were not party to it are still in question. In Washington, arrests of treaty Indians fishing in usual and accustomed places are continuing. Muckleshoot Indians have been arrested this fall on the White River. A new injunction has been obtained by the Department of Fisheries against fishing by Puyallup Indians in the Puyallup River. Clallam Indians have been arrested on the Elwha River. In maintaining this position, is the state prepared to show that the Indians' treaty fishing is being dealt with "as a subject separate and distinct from that of fishing by others"; that the Muckleshoot Indians, the Puyallup Indians, and the Lower Elwha Clallam Indians are "accorded an opportunity to attempt to take, at their usual and accustomed fishing places, by reasonable means feasible to them, a fair and equitable share of all fish which it permits to be taken from any given run" destined for their rivers; that total prohibition of their off-reservation fishing is "the least restrictive [regulation] which can be imposed consistent with assuring the necessary escapement of fish for conservation purposes"; that imposition of this regulation was preceded by hearings at which the tribes and "designated representatives of their members" had the "opportunity to be heard and participate meaningfully in the rulemaking process"; that in promulgating the regulations "the protection of the treaty right to take fish at the usual and accustomed places" was "an object of the state's regulatory policy"?

The Washington Department of Fisheries has announced regulations allowing limited off-reservation fishing for five western Washington tribes. In one case (Squaxin) the Department of Fisheries accepted what the tribe requested; with the Nisqually, regulations drafted by the tribe were accepted by the Department of Fisheries as to manner of fishing but were applied only to a portion of the Nisqually River—the open area off reservation ending right at the place where the locations of the controversial fishermen start; and in the other three cases (Quileute, Hoh, and Suquamish) Indian leaders from those tribes report absence of meaningful discussion or agreement on the regulations.

Asked about implementation of "the wording and spirit" of the *Sohappy* decision, the Department of Fisheries' Director Thor C. Tollefson wrote on September 8, 1969:

The Department interprets [Judge Belloni's decision] in the light of the U.S. Supreme Court's decision in the Puyallup and the Nisqually cases. Those cases held that the State had the right to regulate Indian off-reservation fishing provided Indians were not discriminated against. This resolved an issue which had been so controversial for many years. The Indians now seem to accept the decision, although there are a few exceptions.

Our Department read into the decision of the U.S. Supreme Court the obligation of the Department to provide fishing time and opportunity for Indians at their old and accustomed places if this could be done without serious damage to the salmon runs. As a matter of fact, that had been the Department's position long prior to the Supreme Court decision.[8]

According to press reports the Washington State Sportmen's Council passed a resolution at its quarterly meeting September 23, 1969, asking that Governor Evans and State Fisheries Director Tollefson rescind the special agreements with Indians,

[8] Letter, Thor C. Tollefson to Charles L. McEvers, September 8, 1969.

and declaring that if they do not do so the council will initiate legal action.[9]

The Washington Department of Game states bluntly a harder position than the Department of Fisheries. In response to the same question, John A. Biggs, director, replied in part on September 9, 1969:

The laws of the State of Washington specifically declare the steelhead to be a game fish and specifically prohibits [sic] its sale or its taking for any commercial purpose. The only exception to this law relates to steelhead taken on defined Indian reservations which may be shipped out of the state in the course of interstate commerce, but may not be sold within the state. The special Indian seasons which are being considered are of course at off-reservation locations, areas which do not come within established Indian reservations and, therefore, do not lend themselves to a sale of fish to interstate commerce.

For these reasons I am unable to advise you that the Washington State Department of Game, which has statutory responsibility under the laws of this state for the management and harvest of steelhead trout, is considering any special off-reservation Indian seasons for the taking of steelhead trout. It is our position that lacking a clear-cut mandate from a court of appropriate authority, which takes into account the laws of the State of Washington and in effect declares them to be invalid, that we are powerless to establish such seasons and have no authority of any kind to do so.[10]

In the absence of state law specifically recognizing the Indian salmon and steelhead fisheries in full compliance with the treaties, the legalistic controversy is certain to continue, rooted in the difficulty with which the particular "user interests" historically served by the state come to respect the Indian interest. Meanwhile the matrix of it all—the environmental setting of both man and salmon and the ecological implications of environmental changes—continues to be neglected.

October 21, 1969

[9] "Indian Fishing Pacts Hit," *The Daily Olympian* (Olympia, Wash.), September 25, 1969.
[10] Letter, John A. Biggs to Charles L. McEvers, September 9, 1969.

Appendix 1 | Excerpts from "A Citizen's Letter to His Governor"

The Armed Guards are under instructions to use weapons ONLY to prevent the specific actions by State enforcement officers to (1) trespass upon this property for the purpose of making an arrest or serving a state-issued warrant of arrest; and (2) trespassing for the purpose of confiscating the fishing net emplaced in the river off Frank's Landing and affixed to it.

The Armed Guards are under instructions to not use weapons in any other instances or at any other time. . . .

No one other than myself, Sid Mills, and Chiefy Johns are authorized to be armed at any time, and at all times no one else will be armed . . . all Armed Guards will be visible upon the arrival and approach of State Officers, and all other persons at Frank's Landing will be instructed to move to another part of the property. If more than one person is Armed, all Arms or Weapons will be placed upon the ground—except one.

If State enforcement officers attempt to proceed upon the Property of Frank's Landing after being warned against trespass and entry by the remaining Armed Guard, the weapon will be used against the trespassers. Likewise, if the net is emplaced in the water off Frank's Landing, the weapon will be used against any State Officer placing a hand upon that net. . . .

If State Officers act to violate the two prohibitions we have established against their trespass and act to eliminate the single Armed Guard enforcing it, State Officers will meet with no other armed resistance by any other persons on or at Frank's Landing.

We will honor any and all federal warrants of arrest, search or seizure; but not those issued under authority of the State of Washington or Thurston County Courts.[1]

[1] From Hank Adams, Survival of American Indians Association, to Governor Daniel J. Evans, October 17/21, 1968.

Appendix 2 | State Position on the Squaxin Agreement

Following the agreement between the Squaxin Indians and the State Department of Fisheries in the fall of 1969, the Nimrod Club of Shelton, Washington, directed a letter to Governor Daniel J. Evans protesting the action:[1]

We feel this season is illegal, because it discriminates against all other persons in this State by not allowing them to fish. In May, 1968, U.S. Supreme Court Decision, that Mr. Tollefson cites as his authority to set this season, it states that the State cannot discriminate against the Indians. We feel that in turn the State may not discriminate against any other citizen.

The governor replied as follows:[2]

I can appreciate the feelings of your club, and your reasoning is clear. In fact, the contention of the State of Washington before the U.S. Supreme Court was that Indians had no more rights than any other citizen in off-reservation areas. The Court, however, held that the State must permit the Indians to fish at their usual and accustomed places, but said that the State could regulate in the interests of conservation. We will do so, although we are having

[1] From "Fish Act Protested," *Shelton-Mason County Journal* (Shelton, Wash.), Oct. 24, 1968.
[2] From "Nimrods Get Reply on Indian Fishing," in *ibid.*, Oct. 31, 1968.

problems interpreting the Supreme Court decisions. But the Squaxin case is quite clear-cut.

Perhaps the best approach is to reply to your three points first:

(1) The United States government made a treaty with the Indians which grants them certain rights as Indians. Congress has also made them full citizens (in 1924) so that they have all of the rights of other citizens plus their treaty rights. Further, the treaty is binding upon the states and takes precedence over State law.

(2) The State may regulate where *reasonable and necessary* for conservation. We are well aware that set nets are illegal under State law. However, our own Supreme Court has held that it does not apply to Indians, unless our management experts can show that their ban is for conservation reasons. Set nets can be readily managed to allow proper escapement for spawning. We cannot prove that (in the Squaxin case) the prohibition against set nets is reasonably necessary for conservation and, therefore, must recognize the treaty right.

(3) Salmon preserves are created and maintained under the authority of the Director of Fisheries. The treaty right does prevail, but the Director of Fisheries does have authority over salmon preserves and can regulate the Indian fishing therein.

I would point out that a handful of Squaxin Indians have been fishing in Southern Puget Sound for many years. In agreeing to a set of regulations the State recognized their treaty rights, and the Indians recognized the State's rights to regulate their fishery. This is the first tribe to do so, and we are pleased to be able to arrive at an amicable agreement with them which will protect our fishery resource.

Appendix 3 | Public Law 90–284 (90th Congress; 2d Session, April 11, 1968)

Title IV: Jurisdiction over Criminal and Civil Actions

ASSUMPTION BY STATE

Sec. 401. (a) The consent of the United States is hereby given to any State not having jurisdiction over criminal offenses committed by or against Indians in the areas of Indian country situated within such State to assume, with the consent of the Indian tribe occupying the particular Indian country or part thereof which could be affected by such assumption, such measure of jurisdiction over any or all of such offenses committed within such Indian country or any part thereof as may be determined by such State to the same extent that such State has jurisdiction over any such offense committed elsewhere within the State, and the criminal laws of such State shall have the same force and effect within such Indian country or part thereof as they have elsewhere within that State.

(b) Nothing in this section shall authorize the alienation, encumbrance, or taxation of any real or personal property, including water rights, belonging to any Indian or any Indian tribe, band, or community that is held in trust by the United States or is subject to a restriction against alienation imposed by the United States; or shall authorize regulation of the use of such property in a manner inconsistent with any Federal treaty, agreement, or statute or with any regulation made pursuant thereto; or shall deprive any Indian or any Indian tribe, band, or community of any right, privilege, or immunity afforded under Federal treaty, agreement, or statute with respect to hunting, trapping, or fishing or the control, licensing, or regulation thereof.

ASSUMPTION BY STATE OF CIVIL JURISDICTION

Sec. 402. (a) The consent of the United States is hereby given to any State not having jurisdiction over civil causes of action between Indians or to which Indians are parties which arise in the areas of Indian country situated within such State to assume, with the consent of the tribe occupying the particular Indian country or part thereof which would be affected by such assumption, such measure of jurisdiction over any or all such civil causes of action arising within such Indian country or any part thereof as may be determined by such State to the same extent that such State has jurisdiction over other civil causes of action, and those civil laws of such State that are of general application to private persons or private property shall have the same force and effect within such Indian country or part thereof as they have elsewhere within that State.

(b) Nothing in this section shall authorize the alienation, encumbrance, or taxation of any real or personal property, including water rights, belonging to any Indian or any Indian tribe, band, or community that is held in trust by the United States or is subject to a restriction against alienation imposed by the United States; or shall authorize regulation of the use of such property in a manner inconsistent with any Federal treaty, agreement, or statute, or with any regulation made pursuant thereto; or shall confer jurisdiction upon the State to adjudicate, in probate proceedings or otherwise, the ownership or right to possession of such property or any interest therein.

(c) Any tribal ordinance or custom heretofore or hereafter adopted by an Indian tribe, band, or community in the exercise of any authority which it may possess shall, if not inconsistent with any applicable civil law of the State, be given full force and effect in the determination of civil causes of action pursuant to this section.

RETROCESSION OF JURISDICTION BY STATE

Sec. 403. (a) The United States is authorized to accept a retrocession by any State of all or any measure of the criminal or civil jurisdiction, or both, acquired by such State pursuant to the provisions of section 1162 of title 18 of the United States Code, section 1360 of title 28 of the United States Code, or section 7 of the Act of August 15, 1953 (67 Stat. 588), as it was in effect prior to its repeal by subsection (b) of this section.

(b) Section 7 of the Act of August 15, 1953 (67 Stat. 588),[47] [[47]28 U.S.C.A. § 1360 note.] is hereby repealed, but such repeal shall not affect any cession of jurisdiction made pursuant to such section prior to its repeal.

CONSENT TO AMEND STATE LAWS

Sec. 404. Notwithstanding the provisions of any enabling Act for the admission of a State, the consent of the United States is hereby given to the people of any State to amend, where necessary, their State constitution or existing statutes, as the case may be, to remove any legal impediment to the assumption of civil or criminal jurisdiction in accordance with the provisions of this title. The provisions of this title shall not become effective with respect to such assumption of jurisdiction by any such State until the people thereof have appropriately amended their State constitution or statutes, as the case may be.

ACTIONS NOT TO ABATE

Sec. 405. (a) No action or proceeding pending before any court or agency of the United States immediately prior to any cession of jurisdiction by the United States pursuant to this title shall abate by reason of that cession. For the purposes of any such action or proceeding, such cession shall take effect on the day following the date of final determination of such action or proceeding.

(b) No cession made by the United States under this title shall deprive any court of the United States of jurisdiction to hear, determine, render judgment, or impose sentence in any criminal action instituted against any person for any offense committed before the effective date of such cession, if the offense charged in such action was cognizable under any law of the United States at the time of the commission of such offense. For the purposes of any such criminal action, such cession shall take effect on the day following the date of final determination of such action.

SPECIAL ELECTION

Sec. 406. State jurisdiction acquired pursuant to this title with respect to criminal offenses or civil causes of action, or with respect to both, shall be applicable in Indian country only where the enrolled Indians within the affected area of such Indian country accept such jurisdiction by a majority vote of the adult Indians voting at a special election held for that purpose. The Secretary of the Interior shall call such special election under such rules and regulations as he may prescribe, when requested to do so by the tribal council or other governing body, or by 20 percentum of such enrolled adults.

Bibliography

BOOKS AND GENERAL PUBLICATIONS

Alcorn, Gordon D. *Shadow on the Land*. John Dickinson Lecture. Tacoma, Wash.: University of Puget Sound, 1968.

Anderson, Eva. *Chief Seattle*. Caldwell, Idaho: Caxton Printers, 1944.

Andrew, F. J. and Geen, G. H. *Sockeye and Pink Salmon Production in Relation to Proposed Dams in Fraser River System*. International Pacific Salmon Fisheries Commission, Bulletin XI. New Westminster, B.C., 1960.

Avery, Mary. *Government of Washington State*. Seattle: University of Washington Press, 1966.

Bagley, Clarence B. *History of King County, Wash.*, Vol. I. 4 vols. Chicago, Seattle: S. J. Clarke, 1929.

Balch, Reginald E. *The Ecological Viewpoint*. CBC Radio Lecture Series. Toronto: T. H. Best, 1965.

Ballard, Arthur. *Mythology of Southern Puget Sound*. University of Washington Publications in Anthropology, Vol. III, No. 2. Seattle: University of Washington Press, 1929.

———. *Some Tales of the Southern Puget Sound Salish*. University of Washington Publications in Anthropology, Vol. II, No. 3. Seattle: University of Washington Press, 1927.

Barnett, Homer G. *Indian Shakers*. Carbondale: Southern Illinois University Press, 1957

Binns, Archie. *Northwest Gateway: The Story of the Port of Seattle*. Portland, Ore.: Binfords & Mort, 1941.

Brown, William Compton. *The Indian Side of the Story*. Spokane, Wash.: C. W. Hill, 1961.

Clutesi, George. *Son of Raven, Son of Deer: Fables of the Tse-Shaht People*. Sidney, B.C.: Gray's Publishing, 1967.

217

Cohen, Felix S., ed. *Federal Indian Law*, U.S. Solicitor for the Department of Interior. Wash., D.C.: Govt. Printing Office, 1958.

Collier, John. *Indians of the Americas*. New York: Mentor Books, 1947.

Cressman, Luther S. *Cultural Sequences at The Dalles, Oregon*. Transactions of the American Philosophical Society, New Series, Vol. L, Pt. 10. Philadelphia: American Philosophical Society, 1960.

Curtis, Edward. *The North American Indian*, Vol. IX. 20 vols. Norwood, Mass.: Plimpton Press, 1911.

Denny, Arthur A. *Pioneer Days on Puget Sound*. Seattle, 1888. Exact reprint available from Ye Galleon Press, Fairfield, Wash., 1965.

Dorst, Jean. *Before Nature Dies*. London: Collins, 1969; French ed., Neuchâtel, Switzerland, 1964.

Drucker, Philip. *Indians of the Northwest Coast*. American Museum of Natural History. Garden City, N.Y.: Natural History Press, 1955.

Emmons, Della Gould. *Leschi of the Nisquallys*. Minneapolis: T. S. Denison & Co., 1965.

Fey, Harold E., and D'Arcy McNickle. *Indians and Other Americans*. New York: Harper & Bros., 1959.

Gates, Charles M., ed. *Readings in Pacific Northwest History*. Seattle: University Bookstore, 1941.

Gibbs, George. "Tribes of Western Washington and Northwestern Oregon," in W. H. Dall, *Tribes of the Extreme Northwest*, Vol. I, Pt. 2 of Contributions to North American Ethnology. Wash., D.C., 1877.

Goddard, P. E. *Indians of the Northwest Coast*. Handbook Series, No. 10. New York: American Museum of Natural History, 1945.

Gunther, Erna. *A Further Analysis of First Salmon Ceremony*. University of Washington Publications in Anthropology, Vol. III, No. 5. Seattle: University of Washington Press, 1928.

Haeberlin, Herman K., and Erna Gunther. *The Indians of Puget Sound*. University of Washington Publications in Anthropology, Vol. IV, No. 1. Seattle: University of Washington Press, 1930.

Hagan, William. *American Indians*. Chicago: University of Chicago Press, 1961.

Hawthorn, Audrey, ed. *People of the Potlatch*. Vancouver, B.C.: Vancouver Art Gallery, [1956].

Holbrook, Stewart. *Green Commonwealth*. Published by Simpson Logging Co., Shelton, Wash., 1945.

Hough, Henry W. *Development of Indian Resources*. Denver: World Press, 1967.

Hunt, Herbert, and Floyd Kaylor. *Washington, West of the Cascades*, Vol. I. 3 vols. Chicago, Seattle: S. J. Clarke, 1917.

Isely, Mary B. "A Look at the Washington State Indian Fisheries, As Shown in State Department of Fisheries Statistics." Mimeo-

BIBLIOGRAPHY   219

graphed. Seattle, Wash., American Friends Service Committee, 1969.

Josephy, Alvin. *The Nez Perce Indians and the Opening of the Northwest.* New Haven, Conn.: Yale University Press, 1965.

Landerholm, Carl, ed. *Notices and Voyages of the Famed Quebec Mission to the Pacific Northwest, 1838–1847.* Oregon Historical Society. Portland, Ore.: Champoeg Press, 1956.

Lavender, David. *Land of Giants.* Garden City, N.Y.: Doubleday, 1958.

Leonard, George B. *Education and Ecstasy.* New York: Delacorte Press, 1968.

Loutzenhiser, F. H. and J. R. *Told by the Pioneers.* 3 vols. Olympia, Wash., WPA Project, 1937–38.

Meany, Edmond S. *History of the State of Washington.* New York: Macmillan Co., 1909.

———. *Indian Geographic Names of Washington.* Seattle: Hyatt-Fowells School, 1908.

———. *Origin of Washington Geographic Names.* Seattle: University of Washington Press, 1923.

Meeker, Ezra. *Pioneer Reminiscences of Puget Sound and the Tragedy of Leschi.* Seattle, Wash.: Lowman & Hanford, 1905.

Moore, Milo. *Salmon of the Pacific.* Olympia: Wash. State Department of Fisheries, 1960(?).

———, Ken McLeod, and Don Reed. *Fisheries,* Vol. III. Olympia: Washington State Department of Fisheries, 1960.

Muckleshoot Indians, Pamphlet File. Northwest Collection, University of Washington, Indians of North America Tribes, Oregon and Washington.

Nairn, Ronald C. *International Aid to Thailand—the New Colonialism?* New Haven, Conn.: Yale University Press, 1966.

Phillips, Walter S. *The Chinook Book.* Seattle: R. L. Davis Printing Co., 1913.

Relander, Click. *Strangers on the Land.* Yakima, Wash.: Franklin Press, 1962.

Royce, W. F., D. E. Bevan, James A. Crutchfield, Gerald Paulik, and R. L. Fletcher. *Salmon Gear Limitation in Northern Washington Waters.* University of Washington Publications in Fisheries, New Series, Vol. II, No. 1, 1963.

Scheffer, Victor B. and Rex J. Robinson. "A Limnological Study of Lake Washington," in *Ecological Monographs,* Publication of the Ecological Society of America, Vol. IX. Durham, N.C.: Duke University Press, 1939.

Sicade, Henry. "The Indians' Side of the Story," in *Building A State: Washington 1889–1939.* Tacoma: Washington State Historical Society, 1940.

Smith, Marian W., ed. *Indians of the Urban Northwest.* Columbia University Contributions to Anthropology, No. 36. New York: Columbia University Press, 1949.

———. *The Puyallup-Nisqually.* Columbia University Contributions to Anthropology, No. 32. New York: Columbia University Press, 1940.

Snowden, C. A. *History of Washington.* 4 vols. New York: Century History Co., 1909.

Stevens, Hazard. *The Life of Isaac Ingalls Stevens.* 2 vols. Boston: Houghton Mifflin, 1900.

Swan, James G. *Indians of Cape Flattery.* Smithsonian Institution Publication No. 220. Wash., D.C.: Smithsonian Institution, 1870.

———. *The Northwest Coast.* New York: Harper & Bros., 1857. Reprinted by Ye Galleon Press, Fairfield, Wash., 1966.

Swanton, John R. *Indian Tribes of North America.* Bureau of American Ethnology, Bulletin 145. Wash., D.C.: Govt. Printing Office, 1952.

Thomas, Edward Harper. *Chinook: A History and a Dictionary.* Portland, Ore.: Metropolitan Press, 1935; reprinted by Binfords & Mort.

Underhill, Ruth. *Indians of the Pacific Northwest.* Education Division, U.S. Office of Indian Affairs. Wash., D.C., 1944; Riverside, Calif.: Sherman Institute Press, 1945.

———. *Red Man's America.* Chicago: University of Chicago Press, 1953.

U.S. Public Health Service. *Pollution Caused Fish Kills.* Bulletin 847. Wash., D.C.: Govt. Printing Office, 1964.

Washington State Department of Fisheries. *Indian Fisheries Problem.* Olympia, 1964.

———. *Working Draft: The Ingredients of a Ten-Year Plan.* Olympia, Wash. (1965?).

Watt, Roberta Frye. *Four Wagons West.* Portland, Ore.: Binfords & Mort, 1933.

White, Lynn, Jr. "The Historical Roots of Our Ecological Crises," 133rd Meeting of the American Association for the Advancement of Science. Wash., D.C., Dec. 1966 (mimeo).

Whitebrook, Robert. *Coastal Exploration of Washington.* Palo Alto, Calif.: Pacific Books, 1959.

Whiting, J. S. *Forts of the State of Washington.* Seattle: Kelly Printing Co., 1951.

PERIODICAL ARTICLES

Bagley, Clarence B. "Chief Seattle and Angeline," *Washington Historical Quarterly,* XXII (Oct. 1931)

Bird, Annie Laurie. "William Henson Wallace, Pioneer Politician," *Pacific Northwest Quarterly,* XLIX (April 1958), 61–76.

Buchanan, Charles M. "Rights of the Puget Sound Indians to Game and Fish," *Washington Historical Quarterly,* VI (April 1915), 109–18.

Coan, C. F. "The Adoption of the Reservation Policy in the Pacific Northwest, 1853–1855," *Oregon Historical Quarterly,* XXIII (March 1922), 1–38.

————. "The First Stage of Federal Indian Relations in the Pacific Northwest, 1849–1852," *Oregon Historical Quarterly,* XXII (March 1921), 46–89.

Cunningham, Ross. "Grand Coulee Dam Blamed for Upper River Salmon Kill," *Seattle Times,* Aug. 23, 1954.

Ellis, James R. "Northwest Today" section, *Seattle Post-Intelligencer,* Nov. 13, 1966, p. 3.

Fleming, Elaine. "Among the Indians Fifty Years Ago," *Seattle Times,* Aug. 29, 1965.

Galbraith, John S. "The British and Americans at Fort Nisqually, 1846–1859," *Pacific Northwest Quarterly,* XLI (April 1950), 109–20.

Gosnell, Wesley B. "Causes of the Indian War: A Report to Governor Stevens, Dec. 31, 1856," *Washington Historical Quarterly,* XVII (Oct. 1926), 289–99.

Haines, Francis. "Problems of Indian Policy," *Pacific Northwest Quarterly,* XLI (July 1950), 203–12.

Hobbs, Charles A. "Indian Hunting and Fishing Rights," *George Washington Law Review,* Vol. XXXII, No. 3 (March 1964).

"Indian Fishing Pact Hit," *The Daily Olympian* (Olympia, Wash.), September 25, 1969.

Rigert, Joe. "Hatchery Brings Up Legal Difficulties," *Aberdeen Daily World* (Aberdeen, Wash.), June 17, 1965.

Royal Bank of Canada (Montreal), "Man in the Balance of Nature," *Monthly Letter* (Feb. 1969).

Seattle Post-Intelligencer. Pictorial Review Section, Aug. 4, 1957.

Stevens, Isaac. "Letters of Isaac Stevens, 1857–1858," ed. Ronald Todd. *Pacific Northwest Quarterly,* XXXI (Oct. 1940), 403–59.

UNESCO Courier (Paris, Jan. 1969).

GOVERNMENT DOCUMENTS, REPORTS, AND TREATIES

Columbia River Comprehensive Report on Development. . . . Bureau of Reclamation, U.S. Department of Interior, Wash., D.C.: Govt. Printing Office, 1947.

Executive Orders Relating to Indian Reserves. From May 14, 1855, to July 1, 1902. Compiled by the Indian Office under authority of Act of Congress approved May 17, 1882 (22 Stats., p. 88), Wash., D.C.: Govt. Printing Office, 1902.

Kappler, Charles J. *Indian Laws and Treaties,* Vol. I. 3 vols. Wash., D.C.: Govt. Printing Office, 1903.

Meriam, Lewis, *et al. The Problem of Indian Administration.* Baltimore, Md., 1928.

Report of the Commissioner of Indian Affairs, Accompanying the Annual Report of the Secretary of the Interior for the Year 1858. Wash., D.C.: Wm. A. Harris, 1858.

Report of the Joint Special Committee, appointed under Joint Resolution of March 3, 1865, with an Appendix: Condition of the Indian Tribes. Wash., D.C.: Govt. Printing Office, 1867.

Royce, C. C. *Indian Policy of the United States, and Indian Land Cessions in the United States.* 18th Annual Report, Bureau of Ethnology. Wash., D.C., 1899.

Swindell, Edward G. *Report on Source, Nature, and Extent of the Fishing, Hunting, and Misc. Related Rights of Certain Indian Tribes in Washington and Oregon Together with Affidavits Showing Location of a Number of Usual and Accustomed Fishing Grounds and Stations.* Division of Forestry and Grazing, Office of Indian Affairs, U.S. Department of Interior. Los Angeles, Calif., 1942.

Treaty with Duwamish, Suquamish, etc. (Point Elliott), Jan. 22, 1855. 12 Stat., 927. Ratified March 3, 1855; proclaimed April 11, 1859.

Treaty with Nisqually, Puyallup, etc. (Medicine Creek), Dec. 26, 1854. 10 Stat., 1132. Ratified March 3, 1855; proclaimed April 10, 1855.

U.S. Congress, Senate Committee on Interior and Insular Affairs, Subcommittee on Indian Affairs. *Indian Fishing Rights: Hearing on S.J.R. 170 and S.J.R. 171.* 88th Cong., 2d sess., Aug. 5 and 6, 1964. Wash., D.C.: Govt. Printing Office, 1964.

Washington State. *Transcript of Conference in the Matter of Pollution of Interstate Waters.* 3 vols. 1st sess., Jan. 16–17, 1962. Joint Federal–Wash. State Pollution Control Conference. Published by the State of Washington, Olympia, 1962.

Washington State Department of Fisheries. *Annual Report.* Annual volumes, 1890–1966. Olympia, Wash.

Washington State Department of Game. *Biennial Reports.* Olympia, Wash.

Washington State Pollution Control Commission. *Pollution Effects of Pulp and Paper Industrial Wastes in Puget Sound.* Olympia, Wash., 1967.

Webster, Henry A. Makah Report in *Annual Report of the Commissioner of Indian Affairs.* Wash., D.C.: Govt. Printing Office, 1865.

BIBLIOGRAPHY 223

COURT CASES

Duwamish, Lummi, Whidby Island, Skagit, Upper Skagit, Swinomish, et al. Tribes of Indians v. *U.S.A. Court of Claims of the United States.* LXXIX, 530. Wash., D.C.: Govt. Printing Office, 1935. Documents pertaining to this case are contained in two volumes printed by the Argus Press, Seattle, Wash., available in the Northwest Collection of the University of Washington Library.

Maison v. *Confederated Tribes of the Umatilla Indian Reservation,* 314 F.2d 169 (CA 9, 1963). (Available in Federal Reporter System at all county law libraries and law schools.)

Memorandum Decision No. 158069 by Judge John D. Cochran, May 27, 1965, in *Departments of Game and Fisheries of the State of Washington* v. *The Puyallup Tribe,* in Pierce County Superior Court, Tacoma, Wash.

Puyallup Tribe v. *Department of Game,* 70 Wn.2d 245, 422 P.2d 754 (1967); 391 U.S. 392, 20 L Ed 689 (1968).

Sohappy v. *Smith,* USDC D. Oregon, No. 68–409, and *U.S.* v. *Oregon,* USDC D. Oregon, No. 68–513 (concurrent, 1969).

State v. *Satiacum,* 50 Wn.2d 513, 314 P.2d 400 (1957). (Available in Federal Reporter System at all county law libraries and law schools.)

Tulee v. *Washington,* 315 U.S. 681 (1942). (Available in Federal Reporter System at all county libraries and law schools.)

LETTERS

Biggs, John A. Letter to Charles L. McEvers, Sept. 9, 1969.

Heckman, James L. Letter to Charles L. McEvers, Feb. 16, 1966.

Pautzke, Clarence. Letter to Charles L. McEvers, March 4, 1966.

Smith, Anthony Wayne. Letter to Walter Taylor, Jan. 13, 1966.

Tollefson, Thor C. Letters to Charles L. McEvers, March 3, 1966; Sept. 8, 1969.

Index

Licensing, 87–88
Logging, 159–60, 167
Lone Wolf v. *Hitchcock,* 74–75
Lummi tribe, 197*n*

Magnuson, Warren G.: fishing rights, 108–9, 114, 115; on Fishery Services Division, 144*n*
Maison v. *Confederated Tribes of the Umatilla Indian Reservation* (Ore.), 89, 91, 92, 96, 97, 202–5
Makah tribe: on fishing rights, 117; fisheries programs, 143, 190; on tribal regulations, 178–79; on scapegoat practices, 180–81
Makah Indian Tribe v. *Schoettler,* 88–89, 90
Manypenny, George T., 37–38
Marshall, Chief Justice John, 74
Mason v. *Sams,* 84*n*
Mayfield Dam, 154, 173–76, 180
Maynard, David, 61–62
Medicine Creek, treaty of, 19; terms of, 25–26; changes in, 37–39; reservation size, 42, 53–57; on fishing rights, 82–83; in *Satiacum,* 90; in *Puyallup,* 94; Nisqually under, 98–99; and Muckleshoots, 103; off-reservation fishing, 116; Squaxins under, 133*n*
Meeker, Ezra: on Indian-white relations, 15; on Chinook jargon, 24; on Governor Stevens, 27
Menominee Tribe v. *U.S.,* 78
Meriam Report, 48
Minnesota v. *Hitchcock,* 75*n*
Missionaries, 12–17
Montana Power Co. v. *Rochester,* 79
Moore, Milo, 131
Mossyrock Dam, 173–76, 180
Muckleshoot reservation: established, 37–39; settlement, 39–40; and treaty claims, 40; size of, 56–57
Muckleshoot tribe: naming of, 35;

tribal government, 49, 58–60; state jurisdiction, 51–52; numbers of, 56; fishing sites, 59–60; changes in culture, 66; court cases, 72*n*, 89–90, 94–95, 101–5, 140; constitution, 99–100; tribal status, 99–100, 104; treaty status, 100–4, 109, 111; in fishing disputes, 111, 116; in fisheries program, 143; fishing, 151, 161*n*; arrests, 206
Mud Mountain Dam, 154, 156, 164
The Muckleshoot Tribe of Indians v. *U.S.,* 102

National Congress of American Indians, 114–15, 117
National Indian Youth Council, 108
Neah Bay, treaty of, 19
Neeley's Bridge, 105
Nelson (Muckleshoot chief), 35
Net fishing: arrests for, 108, 110*n*; and river closures, 108; sportsmen on, 119–20; state on, 131, 136; attacks on, 134; effect on runs, 190
Neubrech, Walter, 115
Nez Perce tribe: treaty with, 33–34; in interstate case, 200–1
Nisqually reservation: treaty changes in, 37–39; size of, 42, 55; condemnation, 55–56
Nisqually River: and reservation, 55; as fishing site, 59; steelhead controversy, 83; closing of, 108, 112, 140; demonstrations on, 108, 110, 112, 116; salmon in, 151; changes in, 156, 159; fishing agreement, 207
Nisqually tribe: early, 15; and Treaty of Medicine Creek, 26–27; tribal government, 49, 57–60; under state jurisdiction, 51–52; numbers of, 52–53, 55–56; fishing sites, 59–60, 151; changes in culture, 66; court cases, 86, 92, 94–99, 106; on state regula-